THE DAILY STUDY BIBLE

(OLD TESTAMENT)

General Editor: John C. L. Gibson

TWELVE PROPHETS

Volume 2

THE DAILY STUDY BIBLE

(OLD TESTAMENT)

General Editor: John C. L. Gibson

TWELVE PROPHETS
Volume 2

TWELVE PROPHETS

Volume 2

MICAH, NAHUM, HABAKKUK, ZEPHANIAH, HAGGAI, ZECHARIAH, AND MALACHI

PETER C. CRAIGIE

THE WESTMINSTER PRESS
PHILADELPHIA

Published by
The Saint Andrew Press
Edinburgh, Scotland
and
The Westminster Press®
Philadelphia, Pennsylvania

PRINTED IN THE UNITED STATES OF AMERICA
2 4 6 8 9 7 5 3 1

Library of Congress Cataloging in Publication Data

Craigie, Peter C.
    Twelve prophets.

    (The Daily study Bible series)
    Bibliography: p.
    1. Bible. O.T. Minor Prophets—Commentaries.
I. Title. II. Title. 12 prophets. III. Series: Daily
study Bible series (Westminster Press)
BS1560.C72 1984   224'.9077   84-2372
ISBN 0-664-21813-X (v. 2)
ISBN 0-664-24582-X (pbk. : v. 2)

GENERAL PREFACE

This series of commentaries on the Old Testament, to which Professor Craigie's second volume on the *Twelve Prophets* belongs, has been planned as a companion series to the much-acclaimed New Testament series of the late Professor William Barclay. As with that series, each volume is arranged in successive headed portions suitable for daily study. The Biblical text followed is that of the Revised Standard Version or Common Bible. Eleven contributors share the work, each being responsible for from one to three volumes. The series is issued in the hope that it will do for the Old Testament what Professor Barclay's series succeeded so splendidly in doing for the New Testament—make it come alive for the Christian believer in the twentieth century.

Its two-fold aim is the same as his. Firstly, it is intended to introduce the reader to some of the more important results and fascinating insights of modern Old Testament scholarship. Most of the contributors are already established experts in the field with many publications to their credit. Some are younger scholars who have yet to make their names but who in my judgment as General Editor are now ready to be tested. I can assure those who use these commentaries that they are in the hands of competent teachers who know what is of real consequence in their subject and are able to present it in a form that will appeal to the general public.

The primary purpose of the series, however, is *not* an academic one. Professor Barclay summed it up for his New Testament series in the words of Richard of Chichester's prayer—to enable men and women "to know Jesus Christ more clearly, to love Him more dearly, and to follow Him more nearly." In the case of the Old Testament we have to be a little more circumspect than that. The Old Testament was completed long before the time of Our

Lord, and it was (as it still is) the sole Bible of the Jews, God's first people, before it became part of the Christian Bible. We must take this fact seriously.

Yet in its strangely compelling way, sometimes dimly and sometimes directly, sometimes charmingly and sometimes embarrassingly, it holds up before us the things of Christ. It should not be forgotten that Jesus Himself was raised on this Book, that He based His whole ministry on what it says, and that He approached His death with its words on His lips. Christian men and women have in this ancient collection of Jewish writings a uniquely illuminating avenue not only into the will and purposes of God the Father, but into the mind and heart of Him who is named God's Son, who was Himself born a Jew but went on through the Cross and Resurrection to become the Saviour of the world. Read reverently and imaginatively the Old Testament can become a living and relevant force in their everyday lives.

It is the prayer of myself and my colleagues that this series may be used by its readers and blessed by God to that end.

New College
Edinburgh

JOHN C. L. GIBSON
General Editor

CONTENTS

MICAH

Introduction 1
A Nation in Crisis (1:1)................................ 5
The Sins of Two Cities (1:2–9)......................... 8
A Gazetteer of Judgment (1:10–16)...................... 13
A Word of Woe to the Wicked (2:1–5) 17
On Preaching and Preachers (2:6–13) 20
The Centrality of Justice (3:1–12) 25
Swords into Ploughshares (4:1–5)....................... 30
The Reign of God (4:6–13).............................. 33
"Bethlehem Ephrathah" (5:1–6) 38
Israel's Prospect and Punishment (5:7–15)............ 41
The Lord's Controversy with Israel (6:1–8) 44
Of Crime and Punishment (6:9–16) 47
A Lament for a Lost Society (7:1–7).................... 51
A Postscript: the Continuity of Micah's Message (7:8–20).... 54

NAHUM

Introduction 58
The Judge of Nineveh (1:1–15) 62
The Siege of Nineveh (2:1–13) 67
Nineveh and Thebes (3:1–19)............................ 71

HABAKKUK

Introduction 77
The Prayer of Habakkuk (1:1–4) 81
God's First Response (1:5–11) 84
Habakkuk's Argument (1:12–2:1)......................... 88
God's Response: the Vision (2:2–4) 91
Five Woes to the Wicked (2:5–20) 94
Habakkuk's Psalm (3:1–19).............................. 100

ZEPHANIAH

Introduction 105
The Judgment of Judah (1:1–13) 110

The Day of Wrath (1:14–2:3)............................ 114
The Desolation of Foreign Nations (2:4–15) 118
The Corruption of Jerusalem (3:1–7) 122
Judgment and Survival (3:8–13) 126
A Postscript of Joy (3:14–20)............................ 130

HAGGAI
Introduction 133
August 29, 520 B.C. (1:1–11)............................ 137
September 21, 520 B.C. (1:12–15)........................ 141
October 17, 520 B.C. (2:1–9)............................ 144
December 18, 520 B.C. (2:10–19)........................ 147
The Message to Zerubbabel (2:20–23) 151

ZECHARIAH
Introduction 154

Part I: Chapters 1–8
An Old Message for a New Age (1:1–6).................. 159
Vision in the Night (1:7–17) 162
The Second Vision: Four Horns (1:18–21)................ 167
The Third Vision: A City without Walls (2:1–13) 168
The Fourth Vision: Joshua and the Satan (3:1–10).......... 172
The Fifth Vision: the Lampstand (4:1–14) 176
The Sixth and Seventh Visions (5:1–11) 180
The Final Vision: Four Chariots (6:1–15) 184
The Sermons of Zechariah—I (7:1–14)................... 188
The Sermons of Zechariah—II (8:1–23).................. 192

Part II: Chapters 9–14
The Coming King (9:1–17).............................. 197
The Coming of Redemption (10:1–12) 202
Further Reflections on the Shepherd Theme (11:1–17)....... 206
The Coming Day of God (12:1–14) 211
The Coming of Hope (13:1–9)........................... 215
The Apogee of Apocalypse (14:1–21)..................... 218

MALACHI
Introduction 224
The Love of God (1:1–5) 226
A Critique of the Priesthood (1:6–2:9).................... 230

CONTENTS

Marriage and Divorce (2:10–16) 235
Justice and Judgment (2:17–3:5) 238
The Robbing of God (3:6–12) 241
Good and Evil (3:13–4:3) 244
Postscript: the Coming of Elijah (4:4–6) 247

Further Reading... 249

INTRODUCTION TO THE BOOK OF MICAH

Micah lived in one of the great ages of prophecy in Old Testament times. He was a contemporary of Isaiah in Judah; in Israel, to the north, it was the time in which Amos and Hosea ministered. And yet, by some quirk of history, Micah is less well known today than are his famous contemporaries. Perhaps the relative brevity of his book, or its lack of biographical information, has made him seem less memorable. But we must be careful not to project Micah's contemporary low profile back into the biblical world for, in his own time, he was among the best known of the prophets. A century after his death, his ministry was still remembered in the time of another prophet, Jeremiah (26:18–19).

For all his fame in ancient times, all too little is known of the prophet Micah. He is called "Micah of Moresheth", and many have assumed on the basis of his title that he lived in the village of Moresheth-Gath, a small settlement in the Judean lowlands some twenty miles south-west of Jerusalem. But it is more probable that he was a regular resident of Jerusalem, called "of Moresheth" after the town from which he had come. The name Micah was a common one in Hebrew; if the prophet had continued to live in Moresheth-Gath, he would hardly have been named after the place, though in Jerusalem, naming him after the place of his origin might have distinguished him from other Micahs.

Micah was a prophet in the southern state of Judah, though his message was also addressed, initially at least, to the northern state and its capital Samaria. The period during which he ministered is specified by the reference in 1:1 to the reigning kings of Judah: Jotham, Ahaz and Hezekiah. In general terms, these kings reigned from about 740 to 68 B.C.; Micah's ministry did not necessarily last throughout this whole period of more than half a century, but took place within it. It was a time of uncertainty in Hebrew history. The death of King Uzziah (c. 740/739 B.C.) had marked the end of an extraordinary era in Judah, but to the north the new Assyrian Empire was becoming an ever more powerful threat to the nations in the south. Indeed, in 722 B.C., the Assyrians defeated the northern state of Israel, with its capital city at Samaria. It is probable that Micah's ministry began just a few years before this significant event. And, as he continued to minister in the south, he was addressing a nation living in the perpetual fear of external enemies.

Of the man himself, little is known beyond the words of his prophecies that have been left to us. The book contains no explicit biography, as do those of his contemporaries. He is often described by modern writers as a countryman, not only because of his link with Moresheth, but also because the substance of his preaching addressed the needs of the country folk and their exploitation by rich city dwellers. But such a description is uncertain; though he was certainly familiar with country life, he was more likely to have been a resident of Jerusalem. Other than such uncertain inferences, little is known of Micah beyond the substance of his message.

As with most of the prophetic writings, Micah's little book is not an easy one to read. It contains a collection of his oracles and sermons from different periods of his life. To understand them, one would like to know the time and place at which each message was delivered, but sufficient information rarely remains to enable one to make such informed judgments with certainty. Indeed, it sometimes is difficult to know where each message begins and ends. There has been a certain amount of debate amongst scholars as to whether all the oracles in this book come from Micah himself, or whether some come from an unknown prophet at a later date. Few have doubted the authenticity of chapters 1–3, though many scholars have claimed that the substance of chapters 4–7 must come from a period after Micah's death. Such judgments are very hard to make, given the paucity of evidence and its subjective character. In general, the remarks that follow by way of interpretation are written from the perspective that all seven chapters, with a few minor exceptions, can reasonably be ascribed to Micah, a position held by a number of contemporary scholars. It is certainly not a position that can be proved, yet the weight of the evidence does not compel me to view the last four chapters of the book as coming from a period later than that of the prophet Micah. Only two sections are in serious doubt: (a) 4:1–5 is shared with Isaiah and is of uncertain origin; (b) 7:8–20 appears to be a later postscript to the original book.

THE MESSAGE OF MICAH

As with all prophets, Micah is gripped by an awareness of the living God. His God is real and thus must be recognized in all aspects of human existence. God is relevant not only in those aspects of life that are thought of as "religious", but also in the context of business, the law courts, and every milieu of human relationships. Furthermore, God was not only the covenant God of the chosen people, but also the God of all the nations; his involvement in human affairs impinged not only upon Israel, but also upon the affairs of other nations and their impact upon Israel and Judah.

From the perspective of a penetrating view of God's righteousness and his concern for human relationships, Micah addressed the citizens of Judah, especially Jerusalem, and for a while their neighbours to the north. His vision of the society in which he lived had a kind of X-ray quality to it. Like his contemporary Amos, who ministered in the northern state, Micah could see beneath the polished veneer of his society and pick out the fundamental flaws that lay just slightly beneath the surface. He perceived how the powerful exploited the poor, how the courts of the land had been corrupted, and how rulers and religious leaders alike had failed in the exercise of their responsibilities. And he was fully aware that the continuing practice of religion in the state made things worse, not better, for religious practice coupled with moral turpitude produced only the worst forms of evil and hypocrisy.

Micah's analysis of the moral disease that afflicted his society of necessity propelled him towards offering a prognosis. A righteous God could not overlook such rampant unrighteousness. Inevitably, therefore, a society that continued to practise evil must expect divine judgment. But the judgment, in Micah's view, would not be an abstract or distant reality; he related the inner decline of the nation to the external military threat presented by the Assyrian Empire to the north. Assyria was to be feared, not simply as a powerful foreign enemy, but rather as a potential instrument of God's judgment. He anticipated the destruction of Jerusalem and subsequent captivity, perhaps coming to this conclusion as a consequence of the fate of Samaria which occurred early in the course of his ministry (722 B.C.). To many of his contemporaries, Micah's message must have seemed outrageous, if not heretical; how could a true prophet declare the coming judgment of God's people and the holy city at the hands of a *pagan power*? Yet there was nothing heretical about his pronouncements. On the one hand, he saw that the nation's evil was so gross as to invite such judgment. On the other hand, he perceived that the God of Covenant was fully within his rights to exercise judgment on a covenant people who had totally forgotten their covenantal obligations.

But the message of Micah extends beyond his own time and place to have implications for future generations. In chapter 5, his preaching takes on a futuristic and messianic tone; beyond the judgment, there still remained hope for a new and enduring work of God for his people and the world. In part, the messianic expectations are given substance by the New Testament (see the commentary on chapter 5, below); in part, they remain the substance of future thought, anticipating a world in which the evil of the present age will be no more.

The prophet's message is thus a mixture of light and dark. Not without reason, he has been called the "conscience of Israel"; his words bring out in sharp relief the rampant moral decline of his age. Yet there is also a ray of light, a fragment of hope for a future world; it cannot be fully seen until first the evil of the human species has been dealt with in judgment. But there would come a time, nevertheless, when the instruments of war would be converted to the implements of peace in a world that belonged to God. The prophet's message had a visionary character in its own time; in part that vision has taken on substance in the New Testament, but in part it remains the substance of things hoped for, not seen. And if we would appreciate Micah's book for our own age, we must somehow grasp his vision; it has present implications for action and ethics and it is the stuff of faith for the future.

A NATION IN CRISIS

Micah 1:1

¹The word of the Lord that came to Micah of Moresheth in the days of Jotham, Ahaz, and Hezekiah, kings of Judah, which he saw concerning Samaria and Jerusalem.

The book of Micah, like many other prophetic works, begins with a brief introduction specifying the prophet, the nature of his ministry, and the times in which he lived and worked.

(i) *The key figure is Micah.* His name is an abbreviated form of an expression meaning: "Who is like the Lord?". The words stress the incomparability of the God of the chosen people, and though the name was common enough, it was a suitable name for one engaged in a prophetic ministry. Micah is identified with Moresheth, properly Moresheth-Gath, a country town some twenty miles south-west of Jerusalem, the remains of which can still be seen at the site now called Tell ej-Judeideh.

(ii) *Micah's ministry was that of a prophet.* He is not called a *prophet* explicitly in this context, but the "word of the Lord" came to him, and that is the very essence of all true prophecy. God would speak to his chosen people, but the divine word would be heard in and through the human words of Micah. The substance of Micah's ministry would be that "which he saw concerning Samaria and Jerusalem"; though Micah's religious experience of God may have had a visionary component to it, his ministry as such was to be oral, the public proclamation of God's word.

The subject matter of Micah's public proclamation is here summarized by the names of two cities, Samaria and Jerusalem. Samaria was the capital city of the northern state of Israel, Jerusalem the capital of the southern state of Judah. Though he spoke *about* both cities and nations, Micah spoke primarily *to* the city of Jerusalem and the kingdom of Judah.

(iii) *The historical period.* Micah's ministry took place during the reigns of three Judean kings, Jotham, Ahaz, and Hezekiah. If we are to understand properly the prophet's book, the historical information implicit in these royal names is essential; they specify the general historical period within which Micah ministered and thus enable us to understand the focus and force of his message. By analogy, if we were to study the lives and writings of important 20th-century religious figures, it would be important to know not only *where* they lived, but *when* they lived. Thus, one can read the writings of Dietrich Bonhoeffer profitably without knowing of his time and place in history; but the reading of his works is enriched enormously by the knowledge that he ministered, as the Bible would put it, "in the days of Adolf Hitler". As both the public ministry and private agony of Bonhoeffer were shaped by his times, so too was the ministry of Micah. The names of three kings in verse 1 open the door to a knowledge of the circumstances prevalent in the prophet's world.

In part, the three kings specify simply the period of the prophet; he ministered somewhere between 740 and 687 B.C., and though we do not know the precise limits of his ministry, a period from about 735 B.C. to 700 B.C. is likely. But a knowledge of the time period also provides a knowledge of the historical circumstances, garnered both from biblical sources (notably 2 Kings) and also from external sources recovered through archaeological work, such as the chronicles of Assyrian kings.

The two kingdoms of Israel and Judah were passing through a series of international and internal crises during Micah's lifetime. The young Micah would no doubt have been told of the glorious years in Judah during the reign of King Uzziah, who had died

c. 740 B.C. But when Micah began his ministry, Uzziah's son, Jotham, had become king. He was a decent enough man and carried on in many ways the work established by his father. But Jotham did not have his father's strength and, worse, he did not live in his father's world. In 745 B.C., Tiglath-Pileser III became king of Assyria and set for his nation a course of imperial expansion; Israel and Judah would eventually fall within the Assyrian plans for empire.

The various states located in Syria-Palestine, Israel and Judah among them, anticipated an Assyrian invasion; two of them, Damascus and Israel, formed a coalition to block Assyria's expansion and sought to persuade the state of Judah to join the coalition. Judah refused, and the northern coalition, not wanting any danger in the south while it prepared for a northern attack, invaded Judah, which was now ruled by Ahaz, following Jotham's death. Ahaz, in desperation, appealed to Tiglath-Pileser for help, though such a move was not a popular one in Jerusalem. But events had now been set in motion in which it seemed that Judah was but a pawn, tossed this way and that by the tides of history. Israel, with its capital at Samaria, was defeated and destroyed by the invading Assyrian armies. Judah, though it escaped the calamity that befell its northern neighbour, became little more than a colony of the growing Assyrian Empire. And within Judah, under the weak rule of Ahaz, both spiritual and economic life entered a period of decline. The faith in the true God of the chosen people was lost in one of the darkest periods of apostasy in Judah's entire history.

The prospects for Judah brightened somewhat when Hezekiah became king on the death of Ahaz (c. 716 B.C.). Hezekiah initiated a religious reform, attempting to restore the nation's faith to its ancient purity. And, gradually, he began to move his nation back to a course of independence from Assyrian domination. When Sennacherib became the new Assyrian emperor (704 B.C.), Hezekiah took the opportunity to declare independence once again. But Judah's freedom was short-lived. In 701 B.C., Sennacherib undertook a military expedition into Syria-Palestine, successfully subduing the rebellious states that had sought to regain their freedom. Judah was desolated, and though the city of Jerusalem escaped destruction, Hezekiah was forced once again to recognize Assyria as his master.

Such, in short, were the circumstances through which Micah lived and ministered. They were troubled times in the Middle East, and the fate and survival of the two Hebrew kingdoms hung in the balance. While Micah was still a young prophet, the kingdom of Israel came to an end; Judah survived, though only in a broken and servile condition. And Micah ministered to the people of Judah, addressing both the international crisis of the age and the internal chaos of his nation. We need to recreate in our minds something of the terror of those times if we are to grasp the urgency and power of Micah's message. He was a prophet to a nation in crisis.

THE SINS OF TWO CITIES

Micah 1:2–9

2Hear, you peoples, all of you;
 hearken, O earth, and all that is in it;
 and let the Lord God be a witness against you,
  the Lord from his holy temple.
3For behold, the Lord is coming forth out of his place,
 and will come down and tread upon the high places of the earth.
4And the mountains will melt under him
 and the valleys will be cleft,
 like wax before the fire,
  like waters poured down a steep place.
5All this is for the transgression of Jacob
 and for the sins of the house of Israel.
 What is the transgression of Jacob?
  Is it not Samaria?
 And what is the sin of the house of Judah?
  Is it not Jerusalem?
6Therefore I will make Samaria a heap in the open country,
 a place for planting vineyards;
 and I will pour down her stones into the valley,
  and uncover her foundations.

⁷All her images shall be beaten to pieces,
  all her hires shall be burned with fire,
  and all her idols I will lay waste;
 for from the hire of a harlot she gathered them,
  and to the hire of a harlot they shall return.

⁸For this I will lament and wail;
  I will go stripped and naked;
 I will make lamentation like the jackals,
  and mourning like the ostriches.
⁹For her wound is incurable;
  and it has come to Judah,
 it has reached to the gate of my people,
  to Jerusalem.

The first words that a person speaks create in our minds a deep
and continuing impression of that person's character. We cannot
be sure that these verses contain the first words of Micah's public
ministry, though it is evident that they come from early in his
ministry (before the defeat of Samaria in 722 B.C.). It is clear,
nevertheless, that these opening verses of the book have been
deliberately placed at the head to give us some clear idea of the
substance and tenor of Micah's preaching.

He has a gift with language, articulating clearly and effectively
the substance of his message. And he has the skills of an orator,
first wooing his audience into accepting his line of thought and
then confronting them dramatically with his challenge. He speaks
first his own words as a prophet (verses 2–5), and then explicitly
states the divine words, couched in the first person singular
(verses 6–9). As in other prophetic books, the personal prophetic
word and the direct, divine oracle are intermixed, so that both
directly and indirectly through his servant, God addresses his
people. And the message here declared by the prophet has
several significant themes running through it.

(i) *The nature of God.* Micah begins with a description of the
advent of God to his world that is both cosmic and international in
scope. Although he is addressing specifically the citizens of
Jerusalem, rhetorically he invites all "peoples" (i.e. nations,

verse 2), indeed the whole earth, to listen to what he has to say.
And he invites them all to listen, because God is coming as the
Lord and Judge of all nations to exercise his judgment. Metaphorically, Micah has adapted the language of the law courts to
his purpose; as a judge comes to his court, so too God comes to
his world to exercise judgment on the earth's nations. And his
coming is accompanied by all the phenomena of theophany: the
mountains melt beneath him and the valleys split open at his
presence (verse 4).

In these opening verses (2–4), Micah demonstrates both his
conception of God and his skill as an orator. His conception of
God is cosmic; he is not merely Lord of Judah and Israel, but God
of all nations and the entire earth. And God's universal dominion
entitles him to act as Judge of all the earth. But this conception of
God is used to good purpose; Micah's audience, hearing the
initial words, would no doubt have nodded their approval: God
was indeed universal and had every right to judge the nations.
Having won the initial approval of his audience, Micah then turns
the tables: the Judge of all nations has come to judge Israel and
Judah. Those in the audience who have acknowledged the divine
right to judge the nations cannot now deny God's right to judge
the chosen people.

But what is most remarkable about Micah's conception of God
in these opening verses is the grand vision incorporated within it.
The members of his audience knew that they lived in troubled
times, but they could not see beyond the immediate political and
international crises. They believed in God, but could not trace
the movements of the divine hand in the troubled circumstances
of their time. Micah saw more than did his contemporaries. When
he heard the daily news and observed the events taking place in
his and neighbouring nations, he saw what the unaided eye cannot perceive by itself, that God was moving in judgment. And
one of the things that Micah has to teach us is that lying behind the
internal and international crises of our own times, the sovereign
God is at work.

(ii) *The pattern of divine judgment*. Micah's audience would
have been unsettled by the shift in focus from the international

scene to the more immediate perspective of Judah and Israel. The substance of the prophet's remarks would have been even more unnerving. The principle was clear and well established: sin and transgression culminate in judgment (verse 5). The sins of the two capital cities typified the sins of the two nations; judgment must therefore follow.

But the general message of judgment is given a tone of immediacy by the specific reference to Samaria in verses 6–7, which is expressed as God's own words in the first person. Samaria was an impressive city, having been built by King Omri on a hill, some 300 feet high, set in the midst of the plain of Esdraelon. Yet this impressive city on a hill, noted for its beauty and military strength, would soon be little more than a tell, a hill hiding the remnants of a dead city. The stones of the city walls would topple down into the valley; another generation would come and plant vineyards on the deserted slopes of the hillside.

Micah's words are, on the one hand, a prophecy of the imminent destruction of Samaria, a prophecy that was to be fulfilled dramatically in 722 B.C. when the Assyrian armies destroyed the northern capital. And the hard-nosed realism of this prophecy would have been easily detected by Micah's audience. Samaria had been involved in rebellion against the Assyrians; retribution was inevitable. And Samaria lay north of Jerusalem, lying squarely in the path of any advancing army of Assyria. One did not need to be a prophet to see that Samaria's days were numbered. What Micah saw, and his audience did not, was that Samaria's fall would be God's doing; the Assyrian armies would merely be God's instrument. And what Micah also saw was that Samaria's fate must also be Jerusalem's fate eventually. Judgment was a consequence of sin; that divinely-established pattern must mean that Jerusalem's days were also numbered, at least for as long as Jerusalem, like Samaria, continued in the pursuit of sin.

The pattern that sin must be followed by judgment was there for all to see, yet Micah was one of the few to see it. And like Micah's audience, we can detect the pattern more easily in other generations than in our own, and more easily in other lives than in our own life. But the judgment declared for Samaria has a message, for those who would hear it, not confined to its own time and its immediate environment.

(iii) *The divine agony* (verses 8–9). The note of impending judgment, with which Micah's message begins, could give to the reader a lop-sided impression of God. The judgmental theme may imply only a harsh God, working out through the currents of human history the divine and wrathful purpose. But the closing verses of this opening oracle set a different perspective. They are still expressed in the first person, as were verses 6–7, indicating that God is still the speaker. And they present a quite different picture of God from that which is explicit in the preceding verses.

The God who was first presented as the majestic Judge of the earth's nations (verses 3–4) is now depicted as one distraught with grief. Stripped of formal attire, he goes about in grief and lament. The cries that escape his lips are like the eerie howls of the jackals that travel by night in packs, searching for prey. His lament is like the strange cry of the ostrich (or perhaps the owl: the meaning of the Hebrew word is uncertain), expressive of a pain that is beyond words. And the divine agony, as Micah portrays it, is on behalf of Judah and Jerusalem; God can see clearly enough the end to which his people's sins inevitably propel them. Though he is the agent of judgment, it gives him no pleasure. And thus the prophet draws back a little the veil that hides the face of God. The agony of God's grief is rooted in God's love, for he desires only good for his people. As Ezekiel was to say to a subsequent generation: "As I live, says the Lord God, I have no pleasure in the death of the wicked" (33:11). If we are to understand Micah correctly, we must keep in mind this opening vision of God. He is on the one hand the Lord of judgment, but he is also the one distraught with grief at the possibility that the judgment announced could become a present reality. And no doubt this inner tension had also become a part of Micah's character; the stern announcement of judgment following upon sin was penetrated with that same divine grief that is rooted in love.

A GAZETTEER OF JUDGMENT

Micah 1:10–16

> [10]Tell it not in Gath,
> weep not at all;
> in Beth-le-aphrah
> roll yourselves in the dust.
> [11]Pass on your way,
> inhabitants of Shaphir,
> in nakedness and shame;
> the inhabitants of Zaanan
> do not come forth;
> the wailing of Beth-ezel
> shall take away from you its standing place.
> [12]For the inhabitants of Maroth
> wait anxiously for good,
> because evil has come down from the Lord
> to the gate of Jerusalem.
> [13]Harness the steeds to the chariots,
> inhabitants of Lachish;
> you were the beginning of sin
> to the daughter of Zion,
> for in you were found
> the transgressions of Israel.
> [14]Therefore you shall give parting gifts
> to Moresheth-gath;
> the houses of Achzib shall be a deceitful thing
> to the kings of Israel.
> [15]I will again bring a conqueror upon you,
> inhabitants of Mareshah;
> the glory of Israel
> shall come to Adullam.
> [16]Make yourselves bald and cut off your hair,
> for the children of your delight;
> make yourselves as bald as the eagle,
> for they shall go from you into exile.

This second example that we are given of Micah's preaching continues the tone and themes of the first. The prophet is still speaking of judgment, and though he describes it in the terms of towns and villages to the south and west of Jerusalem, he still seems to be addressing the citizens of the capital city. His purpose in this gazetteer of judgment is not entirely morbid; Micah hopes to awaken in his audience an awareness of the critical times in which they live and thus precipitate a return to the true faith in God. The date of this oracle is uncertain, though it would appear to be much later than the first. If it is correct to interpret the verses as *anticipating* the judgment of towns and villages listed, then it should be dated somewhere in the period 720 to 710 B.C., either late in the reign of Ahaz, or early in the reign of Hezekiah. The external threat at that time was represented by the Assyrian emperor, Sargon. On the other hand, since almost all of the towns and villages listed here were destroyed during Sennacherib's military invasion of Judah in 701 B.C., it is possible (though less probable) that the message may come from that later period.

As a general rule, the reader of the English Bible is not at a serious disadvantage by virtue of not knowing the original languages of Scripture; modern translations of the Bible, such as the RSV, have been excellently done. But there are parts of the biblical text which cannot be translated without losing some of their original power and effect, and these verses (1:10–16) are an example of that disadvantage. Micah, in listing various towns and villages, employs puns and word plays. Sometimes it is the sound of the place name he plays with, sometimes the meaning of the name. And such puns and word plays cannot be translated; in English, the translation may be correct, but the power has been lost.

An analogy may help to illustrate the style of Micah's speech in these verses. Had he been a Scottish prophet, speaking to a Scottish audience of the judgment coming to their native towns and villages, he might have said something like this:

> Crieff will know grief. Forfar will forfeit. Craill will be frail. Wick will be burned. Stornoway will be blown away. Edinburgh will be no Eden. For Tain, there will only be pain.

I cannot claim for the analogy the artistic merit of Micah, but it illustrates, nevertheless, the prophet's use of language. For some towns, he uses a pun, for others a play on the sound of the town's name, for yet others he draws out the meaning implicit in the name as such. And the listing of the names one by one would catch the attention of his audience: the words would easily stick in their minds, as familiar names were delivered in striking phrases. But, of course, the prophet's purpose was a deeper one. If the basic message of judgment were communicated, then perhaps the audience would also perceive Jerusalem's danger and turn back to the faith in God.

Space does not permit an elaboration on each pun and word play; a couple of illustrations will suffice. (a) "In Beth-le-Aphrah, roll yourselves in the dust" (verse 10). The place name means "House of Dust", and the word play, rolling in dust, points to coming mourning as a consequence of judgment. (b) "The houses of Achzib shall be a deceitful thing" (verse 14). *Achzib*, in Hebrew, means "lying, deceitful". In this manner, Micah takes his audience on an imaginary tour of the towns and villages of the Shephelah, the region of Judah lying west of the mountainous central region of the land and east of the coastal plain. And the sheer number of the towns and villages referred to must have had a chilling effect on the audience; the anticipated judgment would be very extensive.

The climax of the prophet's message is reached in verse 16. Addressing now the citizens of Jerusalem, he invites them to lament for their "children", namely the towns and villages that looked to Jerusalem as their capital city. But, by implication, they were to lament not only for others, but also for themselves, for the fate of the capital city was to be seen clearly in that of its satellite cities. Without its satellites, Jerusalem would no longer be a capital. Thus does Micah, who came from the region described in his own gazetteer of judgment, communicate to the citizens of Jerusalem their own impending fate. And he does so in a way that illustrates the importance of the regions to the nation's centre; when the regions were gone, there could be no centre.

Although these verses express the same general message of judgment as do 1:2–9, they shed nevertheless at least two new rays of light on the overall situation.

(i) *Judgment is close at hand.* In the prophet's earlier ministry (1:2–9), he had indicated that Samaria's fate would eventually also be Jerusalem's fate. The passage of time had shown clearly enough what Samaria's fate had been: total defeat and disaster. And now the prophet indicates that judgment is even closer to hand; Samaria was in a neighbouring nation, but the towns and villages listed here were actually in the territory of Judah, on Jerusalem's very doorstep. As the end was coming bit by bit to other places, inevitably it was drawing closer to Jerusalem.

And yet the sense of judgment's progress between these two messages in chapter 1 is essentially a sign of God's mercy and long-suffering. A decade or two had passed from the time of the prophet's first preaching to that contained in verses 10–16; still God warned his people, but still the judgment had not come. Just as in the first oracle the agony of God revealed his love for his people, so in these verses the long-suffering and patience of God reveal the persistence of his love. Judgment is a natural and inevitable response to sin, but the delay in judgment may be a sign of God's mercy and desire that judgment be averted.

(ii) Between 1:2–9 and 1:10–16 a period of one or two decades of the prophet's ministry has been telescoped. We can read the chapter in a few minutes, but lying behind the words are years of faithful service and ministry. We do not know the circumstances of Micah's life during this period, as we do for other prophets such as Jeremiah. We may surmise that it was not an easy life, and that Micah had to learn his own patience and long-suffering. In a strange way, one of the more heroic aspects of Micah's book is that he tells us so little about himself. He is not concerned to perpetuate his own memory in the pages of human history, but only to be faithful in his service of God. That faithfulness was to be found in declaring God's word, from one decade to another. And while we, the readers of his words, may sense the growing momentum of judgment, we cannot so easily grasp the weeks and years of faithful service lying behind the written word.

A WORD OF WOE TO THE WICKED

Micah 2:1–5

> [1]Woe to those who devise wickedness
>   and work evil upon their beds!
>   When the morning dawns, they perform it,
>   because it is in the power of their hand.
> [2]They covet fields, and seize them;
>   and houses, and take them away;
>   they oppress a man and his house,
>   a man and his inheritance.
> [3]Therefore thus says the Lord:
>   Behold, against this family I am devising evil,
>   from which you cannot remove your necks;
>   and you shall not walk haughtily,
>   for it will be an evil time.
> [4]In that day they shall take up a taunt song against you,
>   and wail with bitter lamentation,
>   and say, "We are utterly ruined;
>   he changes the portion of my people;
>   how he removes it from me!
>   Among our captors he divides our fields."
> [5]Therefore you will have none to cast the line by lot
>   in the assembly of the Lord.

The general themes of the prophet's preaching, as illustrated in the two oracles contained in chapter 1, are now supplemented by an example of the prophet's preaching that is much more specific. Micah addresses a particular group of people, the wealthy landowners, and identifies a particular crime, the illegal appropriation of land. Finally, he specifies what would be the divine punishment on the perpetrators of the crime. The date of this oracle cannot be determined with precision; it may nevertheless be dated generally in the reign of Jotham or Ahaz, and the oracle typifies one of the major social thrusts of Micah's ministry.

(i) *The crime* (verses 1–2). The crime begins with coveting and culminates in the appropriation of farm lands and estates.

The criminals are described in colourful terms. At night, when decent folk are sleeping, they lie in their beds working out schemes by which they can increase their land-holdings. Then they are up at the crack of dawn, and they have the power and influence to convert their nocturnal schemes into daytime practice. They are hungry for land, fields and houses, because land represents both power and wealth. And only one thing stands in the way of further acquisitions: the owner of the land! But owners can be bullied, cheated, and oppressed, until at last they are willing to turn over their land for a song. And the greater one's holdings of land, the easier it is to acquire more. It is a crime both ancient and modern to which Micah points the finger of condemnation: in all ages, from Micah's to our own, men and women have hungered for land and gold, as the two possessions which seem to offer the most enduring worth.

The prophet's condemnation of the crime is uttered fearlessly; he does not hesitate to call it what it is, "wickedness" and "evil" (verse 1). And perhaps his background in the country region of Moresheth gave him particularly acute insight into the nature of the crime and its social consequences. In the city of Jerusalem, it may have seemed simply to be the operation of big business: wealthy men were increasing their land-holdings. But in Moresheth and the country towns, it was oppression, not business. The small landowner, who could provide for himself and his family, was suddenly destitute. Where once he was self-sufficient, he now became dependent on others, his livelihood lost to the unscrupulous dealers in real estate. And the small landowner lost not only his own livelihood, but also his "inheritance" (verse 2), that which he might have bequeathed to his children for their future support and survival. What we see condensed into these verses is one of the signs of the breakdown of Judah's social structure. The greed of the wealthy created a category of "new poor". A section of society that once fended for itself now could no longer do so; the nation's socio-economic foundation was crumbling.

(ii) *The punishment* (verses 3–5). The punishment, expressed as the direct words of God, expressly matched the crime. Just as the land barons dreamed their expansionary dreams at night, so too was the Lord devising an appropriate recompense for them. The nature of the recompense appears in the words of the taunt-song incorporated in verse 4. Those who had acquired wealth and power by taking land from others would lose it just as quickly when their land was taken from them. The divine agent of judgment was God, but Micah appears to envisage a foreign enemy, presumably the Assyrians, as the immediate instrument through whom the lands would be removed from the wealthy. And there is an irony in the judgment: to paraphrase, the wealthy land-owners will complain at their judgment: "Look at what's happening! These foreigners are taking our lands and dividing them up among themselves! How can God let them do that?" And the wealthy landowners would not only lose their immediate holdings in land, but would also forfeit any future rights to land in Israel, as is implied by the somewhat obscure substance of verse 5.

The punishment is not only suitable to the crime by virtue of being the same in kind, but also because it hurts the criminals at their most vulnerable point. Those who had a desperate greed for land and power had made their personal goals a kind of god. And those who would worship land in its acquisition would also learn the emptiness of land in its loss.

(iii) *The moral.* The moral, stated simply, is that the punishment fits the crime. But Micah's words go deeper than that; for he has placed his finger not only on the pulse of his own times, but also of the times in which we live. Human beings are by definition mortal and impermanent, and yet all have a deep-seated desire within for permanence, for a sense of belonging in this world. This desire is not in itself wrong; it is part and parcel of the human condition and is recognized frequently in the Bible. The importance of land runs throughout the Old Testament story. The patriachs longed for a land of their own. During the Hebrew kingdoms, the people possessed their own land for a while. In the exile, they mourned for a land from which they were cut off.

Land not only provided a sense of permanence, of belonging in this world, but it also made possible survival: land provided the sustenance by which life could be maintained. The complexity of modern society is such that it is easy to forget that life, in the last resort, depends upon the land, upon the crops and cattle that provide our essential foodstuffs. And yet it is most commonly among the city-dwellers, those without land in the true sense, that the hunger for land may grow. And what starts as a natural desire, rooted deep in the complexity of the human soul, may quickly grow to greed; once exercised, the greed may become an uncontrollable force. The desire for land grows insatiably, though one is rarely healthier or happier for its possession. It was evident in Micah's time, and a reading of human history will reveal the same tortuous trait in human nature in most epochs, and in most regions of the world. At a national level, the desire for the acquisition of land has been the cause of many wars. At a more individual level, the desire for land may be seen to have shaped much of the development and settlement of North America. And at a social level, the rapacious greed for land has been a frequent cause of social collapse and the decline of nations.

All this underlies Micah's message. He is not in any sense a socialist, though he speaks fearlessly against the wealthy land-grabbers of his time. He is concerned primarily with justice in society and perceives clearly enough that covetousness and oppression are forms of sickness undermining a society's health. But his social critique is balanced by a theological critique. He does not merely point out that the actions of wealthy land acquirers undermine the fabric of society. He also asserts that such actions invite, indeed demand, the judgment of God. And the shape of judgment is such that it shatters the illusions of those who think that the possession of land can impart permanence to the citizens of this world.

ON PREACHING AND PREACHERS

Micah 2:6–13

> [6]"Do not preach"—thus they preach—
>   "one should not preach of such things;
>   disgrace will not overtake us."

⁷Should this be said, O house of Jacob?
   Is the Spirit of the Lord impatient?
   Are these his doings?
 Do not my words do good
   to him who walks uprightly?
⁸But you rise against my people as an enemy;
   you strip the robe from the peaceful,
 from those who pass by trustingly
   with no thought of war.
⁹The women of my people you drive out
   from their pleasant houses;
 from their young children you take away
   my glory for ever.
¹⁰Arise and go,
   for this is no place to rest;
 because of uncleanness that destroys
   with a grievous destruction.
¹¹If a man should go about and utter wind and lies,
   saying, "I will preach to you of wine and strong drink,"
   he would be the preacher for this people!

¹²I will surely gather all of you, O Jacob,
   I will gather the remnant of Israel;
 I will set them together
   like sheep in a fold,
 like a flock in its pasture,
   a noisy multitude of men.
¹³He who opens the breach will go up before them;
   they will break through and pass the gate,
   going out by it.
 Their king will pass on before them,
   the Lord at their head.

It is not possible to preach with Micah's bluntness without evoking some sort of opposition. We may suppose that the wealthy
landowners, discomfited by the open criticism of their business
dealings, did their utmost to muzzle Micah. But the best way to
deal with a preacher is to set other preachers upon him. And lying
behind verses 6–11, we must imagine the confrontation between
Micah and the false prophets, each in their preaching contradict-

ing the other. The false prophets were apparently in alliance with
the landowners. And the latter, in turn, must have reasoned: "If
one man's preaching can cause such difficulty, let us finance a
dozen preachers who can support us in our endeavours!"

Thus Micah is faced with a double task. Not only must he
continue his ministry against the wealthy and their comrades who
would exploit the poor and extol injustice; he must also cope with
the army of preachers whose public proclamations supported
their patrons. In verses 6–11, we have an example of this double
thrust in Micah's ministry. First, he engages in combat with the
false prophets, showing the shallowness of their preaching
(verses 6–7, 11). Second, he continues to preach against the
patrons of the false prophets, whose acts of oppression must be
identified (verses 8–9) and whose judgment must be announced
(verse 10). The chapter concludes with a short and separate
oracle (verses 12–13), which is not directly related to the preceding verses; rather, it rounds out the cross-section of Micah's
preaching which has been provided in chapters 1–2.

(i) *False preaching* (verses 6–7, 11). There are some difficulties with respect to the translation and punctuation of verses
6–7, and hence some uncertainty with respect to the precise
meaning. As rendered in the RSV, the sense seems to be as
follows. The message of the false preachers is summarized in
verse 6; Micah's response is given in verse 7. Finally, in verse 11,
Micah's scathing summary of the value of the false prophets is
stated.

The essence of the false preaching of Micah's opponents can be
reduced to two elements. First, they attempted to silence him:
"Do not preach . . . ." Second, they sought to counter Micah's
message by offering the solace of their own half-baked platitudes:
"disgrace will not overtake us." False prophets, realizing full well
that their source of income was their wealthy patrons, had a duty
to try to silence any whose words would make their masters
unhappy. The essence of true prophecy was the declaration of the
word of the Lord; the substance of false prophecy was the proclamation of the words of the prophet's masters. But the credi-
bility of the false prophets was to be found in the fact that much of
what they said was true, albeit a half-truth. They were quick to

mention and stress the ancient promises of blessing God had given to his people; they failed to mention that the promised blessing was contingent upon obedience and righteousness. The false prophets served their masters well; the great land barons were consoled by sermons suggesting their wealth was a sign of God's blessing, but their paid preachers were wise enough never to choose "justice" or "righteousness" as the text of their sermons.

False prophets with their feeble preaching will ever be with us. And though Micah had no difficulty in identifying them, they are not always easy to discern. They can quote Scripture glibly along with the best masters of the pulpit, and their words offer soothing consolation. But ultimately they offer only a placebo; they have no medicine for the soul. As Micah has it, they "utter wind and lies" (verse 11); they might as well be advocates of booze and drunkenness for all the good they do, but they are more subtle, veiling their platitudes with pious words and biblical quotations. But in the last resort, false preaching can only prosper where people want to hear it. The success of the confidence trickster is always rooted in the greed of his victim; likewise, the popularity of the false preacher springs from the evil within those who love to hear his words.

(ii) *True preaching* (verses 8–10). Micah now returns to his principal theme, the critique of the land barons and their oppression of the weak. By their actions, they have become an enemy of the people of God (verse 8); none are safe from their avaricious designs. Peaceful citizens find that they have lost their cloak, a garment by day and a blanket by night. (The allusion is no doubt to the practice of lending money to a poor person and taking the borrower's cloak as collateral. But the law required the cloak to be returned to the person at night, see Deuteronomy 24:10–13; the critique of Micah suggests an abuse of the ancient law.) Women, probably widows, were driven from their homes when their property passed to the hands of purchasers; young children, innocent of all that was going on, lost forever their "glory", namely the inheritance of land that should by right have been theirs.

Having once again documented the misdeeds, Micah continues as before to specify the nature of God's judgment (verse 10). Those who by their actions had made others leave their homes would be required to "arise and go". The greed of the land-grabbers did not only destroy others, widows and children, but would eventually return in the divine scheme of things to destroy themselves.

What is most striking about this example of Micah's preaching is that it has retained its full vigour, losing none of the sharp ring of truth. It is presented in the context of opposition, both from the wealthy and their false prophets. But where a timid preacher might back down in the face of opposition, or soften his statements somewhat, Micah continues boldly to proclaim an unadulterated truth. He will not weaken the word, for it is God's word. He will not cease from preaching while injustice continues to flourish. He will not desist while the weak members of this society continue to be exploited. Thus, not least of the hallmarks of true preaching is that it is delivered with courage. The preacher of the truth seeks only God's approval and cannot be swayed by the reaction and opposition to his words.

(iii) *Preaching on future hope* (verses 12–13). As has been noted, the two concluding verses in chapter 2 are not directly related to the preceding passage. Rather, these verses round out the anthology of Micah's preaching contained in the first two chapters of the book. In all probability, these verses reflect a later period in Micah's ministry than the preceding passages; they presuppose a date around 701 B.C. in the time of Sennacherib's ruthless military expedition into Judah (see further the commentary on 1:1). Although the verses have a messianic ring to them (and sometimes have been interpreted in this light), their focus initially was more immediate. When the disaster of judgment came, nevertheless, a remnant would be spared; they would huddle in the fortress of Jerusalem to which they had fled, and the enemy would be kept at bay. Eventually, when the enemy departed, the survivors would come out of the city again, their king passing out before them (verse 12).

This theme from Micah's preaching illustrates a more pastoral perspective, namely God's care for his people even in a time of disaster. The prophet had little that was positive to say in his condemnation of the nation as a whole and his critique of injustice and oppression. But the wrath of God against the wicked was continually balanced by his concern for the oppressed. The wealthy landowners, as a consequence of their evil, would take to the road of exile; but those who had remained faithful would experience God's protection and compassion in the coming trial. The word of condemnation and the word of consolation go hand in hand, but consolation may only be heard by those who have retained their trust in God.

THE CENTRALITY OF JUSTICE

Micah 3:1–12

¹And I said:
  Hear, you heads of Jacob
    and rulers of the house of Israel!
  Is it not for you to know justice?—
    ²you who hate the good and love the evil,
  who tear the skin from off my people,
    and their flesh from off their bones;
³who eat the flesh of my people,
    and flay their skin from off them,
  and break their bones in pieces,
    and chop them up like meat in a kettle,
    like flesh in a cauldron.

⁴Then they will cry to the Lord,
    but he will not answer them;
  he will hide his face from them at that time,
    because they have made their deeds evil.

⁵Thus says the Lord concerning the prophets
    who lead my people astray,
  who cry "Peace"
    when they have something to eat,
  but declare war against him
    who puts nothing into their mouths.

⁶Therefore it shall be night to you, without vision,
and darkness to you, without divination.
The sun shall go down upon the prophets,
and the day shall be black over them;
⁷the seers shall be disgraced,
and the diviners put to shame;
they shall all cover their lips,
for there is no answer from God.
⁸But as for me, I am filled with power,
with the Spirit of the Lord,
and with justice and might,
to declare to Jacob his transgression
and to Israel his sin.

⁹Hear this, you heads of the house of Jacob
and rulers of the house of Israel,
who abhor justice
and pervert all equity,
¹⁰who build Zion with blood
and Jerusalem with wrong.
¹¹Its heads give judgment for a bribe,
its priests teach for hire,
its prophets divine for money;
yet they lean upon the Lord and say,
"Is not the Lord in the midst of us?
No evil shall come upon us."
¹²Therefore because of you
Zion shall be ploughed as a field;
Jerusalem shall become a heap of ruins,
and the mountain of the house a wooded height.

Justice is the mortar which holds together the structure of human society. In Micah's day, the structures were falling apart, chaos was in ascendancy, and underlying the whole shambles was the triumph of injustice. "Justice," Disraeli said in a speech to the House of Commons (1851), "is truth in action." Injustice, as Micah saw so clearly, was falsity in action throughout every key realm of society. And so, not unnaturally, the polarity of justice and injustice was a central theme in the prophet's preaching. It was not enough to condemn specific crimes, such as the un-scrupulous acquisition of land by the powerful and wealthy; it was also essential to address the fundamental structures of his society which should have checked and controlled such iniquitous acts.

We are provided in this chapter with three short samples of Micah's preaching on this theme, each linked by the key word *justice* (verses 1, 8, 9). First, he addresses the administration of justice in the courts (verses 1–4); second, he speaks of the absence of justice in the ministry of false prophets (verses 5–8); and finally he examines the theme of justice with respect to the actions of Judah's government as a whole (verses 9–12). These oracles from Micah's prophetic ministry are to be dated in the early years of the reign of King Hezekiah. It is not certain, but it is possible, that they were in some measure influential in precipitat-ing Hezekiah's various reforms.

(i) *The absence of justice in the courts* (verses 1–4). In prin-ciple, justice should be the norm by which a society functions; when an act of injustice occurs, it ought to be possible for a plaintiff to take his case to court and seek the restoration of justice. Thus, in Micah's time, a person whose land had been unjustly appropriated ought to have had access to Judah's courts, there to seek the return of what was rightfully his own. But when the courts are corrupt, when injustice becomes the norm of legal activity, there can be no protection for the weak, and justice itself dies a natural death. Such was the situation in Micah's Jerusalem: the cancer of injustice had spread from the market-place to the courtroom. The wealthy and powerful could buy the "justice" they wanted; for the poor and weak, only injustice was dispensed.

Micah's critique is scathing: the persons who should have known justice and operated according to its principles (verse 1), in reality hated what was good and loved what was evil (verse 2). In a blood-curdling metaphor, Micah caricatures the actions of the officers of the courts: they were hungry butchers, skinning the flesh of the weak for a tasty morsel to eat, breaking their bones and popping them into the stock pot to prepare a tasty soup. The officers of the court had no concern for others, no passion for justice; the horizon of their ambitions was merely to fulfil their own hungers and desires. And so the prophet declares a word of judgment (verse 4), in which again it is clear that the punishment will fit the crime and justice will eventually be done. When the time of judgment finally came, they would cry to God for mercy, but would receive no answer, just as they themselves had failed to respond to the cries for justice uttered in their courts of lawlessness. But there is a twist in the judgment. When the judges refused to hear the pleas of the oppressed, they were acting unjustly; when God refused to hear their pleas, he would be acting in full justice.

There is an underlying current of passion running through Micah's words to the officers of the law. In part, his passion was rooted in concern for the plight of the poor and oppressed, but it runs deeper than that. God was by nature a God of justice; the covenant people could only survive if they extolled justice in their community. The decline of justice in any human society is like the declining pulse of a gravely ill patient; when the pulse of justice is finally lost, the society dies. Micah perceived that the departure of justice from his nation's courts was a sign of the end, as it must be for any nation that abandons justice.

(ii) *The absence of justice in the popular prophets* (verses 5–8). Just as the people of Micah's time turned to the courts for justice, so too they turned to the prophets for guidance in their daily lives. They should have been able to approach the prophets, seeking through them to hear God's word. But the clergy had become as corrupt as the judiciary. Those who paid the prophet a hefty fee would hear a pleasant word from God: "Peace. Everything will be just fine!" But the poor, unable to meet the prophet's insatiable desire for profit, would be met with angry and abusive words (verse 5).

Micah therefore condemns the false prophets. His condemnation makes it clear that he does not doubt their vocation, does not question their gift of prophecy. Rather, he condemns the abuse of the prophetic vocation, the prostitution of the divine gift to personal and profitable ends. The divine judgment would take the form of the cancellation of the prophetic gift. No more the visions of night-time, no more the divination that penetrated future darkness, no more the honour of office, but finally only disgrace and shame, as clients asked for a word from God, but no word could be given (verses 6–7). In contrast, Micah affirmed that his own prophetic word was marked by God's power and spirit; in justice, he spoke to Israel of its injustice. He was not boasting, but rather was affirming the integrity of his ministry when faced with a plethora of false prophecy.

The notion of approaching a prophet to ask for a word from God may seem somehow alien to us in the 20th century, but we must not forget that the people of Micah's time had no Bible, no written Word to which to turn and seek divine guidance. The prophets fulfilled that role. It was an essential role, not to be condemned; what Micah condemns is the thoroughgoing injustice of limiting access to the Word of God only to those rich enough to pay for it. In this and a multitude of other ways, legitimate vocation may be converted into illegitimate trade. It is not only the members of the judiciary that are vulnerable to corruption; the clergy are equally vulnerable, and their perversion is no less an act of injustice.

(iii) *The absence of justice in government* (verses 9–12). Now the scope of Micah's denunciation is broadened to incorporate all aspects of Judah's government. Injustice was rampant among the rulers, among the judges, among the priests, and among the prophets. The judges hated justice. The members of government embarked on expansionary building programmes, but they built "with blood" (verse 10), their funds and labour extorted from the poor and weak. Priests were supposed to offer instruction, but they converted their vocation into a well-paid profession, teaching only those who could afford to pay. Prophets, as we have already seen (verses 5–8), sold their services to wealthy clients. And yet, despite this pervasive sickness of injustice, all was done beneath the smug shield of religious hypocrisy: "Is not the Lord in the midst of us?" (verse 11*b*). So again Micah announces judgment: Jerusalem, like Samaria before it (1:6), would become a heap of ruins. The city that had become the world's capital of injustice did not deserve to survive.

If we read these four verses casually, we may fail to perceive the reaction they must have caused in Jerusalem. The people thus condemned so forcibly in public would hardly have welcomed Micah's message. Indeed, we may speculate that attempts were made to silence the prophet. But Hezekiah, at least, had wisdom and attempted to respond to the prophetic ministry. Nevertheless, Micah's preaching caused such a commotion in Jerusalem that it was remembered clearly by the city's inhabitants a century later in the time of Jeremiah (26:17–19). Despite the absence of historical information in the Book of Micah, the incident summarized in Jeremiah gives us some clue as to the effectiveness and difficulty of the prophet's work in Jerusalem.

I began this section of commentary with a quotation of Benjamin Disraeli and will end it in the same way. Addressing the House of Commons in 1871, he said, "We have legalized confiscation, consecrated sacrilege, and condoned high treason." One suspects that he was familiar with Micah! But injustice was not peculiar to Micah's age; it is a disease which would permeate every age and every segment of human society, and which must by every means be eliminated.

SWORDS INTO PLOUGHSHARES

Micah 4:1–5

1It shall come to pass in the latter days
    that the mountain of the house of the Lord
shall be established as the highest of the mountains,
    and shall be raised up above the hills;
and peoples shall flow to it,
2   and many nations shall come, and say:
"Come, let us go up to the mountain of the Lord,
    to the house of the God of Jacob;
that he may teach us his ways
    and we may walk in his paths."
For out of Zion shall go forth the law,
    and the word of the Lord from Jerusalem.

³He shall judge between many peoples,
   and shall decide for strong nations afar off;
and they shall beat their swords into ploughshares,
   and their spears into pruning hooks;
nation shall not lift up sword against nation,
   neither shall they learn war any more;
⁴but they shall sit every man under his vine and under his fig tree,
   and none shall make them afraid;
   for the mouth of the Lord of hosts has spoken.

⁵For all the peoples walk
   each in the name of its god,
but we will walk in the name of the Lord our God
   for ever and ever.

From time to time, as one browses through the multitudinous writings that comprise the literature of the human race, one comes across a passage that is so striking in its vision and its distillation of human hope, that immediately it becomes a classic. These five verses in Micah belong to that rare category of literature; they contain such a vision of the world as it might be that, from Micah's day to our own, the words have continued to capture human imagination. And thus it is initially a little disturbing to discover that there can be no certainty concerning whether Micah actually wrote these words. The same passage occurs in Isaiah (2:2–4), virtually identical but for the fact that Isaiah has no counterpart to Micah's verse 4. And in a later age, the passage was still well known, as is evident from Joel's adaptation of verse 3 (Joel 3:10). Did Micah write the words, only to be quoted by Isaiah? Or did Micah quote Isaiah? Or did both quote from some more ancient source, perhaps a no longer extant psalm similar to Psalm 46:8–10? We cannot be certain, though the third possibility is most likely. But from the substance of the passage we can see clearly enough why both prophets should have desired to use it.

Micah ministered during a time in history characterized both by the threat of war and the awful reality of warfare. And in the preceding passage, he had spoken of the destruction of Jerusalem as an act of divine judgment (3:12). Now either Micah or his editor has juxtaposed a passage that reveals the other face of the coin that was Jerusalem's future. The city of Jerusalem deserved judgment, given the evil actions of its government; yet in the more distant future, Jerusalem could become the capital of a new kind of world order.

The vision is set in the "latter days" (verse 1), an unspecified time in the remote future. The visionary canvas is dominated by a mountain on which is set the "house of the Lord", the perpetual symbol of God's presence in the world. And from every corner of the landscape representatives of the world's nations approach the mountain of the Lord, there to ask instruction concerning the way in which they must walk. From the mountain the law is issued, namely God's word by which human beings and nations may be instructed concerning how to live. And that law in turn precipitates a revolution in human society: the instruments of war would be beaten into implements of peace and the nations would practise war no more. The terror of violence and battle would become a thing of the past: "they shall sit every man under his vine and under his fig tree, and none shall make them afraid" (verse 4). In the new world, nations would walk together in harmony, each walking in its own faith, but Israel walking in a renewed faith in its one true God.

One of the reasons for the beauty of this passage is that it is totally out of harmony with the reality of our world, yet fully in harmony with what we would like the world to be. In Micah's time, there was strife within the nation and war without, and yet the longing for peace and harmony did not die. Jerusalem, the "City of Peace", was corrupt, and the object of Micah's prophecies of condemnation. Yet still he could see what it might be—the focal point of peace! And had the vision come to fruition, then the very *raison d'être* of the chosen people would have been fulfilled; all the world's nations would have been blessed through Israel (Genesis 12:3). Thus, we may begin to perceive the reason for Micah's use of these words. He holds out to his people a vision, intending thereby to remind his people of the true purpose for which they had been called. And in a time of hopelessness, he holds out to them hope, affirming with an unshaken faith that, beyond the violent realities of the time, a better world was possible.

We will only grasp and be grasped by these words if we move from the surface to the vision they embody. A few persons of our time have caught the vision: Mahatma Gandhi, Martin Luther King and a few others have glimpsed the world as it might be and allowed the vision to penetrate their efforts to change the world as it is. The vision, if it is truly grasped, must be invigorating, awaking our energy to transform the world that we know. We have not grasped the vision if we simply label it "prophecy", affirming that one day it will certainly come to pass, and perhaps speculating idly on whether it will be in this century or the next. The vision implies action: we must rework our swords into ploughshares.

THE REIGN OF GOD

Micah 4:6–13

⁶In that day, says the Lord,
   I will assemble the lame
and gather those who have been driven away,
   and those whom I have afflicted;
⁷and the lame I will make the remnant;
   and those who were cast off, a strong nation;
and the Lord will reign over them in Mount Zion
   from this time forth and for evermore.

⁸And you, O tower of the flock,
   hill of the daughter of Zion,
to you shall it come,
   the former dominion shall come,
   the kingdom of the daughter of Jerusalem.

⁹Now why do you cry aloud?
   Is there no king in you?
Has your counsellor perished,
   that pangs have seized you like a woman in travail?
¹⁰Writhe and groan, O daughter of Zion,
   like a woman in travail;
for now you shall go forth from the city
   and dwell in the open country;
   you shall go to Babylon.

There you shall be rescued,
>   there the Lord will redeem you
>   from the hand of your enemies.

11Now many nations
>   are assembled against you,
>   saying, "Let her be profaned,
>   and let our eyes gaze upon Zion."
12But they do not know
>   the thoughts of the Lord,
>   they do not understand his plan,
>   that he has gathered them as sheaves to the threshing floor.
13Arise and thresh,
>   O daughter of Zion,
>   for I will make your horn iron
>   and your hoofs bronze;
>   you shall beat in pieces many peoples,
>   and shall devote their gain to the Lord
>   their wealth to the Lord of the whole earth.

During the course of a long life, the thought of a writer or prophet may change. In part, the change is a consequence of the maturing process in the person's mind; in part, it is a result of changes in external circumstances which require a different response from the prophet or writer.

In the verses we are now examining, the change is very evident from the substance of the earlier chapters of Micah. The social critique of the prophet is no longer present; instead, the words have a more futuristic ring to them. Indeed, the change is so substantial that many interpreters claim that these verses (and others in the last chapters of the book) do not contain the authentic words of Micah, but should be interpreted as later editorial additions from a different source. As we shall see, there may be an element of truth in this perspective, but in general it presuposes too rigid and static a view of Micah's thought and preaching. He lived a long life, and a degree of change and development in his thought is to be expected. But more importantly, Micah's world was subject to radical change. Internally, his nation passed

from the relatively positive years of King Jotham to the dark
years of Ahaz; his successor, Hezekiah, set the nation on a more
positive path once again. Externally, too, circumstances were
constantly changing; the threat of war was followed by times of
peace, but by 701 B.C., with the Assyrian armies already in Judah,
and Jerusalem under siege, many must have thought that the end
had finally come. These were the conditions that provided the
context for Micah's thought and preaching; as circumstances
changed, so too did his message, in order that it might meet the
continuing needs of his people.

In this section of the book, we have three short oracles, or
portions of oracles, linked by the common theme of Zion
(Jerusalem). Although we cannot be certain of their authenticity,
there are no compelling reasons for rejecting their origin with the
prophet Micah. The oracles would seem to reflect the period
around 701 B.C., when the citizens of Jerusalem, Micah included,
must have anticipated Jerusalem's final end. In such a dark context, the oracles offer a future hope and vision with respect to the
reign of God. The three units have a generally similar theme, but
differ somewhat in their precise substance.

(i) *The restoration of dominion* (verses 6–8). The point of
reference is an undetermined time in the future: "In that day"
(verse 6), God will restore both his people and his dominion. The
scene depicted in the words is one of post-war chaos; the survivors of conflict are wounded and homeless, the remnant of a
once proud nation. God would take this desperate rabble of
displaced persons and make them once again the citizens of a
strong nation in which the Lord would reign.

The message was one of future hope that made some sense out
of present misery. With the nation in ruins and the capital city
hanging on grimly in its fight to survive, there must have been
many honest souls in Jerusalem who thought that the reign of
God in Judah had come to an end. A once mighty nation had been
reduced to a ragged remnant. But to such dispirited people,
Micah offered a view of the future in which the "former dominion" (verse 8) would return to Jerusalem. It is a common feature
of the prophets that, in the peaceful days of complacency, they

proclaimed judgment, but when judgment came they pointed to a future beyond the awful present, in which God's mercy would be experienced once again.

(ii) *Ruin and redemption* (verses 9–10). The curious feature in these verses is the reference to exile in Babylon (verse 10). Judah's enemy in Micah's time was Assyria, and it was to be another century before Babylon threatened Judah, and eventually deported many of its citizens to exile there. And so some interpreters have claimed that these two verses are late, from the time of the Exile, and have been added to Micah's book by a later hand. Others have claimed that simply the line referring to Babylon is a later addition, namely that it is a gloss, or marginal note, explaining to the reader what actually happened at a later date. But both these interpretations have difficulties; our knowledge of later history tempts us to "read it back" into these verses. But the verse does not state that Jerusalem would be conquered by Babylon, only that some of its citizens would go there in exile.

It is in fact not unreasonable to suppose that the reference to Babylon was original to Micah's message. We know from other sources that, when the Assyrians conquered Samaria (in Micah's lifetime), they brought to the northern capital people from Babylon to colonize it (2 Kings 17:24). And perhaps Micah is simply reversing this situation; if they were to conquer Jerusalem, was it not probable that they would take Judah's citizens to Babylon? It was an effective military policy for keeping colonial regions under control. If this interpretation is correct then we perceive how, in the light of later history, the words would have taken on a new meaning (certainly not that which was initially intended by Micah) in the light of actual exile in Babylon in the 6th century B.C. And perhaps that sense of fulfilled prophecy was one of the reasons why, in a later age, Micah retained his esteem as one of Judah's greatest prophets.

The difficulty of interpreting these verses should not blind us to their central message. The prophet affirms that his people would indeed experience ruin and despair, but that beyond the disaster the prospect of redemption remained. When we are in the midst of crisis and suffering, we cannot easily see beyond it to the possibility of redemption. But there the prophets come to our aid. They remind us that the crisis may be of our own making, but that the redemption beyond will be an act of God. The redemption promised by the prophets is not that there will be no ruin, but that deliverance and freedom will come from that ruin.

(iii) *Victory beyond defeat* (verses 11–13). The third oracle begins on a note that must have evoked in its audience a sense of their present situation, though once again the focus is on the future. "Many nations are assembled against you" (verse 11); if the oracle is to be dated c. 701 B.C., the multi-racial armies of Assyria were already camped on the doorstep of Jerusalem. But the focus seems rather to be a future occasion on which the tables would be turned: the armies assembled outside Jerusalem, already savouring the taste of victory, would be conquered by "Zion" (verse 13) and the reign of God throughout the world would be established. The tone of these verses is thoroughly militaristic, a far cry from the peaceful perspectives on international harmony contained in 4:1–5. But the theology, in this context, is that of judgment. Just as Jerusalem, in its present travail, was experiencing judgment at the hands of foreign nations, so too would those nations fall eventually beneath the same ban of judgment. All such acts of judgment, whether of Israel or foreign nations, would establish beyond doubt the ultimate sovereignty and reign of God in the world.

It is easier to read prophecies such as these than to know precisely what they mean and how they might be applied to our present world. Yet for all the difficulties in interpreting the details, we can summarize Micah's theology at this point in skeletal form. (a) Depite the terror and reality of the power of human nations, the power of God will ultimately be sovereign in this world. (b) History is not an accidental or random process; contemporary crises can be understood in judgmental terms, that is to say, a consequence of previous evil. (c) The crises of individual or national experience, however final they appear to be, are not necessarily terminal; redemption is possible on the further side of ruin.

"BETHLEHEM EPHRATHAH"

Micah 5:1–6

¹Now you are walled about with a wall;
    siege is laid against us;
  with a rod they strike upon the cheek
      the ruler of Israel.

²But you, O Bethlehem Ephrathah,
      who are little to be among the clans of Judah,
  from you shall come forth for me
      one who is to be ruler in Israel,
  whose origin is from of old,
      from ancient days.
³Therefore he shall give them up until the time
      when she who is in travail has brought forth;
  then the rest of his brethren shall return
      to the people of Israel.
⁴And he shall stand and feed his flock in the strength of the Lord,
      in the majesty of the name of the Lord his God.
  And they shall dwell secure, for now he shall be great
      to the ends of the earth.

⁵And this shall be peace,
      when the Assyrian comes into our land
      and treads upon our soil,
  that we will raise against him seven shepherds
      and eight princes of men;
⁶they shall rule the land of Assyria with the sword,
      and the land of Nimrod with the drawn sword;
  and they shall deliver us from the Assyrian
      when he comes into our land
      and treads within our border.

During the Christmas season, we frequently read these verses from Micah; they evoke for us the memory of the town in Judah where Jesus the Messiah was born. And the Christian tradition of reading Micah's words in a messianic manner is a good one; it goes back to St Matthew's Gospel, in which Micah is quoted in the nativity story (Matt. 2:6). Matthew and the early Christians had adopted the messianic interpretation of Micah that was common in their day; they differed from their Jewish contemporaries only in applying the ancient words to the birth of Jesus. And yet one suspects that, if through some trick of time, Micah could have re-entered the first century A.D., or even our own century, he would have been astonished at the meaning imparted to his words. It is not that Micah's words have been changed, or even perverted from their original sense; rather, with the passage of time, they have taken on new and deeper meaning in a manner that Micah himself could hardly have anticipated. And if we are to understand these words correctly, we must first seek to grasp their import in Micah's own time, before passing on to reflect on their meaning in the light of the birth of Jesus.

First and foremost, the prophet spoke to his own people in the midst of a very present crisis. The crisis is reflected in the verses which surround the central part of the prophecy (verses 1, 5–6): the city of Jerusalem was under siege (the date being c. 701 B.C.) and the threatening enemy was Assyria. The Davidic ruler of Israel, King Hezekiah, was in the city, but seemed to be totally ineffective against the external threat; the besieging enemy had struck him upon the cheek (verse 1), the sign of gross insult.

In the midst of this threat to Jerusalem, with the Davidic king unable to do anything, Micah declares an oracle containing hope for his people. He declares that a new ruler would be born in Bethlehem, in the region of Ephrathah, which was the traditional home of David's royal family (1 Sam. 17:12). The pastoral imagery of verse 4 recalls David's shepherd origins; the new ruler, when he was born, would be a shepherd of God's people. Under his dominion the people of Israel, who were threatened with immediate disaster at the time of Micah's speaking, would dwell in security for ever. We cannot read Micah's mind, but we may suppose that he expected the deliverance of which he spoke to come within the foreseeable future, perhaps a few decades. The enemy from whom he anticipated deliverance was Assyria (verses 5–6); when the child was born and had grown, he would assume the role of the nation's leader and deliverer.

Now it is to be noted that nowhere is the child to be born of Davidic lineage called *Messiah* (indeed, the word is rarely used in the Old Testament). But with the passage of time in Hebrew history, these verses began to take on new meaning in the Jewish community. The oppression of foreign enemies did not desist, and yet the new King of the line of David did not appear, to bring deliverance and security. And so Micah's message took on new perspectives. The prophet's sense of the future was elongated, and yet the hope of immediate fulfilment did not decline, for oppression and external enemies continued to characterize the reality of Israel's historical existence. One day, the hope persisted, the ruler of whom Micah spoke would come, and then there would be freedom from enemies and a life lived in security.

Matthew's quotation of Micah's prophecy has set it in a new perspective for the Christian reader of the Old Testament. The deliverer has come to this world in the person of Jesus; like David, Jesus is the new Shepherd of God's sheep, offering security from external enemies and a life of security. Jesus, of the Davidic line, is above all a gift of God to this world. To those who feel shut in on every side, like the besieged citizens of Jerusalem who first heard these words, Jesus brings the prospect of deliverance and security. And that is the essence of the Christmas message: God makes a gift to a besieged world through whom deliverance may come.

But there is a sting in the tail of these words, as so often in the message of the prophets. Micah spoke of deliverance from the oppressor, from Assyria. And yet the tragedy of so much of Christian history is that the delivered people have become the oppressors, have donned the uniform of Assyria. In the name of this Davidic King, Jesus the Messiah, supposedly Christian persons and nations have set out on the road to war and oppression. And among those who have suffered at the hands of Christian violence are the Jews from whom we have received these ancient words of hope. The message of the Messiah, which is Micah's legacy to us, must constantly be remembered in the context of the same prophet's vision of universal harmony (4:1–5); then we shall know that deliverance and peace must walk hand in hand.

ISRAEL'S PROSPECT AND PUNISHMENT

Micah 5:7–15

> 7Then the remnant of Jacob shall be
>   in the midst of many peoples
> like the dew from the Lord,
>   like showers upon the grass,
> which tarry not for men
>   nor wait for the sons of men.
> 8And the remnant of Jacob shall be among the nations,
>   in the midst of many peoples,
> like a lion among the beasts of the forest,
>   like a young lion among the flocks of sheep,
> which, when it goes through, treads down
>   and tears in pieces, and there is none to deliver.
> 9Your hand shall be lifted up over your adversaries,
>   and all your enemies shall be cut off.
>
> 10And in that day, says the Lord,
>   I will cut off your horses from among you
>   and will destroy your chariots;
> 11and I will cut off the cities of your land
>   and throw down all your strongholds;
> 12and I will cut off sorceries from your hand,
>   and you shall have no more soothsayers;
> 13and I will cut off your images
>   and your pillars from among you,
>   and you shall bow down no more
>   to the work of your hands;
> 14and I will root out your Asherim from among you
>   and destroy your cities.
> 15And in anger and wrath I will execute vengeance
>   upon the nations that did not obey.

The manner in which the prophetic books have been compiled leads sometimes to the appearance of strange contradictions or contrasts between one passage and another. In the passage we are now considering, there are two quite distinct sections. The first (verses 7–9) speaks of the future role of Israel's remnant in very glowing and positive terms. The second (verses 10–15) seems to be totally negative in its anticipation of Israel's thoroughgoing judgment. The contrast is apparent rather than real. The seven short chapters of Micah have preserved for us only a fragment of a lifetime's ministry that extended over several decades. And within the book we read short passages, now lying alongside one another, that originally would have been delivered under quite different circumstances and at different times. Such is the case with the two sections which we are now examining, but when the meaning of each is grasped, the respective passages will be seen to be complementary rather than contradictory.

(i) *Israel's bright prospects for the future* (verses 7–9). The time period presupposed by this short passage is once again the year 701 B.C., when the Assyrian armies were in Judah and the nation had little hope for the future. At the time Micah spoke these words, only a remnant survived and hope had almost died. The nation of the chosen people had preserved traditions going back to the time of Abraham, that they would be as numerous as the sands of the sea, and that through them all the nations of the world would be blessed. But such ancient hopes had a hollow ring in 701 B.C. The northern kingdom had already been lost in 722 B.C., and Judah to the south was on the verge of collapse. Had all been in vain? Had the dreams that had been nourished and passed on from one generation to another since the time of the patriarchs been mere delusions? To the remnant in Jerusalem, torn by this sense of despair, Micah brings a message; he employs two similes to communicate his meaning.

(a) Despite present circumstances, the chosen people would once again be like God's dew and showers, bringing God's bounty to the parched earth of the world's nations (verse 7). (b) Despite present weakness and the shadow of defeat, the nation of the chosen people would in the future be like a lion, powerful and fearless amongst the world's nations (verse 8). The two similes seem at first totally opposite in nature, but they bring out clearly the dual character that had always been integral to the purpose of

Israel: "I will bless those who bless you, and him who curses you I will curse" (Genesis 12:3).

The prophet is addressing the human form of the "remnant mentality". In strictly human terms, the fragmented community that survived in Jerusalem reasonably believed that the purpose of their election had been lost. They had a miserable past; there were too few of them left to change the future. But God, through his prophet, revolutionized the remnant mentality. The sheer number of survivors was not important; if there was any hope for the future, it would be found in God's strength, not in a bulging census report. And Micah affirms unequivocally that there remained yet a future, despite the calamity of present circumstances. And our own human tendency to a remnant mentality, and the Church's natural recourse to an inferiority complex, needs always thus to be turned around. Such negative thinking is based on the wrong foundation; it is not the number of people that counts, but God's capacity to work through his people for the blessing of the world.

(ii) *Israel's punishment* (verses 10–15). This short oracle is to be dated, in all probability, somewhat earlier than the one that immediately precedes it. The time would seem to be early in Hezekiah's reign; preparations are afoot for war with Assyria, but the enemy is not yet in the land. The national self-confidence has yet to be punctured by the events of 701 B.C., and the military preparations give the nation a kind of blind buoyancy, the hope that all will be well. But, as Micah sees, the nation's confidence is sadly misplaced. All round, preparations are undertaken on the assumption that the enemy is Assyria; only Micah perceives that Judah's true enemy, given its evil character, is none other than God.

The message that the prophet brings is designed to shatter the nation's ebullient mood. Building up the military and pouring funds into building new "panzer divisions" of cavalry would do no good, for God would destroy them (verse 10). The fortified cities and strongholds, the soothsayers who advised the military establishment, the images and idols of false religion—all of these things would be destroyed on the day of judgment. None of them could deliver Judah from the doom that was coming.

As Robert Burns observed, "the best laid schemes o' mice an' men gang aft a-gley." The fieldmouse that builds its home in the stalks of wheat sees it cut down by the harvesters. The nation that bases its national security on military establishment and false faith will see it all collapse when the harvest of judgment begins. For Micah, there is only one continuing source of strength and security, God. But before that true foundation can be found, all others must be swept away in judgment.

THE LORD'S CONTROVERSY WITH ISRAEL

Micah 6:1–8

¹Hear what the Lord says:
  Arise, plead your case before the mountains,
    and let the hills hear your voice.
²Hear, you mountains, the controversy of the Lord,
    and you enduring foundations of the earth;
  for the Lord has a controversy with his people,
    and he will contend with Israel.

³"O my people, what have I done to you?
    In what have I wearied you? Answer me!
⁴For I brought you up from the land of Egypt,
    and redeemed you from the house of bondage;
  and I sent you before Moses,
    Aaron, and Miriam.
⁵O my people, remember what Balak king of Moab devised,
    and what Balaam the son of Beor answered him,
  and what happened from Shittim to Gilgal,
    that you may know the saving acts of the Lord."

⁶"With what shall I come before the Lord,
    and bow myself before God on high?
  Shall I come before him with burnt offerings,
    with calves a year old?
⁷Will the Lord be pleased with thousands of rams,
    with ten thousands of rivers of oil?
  Shall I give my first-born for my transgression,
    the fruit of my body for the sin of my soul?"

⁸He has showed you, O man, what is good;
    and what does the Lord require of you
  but to do justice, and to love kindness,
    and to walk humbly with your God?

Micah begins this remarkable speech in language which would
have immediately conjured up in the minds of his audience a
courtroom setting. He employs the formal language of the law:
"Arise, plead your case" (verse 1). But it is no ordinary courtroom of which he speaks. The judge is God and Micah is his
counsel, speaking on his behalf. And before the defendant is
called to the stand to hear the charges, an impressive slate of
witnesses is summoned. Metaphorically, the counsel summons
the mountains and hills, and "the enduring foundations of the
earth", to hear the case that is to come before the court. Only
when the members of the court are formally assembled is the
defendant announced: God has a case to bring against Israel!

Before the members of the court, God makes his case concerning his chosen people. The actual charge is implied rather
than explicitly stated: Israel has grown tired of God and chosen to
go its own way. But why, God asks? Has he let them down?
Consider the evidence of history, he suggests to the court. When
Israel was enslaved in Egypt, he gave his people freedom. When
they were without leaders, he gave them Moses, Aaron, Miriam,
and others. When their very existence was threatened in Moab by
King Balak, he rescued them yet again. When they crossed the
River Jordan, from Shittim to Gilgal, he was with them once
again, protecting them and leading them. Clearly the evidence
presented to the court substantiates the fact that whatever the
reason for Israel's failure, it cannot be blamed on God.

The defendant then addresses the court. Israel does not dispute
the crime of which it is guilty, nor the evidence that has been
presented; the accused simply addresses a question to the court.
In short, "What must I do to set things right?" But the very
phrasing of the question betrays the fact that the defendant still
does not really understand what is going on. Israel assumes that
the solution to its crime is somehow to be found in ritual activity;

but what exactly would God like? And here Micah caricatures his nation though, like most caricatures, it is rooted in truth. Would God perhaps like burnt offerings, yearling calves? Surely that should satisfy his wounded dignity. Or perhaps thousands of rams and millions of gallons of oil, Israel suggests, with childlike naïvety. If that isn't enough, Israel says, I could even sacrifice my first-born son! Nothing is too much for God!

Micah perceived that his nation had lost the very essence of the faith. Ritual had become an end in itself, not an external manifestation of the nation's primary relationship with God. The whole sacrificial system and worship of the temple had been debased into a kind of national insurance policy: we can sin as we wish, the leaders thought, so long as we are up to date with our insurance premiums at the temple. With extraordinary nerve, the nation suggested to the court that the sins of hypocrisy could be atoned for by further hyprocisy on an even grander scale!

The court is concluded by the words of God's counsel (verse 8). There is no mystery as to what God requires, and it has nothing to do with sacrifice and offering. God requires three things of Israel, Micah affirms, and the three are as pertinent today as they were in Micah's time.

(i) *Do justice*. No amount of frenzied temple activity could fill the vacuum of justice. While injustice ruled in Israel, every moment of temple worship was a mockery of Israel's faith. God was just and had always acted in justice with his people; in return he required them to act and live in justice. And, as Micah's earlier preaching has indicated, justice was notable by its absence in Israel. Yet justice is a paramount virtue, without which human beings cannot live together in the manner that God intended.

(ii) *Love kindness*. Kindness, or *loving-kindness* as the Hebrew word is frequently translated, is again one of the principal attributes of God in the Old Testament. As God always acted towards his people in loving-kindness, so too he required them to act thus toward one another. Loving-kindness, though intimately related to justice, goes beyond the first virtue; it gives, where no giving is required, it acts when no action is deserved, and it penetrates both attitudes and activities. It is a part of the virtue extolled by St Paul in his extraordinary hymn to love (1 Cor. 13:1–13).

(iii) *Walk humbly with your God*. It is the daily walk in relationship with God that lies at the heart of religion; the ritual of the temple could give expression to the vitality of that walk, but it could never replace it as the centre of Israel's faith. And the humble walk with God went hand in hand with the practice of justice and the love of kindness. This triad of virtue forms the foundations of the religious life; this was what God required of Israel.

Although we may learn deeply from each of the three parts of the prophet's message, it is the collective whole which is most vital. And when we sense ourselves, in moments of introspection, to be in God's court and wonder what he requires of us, it is to these three foundations that we must return. There is a human tendency within us, when faced as was Israel with the catalogue of our shortcomings, to turn to intense forms of religiosity. We should be in church more; we should spend hours in agonizing prayers of repentance; we should give all that we have to God; and so it goes on, until the fanatic is produced within us, but still without the heart of true religion. "What does the Lord require of you but to do justice, to love kindness, and to walk humbly with your God." At first it does not sound like much, but it is more than enough for one lifetime.

OF CRIME AND PUNISHMENT

Micah 6:9–16

9The voice of the Lord cries to the city—
　　and it is sound wisdom to fear thy name:
　"Hear, O tribe and assembly of the city!
10Can I forget the treasures of wickedness in the house of the
　　wicked,
　　and the scant measure that is accursed?
11Shall I acquit the man with wicked scales
　　and with a bag of deceitful weights?

¹²Your rich men are full of violence;
    your inhabitants speak lies,
    and their tongue is deceitful in their mouth,
¹³Therefore I have begun to smite you,
    making you desolate because of your sins.
¹⁴You shall eat, but not be satisfied,
    and there shall be hunger in your inward parts;
  you shall put away, but not save,
    and what you save I will give to the sword.
¹⁵You shall sow, but not reap;
    you shall tread olives, but not anoint yourselves with oil;
    you shall tread grapes, but not drink wine.
¹⁶For you have kept the statutes of Omri,
    and all the works of the house of Ahab;
    and you have walked in their counsels;
  that I may make you a desolation, and your inhabitants a hissing;
    so you shall bear the scorn of the peoples."

On a market day in ancient Jerusalem there would have been a great bustle of activity. The resident merchants would prepare themselves for a full day of business, and the country folk would come flocking into the city from their rural residences. Goods would be bought and sold, and the small farmers would sell their produce, or barter it for the necessities of their simple country life. The city's streets would be full and the ancient equivalent of cash registers would ring all day long. It was a day for business, a busy day.

On just such a day, Micah delivered the powerful words of this short passage. He knew the city, his current residence, but he also knew the country from which he had come, with its honest farmers and labourers. And Micah was also aware that a market day in Jerusalem, though essential to the economy and to the lives of those who would be there, was a day in which unscrupulous merchants could make a mint for themselves. For a market day was a wonderful opportunity for the rich to become richer and the weak and naive to be exploited.

Thus, to the assembled throngs doing business in the city, Micah delivered a message from God. He was speaking in his prophetic role directly on God's behalf ("the voice of the Lord cries to the city", verse 9); his words were addressed to the "tribe and assembly", namely all the people of Judah, citizens of Jerusalem and country residents alike, who were assembled in the city for business. As with other oracles of this kind, there are two principal parts to the prophet's message: first, he specifies the crimes of which so many in the audience are guilty, and second, he declares a word of judgment from God.

(i) *The crimes of commerce* (verses 10–12). Commerce is not in itself an evil activity, but human nature being what it is, this most fundamental of the various forms of human interaction may easily be abused. Great fortunes could be made by astute businessmen, but Micah describes the fortunes being made in Jerusalem as "treasures of wickedness" (verse 10). All kinds of schemes were employed to make an unjust profit. The weigh scales were rigged so that a merchant buying goods from a farmer paid less for the goods than they were worth. The stone weights in the merchant's bag that were stamped "16 ounces" (or the ancient equivalent) were underweight or overweight, depending on whether the merchant was selling or buying. If a customer complained, the wealthy merchants threatened violence (verse 12). And truthfulness, so essential to honest business, had been abandoned; if a lie helped to earn a fast shekel, then lying was the order of the day.

Such was the nature of business in Jerusalem in Micah's day. There is always a tendency for commerce to slide into such a state of corruption, but normally it is controlled by other checks and balances in society. If the laws are maintained and the courts are free from corruption, such business practices as Micah describes cannot flourish. If the government is doing its job and the clergy are maintaining their responsibilities, the social and moral health of a nation can be maintained. But, as Micah has already made clear, the corruption was widespread, having penetrated the judiciary, the clergy, and even the nation's government. And so it is hardly surprising that the commercial world had also sunk to corruption.

(ii) *The punishment of commercial crime* (verses 13–16). Micah begins immediately by describing all that is going on with the label "sins"; there are no mitigating circumstances, no concessions to "standard business practice", and no attempts to spare the feelings of those being condemned. Sin is sin, and must be declared as such. And sin has its consequences in the divine scheme of things, which the prophet now spells out in horrifying detail. Food acquired by illegal means will no longer satisfy human hunger. The profits won from illegal transactions will be put away in savings accounts, but somehow the savings will be dissipated and disappear. The seed of harvest will be sown, but no harvest will be reaped. The olives will be trampled in the press, but the labour will produce no olive oil. The grapes too will be trodden in the press, but there will be no wine, nothing to gladden the heart at the end of the labour. The somewhat obscure allusion to Omri and Ahab (verse 16) probably refers to the once thriving commerce in the city of Samaria which those two kings had built; but Samaria, for its sins, had been destroyed, and the merchants of Jerusalem were setting their own city on the same path towards destruction.

This message of the prophet is in a way a kind of commentary on the preceding message, that what God required of Israel was that they "do justice, love kindness, and walk humbly with God" (verse 8). The activities of the market-place had become pervaded by injustice. The rapacious merchants had hearts of steel and knew no sentiment of kindness toward their customers. And if any of them still walked with God, their god was Mammon.

The message of Micah has lost none of its urgency in the 20th century. Commerce is always with us, as it must be, and its activities are regulated by law. But at bottom, the integrity of commerce must rest with its practitioners, not with the law. When justice and kindness are among the virtues of business practice, and when these balance the desire for profit and expansion, men like Micah will finally be out of work. And that is one kind of unemployment which the business community may reasonably choose as a goal.

A LAMENT FOR A LOST SOCIETY

Micah 7:1–7

¹Woe is me! For I have become
 as when the summer fruit has been gathered,
 as when the vintage has been gleaned:
there is no cluster to eat,
 no first-ripe fig which my soul desires.
²The godly man has perished from the earth,
 and there is none upright among men;
they all lie in wait for blood,
 and each hunts his brother with a net.
³Their hands are upon what is evil, to do it diligently;
 the prince and the judge ask for a bribe,
and the great man utters the evil desire of his soul;
 thus they weave it together.
⁴The best of them is like a brier,
 the most upright of them a thorn hedge.
The day of their watchmen, of their punishment, has come;
 now their confusion is at hand.
⁵Put no trust in a neighbour,
 have no confidence in a friend;
guard the doors of your mouth
 from her who lies in your bosom;
⁶for the son treats the father with contempt,
 the daughter rises up against her mother,
 the daughter-in-law against her mother-in-law;
 a man's enemies are the men of his own house.
⁷But as for me, I will look to the Lord,
 I will wait for the God of my salvation;
 my God will hear me.

The scene now shifts from the public Micah, ministering in the market-place, to the private Micah, lamenting the sorry estate to which his nation has fallen. The citizen in the street, who heard the prophet preach, may have perceived only the rather harsh exterior of this stern servant of God, but behind the public shield lay the heart of a passionate man, one who was profoundly distressed by the moral condition of the nation to which he belonged. The words of his sorrow are in the familiar form of the psalms of lament; speaking individually and privately, he gives vent to his deepest feelings of disappointment.

Micah begins the description of his feelings with a simile of frustration (verse 1). He is like a man who has entered an orchard, hoping for a ripe fig to appease his appetite; but the orchard has no fruit, for all of it has been gathered. Or he is like a man who has entered a vineyard, hoping to find a refreshing bunch of grapes; but all the grapes have been picked and no fruit remains. His frustration lies not simply in the absence of fruit and continuing hunger, but in the fact that the places that should have had fruit have been stripped bare. Such was his city, Jerusalem; the branches that should have been laden with the fruits of righteousness and justice had long since been stripped.

He laments first the general corruption of the society (verses 2-4). There are, it seems, no honest persons left. Instead, society is populated by violent and ruthless persons, each one set upon the exploitation of a neighbour. The people he sees are not lazy: they are diligent and dedicated in the pursuit of evil (verse 3), and that is the closest they come to nobility or virtue! The rulers and judges take bribes freely, for they have long since abandoned justice in the pursuit of profit. If a powerful man desires some criminal goal, he does not veil his objective, but talks of it openly, seeking advice as to how his end can be achieved. The best of the bunch are useless, prickly like briers and as twisted as a thorn hedge (verse 4); but here the prophet's simile reminds him that briers and thorns burn splendidly in the fire! The day of judgment for such persons must surely be close at hand.

Then Micah turns the focus of his lament from the character of society as a whole to that part of it which is more immediate to his daily existence (verses 5-6). In a sad crescendo of misery, he notes that you cannot trust a neighbour or a friend, and that even the members of an immediate family no longer live together in mutual trust and respect. Parents, children, relatives—all have been infected by the same plague of evil that has corrupted society as a whole.

The words of the prophet's lament are filled more with grief than with judgment, more with sorrow than with vindictiveness. What he saw all around him was such a terrible shame! A nation with such great possibilities had descended to this. A people to whom had been entrusted special revelation concerning the nature of righteousness and justice had abandoned its birthright. And, saddest of all, the pursuit of evil brought no joy, promised no happiness to its practitioners in the short span that is human life. It brought only its own sorry rewards, namely the clouds of divine judgment and justice that now hung so low over the nation's horizon.

But Micah's lament, for all its enervating grief, ends on a positive and constructive note. Despite the moral ruin and decay that he perceives on every side, he affirms that he will continue to trust in God and continue to pray to him (verse 7). Lament does not lead to personal despair, as well it might have done. With great effort, the prophet rises above his despondency and continues to serve the God by whom he had been called.

In the words of this lament, we sense in Micah the profound sensitivity that characterized the spirit of so many of Israel's prophets. They were not merely serving a nation, fulfilling their vocation; they were deeply involved in their task, emotionally tied to the fate of the people whom they served. And the depth of the prophet's emotion is tied, in part, to the clarity with which he saw his nation's sickness. Those who do not see society's sickness and grief cannot lament it with passion. And many do not see clearly the prevalence of injustice in society precisely because they lack a wholehearted commitment to justice. Only when, with Micah, we practise justice and love kindness, are we likely to see how absent those virtues are from our society. And then can we not only enter into the spirit of the prophet's lament, but also join him in a new commitment of faith (verse 7).

A POSTSCRIPT: THE CONTINUITY OF MICAH'S MESSAGE

Micah 7:8–20

⁸Rejoice not over me, O my enemy;
　　when I fall, I shall rise;
when I sit in darkness,
　　the Lord will be a light to me.
⁹I will bear the indignation of the Lord
　　because I have sinned against him,
until he pleads my cause
　　and executes judgment for me.
He will bring me forth to the light;
　　I shall behold his deliverance.
¹⁰Then my enemy will see,
　　and shame will cover her who said to me,
　　"Where is the Lord your God?"
My eyes will gloat over her;
　　now she will be trodden down
　　like the mire of the streets.

¹¹A day for the building of your walls!
　　In that day the boundary shall be far extended.
¹²In that day they will come to you,
　　from Assyria to Egypt,
and from Egypt to the River,
　　from sea to sea and from mountain to mountain.
¹³But the earth will be desolate
　　because of its inhabitants,
　　for the fruit of their doings.

¹⁴Shepherd thy people with thy staff,
　　the flock of thy inheritance,
who dwell alone in a forest
　　in the midst of a garden land;
let them feed in Bashan and Gilead
　　as in the days of old.

¹⁵As in the days when you came out of the land of Egypt
　　I will show them marvellous things.

[16]The nations shall see and be ashamed of all their might;
    they shall lay their hands on their mouths;
        their ears shall be deaf;
[17]they shall lick the dust like a serpent,
    like the crawling things of the earth;
    they shall come trembling out of their strongholds,
        they shall turn in dread to the Lord our God,
        and they shall fear because of thee.

[18]Who is a God like thee, pardoning iniquity
    and passing over transgression
        for the remnant of his inheritance?
He does not retain his anger for ever
    because he delights in steadfast love.
[19]He will again have compassion upon us,
    he will tread our iniquities under foot.
Thou wilt cast all our sins
    into the depths of the sea.
[20]Thou wilt show faithfulness to Jacob
    and steadfast love to Abraham,
as thou hast sworn to our fathers
    from the days of old.

This short book of Micah containing the words of prophecy ends, curiously enough, with a psalm. The psalm has some similarity to those in the Psalter; it is a communal lament, expressing grief at the present disaster and hope for a brighter future. The substance of the psalm is such that most scholars doubt that it is the work of Micah, and they are probably correct. The style is quite different, and the judgments of which Micah spoke seem to have passed from threat to reality. Such questions of authorship are always disputed, but in this instance, it seems reasonable enough to interpret the concluding verses of the book as a postscript, added no doubt by those who preserved Micah's message through subsequent generations and took its substance to heart.

Those who used the psalm were, like Micah before them, citizens of Judah and Jerusalem. But whereas Micah spoke of the judgment that would come, those who used this psalm spoke from the actual experience of judgment. What Micah prophesied had come to pass; the divine wrath had not been averted. Judah had fallen and sat in darkness (verse 8), God's indignation was being experienced (verse 9), the city's walls had collapsed and needed rebuilding (verse 11), and the nation of Judah no longer had land, only hopes for the future. But the actual advent of judgment had not rendered the prophet's words obsolete; rather his message had been vindicated, but now it offered new hope for the future. The reason is clear: Micah's preaching had made it very plain why disaster had come, but knowing the reason for the disaster provided also hope that God's ancient covenant with his people could be restored.

The psalm as such falls into four main sections. (a) The implied speaker in the first section is Zion, the personified city of Jerusalem (verses 8–10). Zion speaks from the humiliation of defeat, but with the awareness that its current disastrous condition is a result of God's punishment for sin. The words of lament are muted by the overtones of hope, the anticipation of mercy that lies beyond the experience of judgment. (b) The second section (verses 11–14) is in the form of an announcement, spoken in a temple liturgy by the priest or prophet of God. The messenger declares that it is time for new action: the collapsed walls of the city are to be rebuilt, the old national boundaries renewed and extended, the people are to be tended as sheep once again in the land of their inheritance. (c) In the third section (verses 15–17), the people (or Zion) speak once again, taking up the confidence of the messenger's announcement and anticipating the restoration of their nation in the sight of other nations. (d) The psalm concludes with a hymn of praise, emphasizing the incomparability of the Lord in his mercy and love (verses 18–20). God's anger is not permanent, but would be superseded by his mercy and love. The sins of Israel which had precipitated such ruin would be cast into the depths of the ocean, lost forever to the memory of God.

The postscript to this remarkable book of Micah speaks to us in several ways about the meaning of the prophet's ministry as a whole.

(i) Micah, at the end of his lifetime, could not have died with any confidence that his mission had been successfully fulfilled. He had preached faithfully, but his city and nation had not yet turned aside the threat of judgment. He had spoken of justice and love, but there had been few signs of a radical social revolution. He had proclaimed future hope and restoration but, if it were to come about, it lay beyond the horizons of his own mortal existence. From a human point of view, it might be said of Micah that he served faithfully, but did not seem to achieve a great deal. And yet lasting achievements can rarely be measured in the span of a single life. And many persons who are eventually granted a measure of success do not live long enough to know it.

The very existence of the postscript is a monument to Micah's success. There were those of a later generation who understood what he said and acted accordingly. They left for us not only a tribute to God's mercy, but also an appropriate word of thanks to one of God's faithful servants.

(ii) The postscript also reminds us of the value of Scripture for ourselves and our time. The prophets spoke first and foremost to their own people in their own time, but their words were preserved because someone had the wisdom to see that their relevance was not confined to the current generation. Micah's words are no less relevant to the 20th century A.D. than to the 8th century B.C., the time of their delivery, or the 6th century B.C., the time of the postscript. For every generation needs to know of the importance of justice and the centrality of loving-kindness; every age needs to have its social conscience pricked by Micah's penetrating words. And thus, as we read the ancient Scriptures and seek to apply them to our own lives and our contemporary world, we are standing firmly in the tradition of those who left us the postscript to Micah's book.

(iii) Micah himself focused on sin and judgment; he revealed to us the harsh face of a God who cannot countenance evil and injustice. But to those who responded to Micah's words, like those who left the postscript, the other side of the countenance of God was revealed.

> He does not retain his anger for ever
> because he delights in steadfast love.
> He will again have compassion on us,
> he will tread our iniquities under foot.

(verses 18–19)

INTRODUCTION TO THE BOOK OF NAHUM

Some books, although they may be read in the comfort of the living-room, contain such passionate and violent sentiments that they create a sense of unease in the reader's frame of mind. Nahum is such a book: the winds of war blow through its pages and its undertones are those of violence and vengeance. This is not a tasteful book, not an easy one to comprehend in the calmness of the study; in order to understand its force and power, one must first attempt to enter Nahum's world.

Just as Nazi Germany still evokes the images of terror in the minds of those Jewish people who survived the holocaust, so too in Nahum's world Assyria was the embodiment of human evil and terror. Of all the oppressive imperial powers that have stained the pages of human history from the past to the present, Assyria claims a place of pre-eminence among evil nations. It was a nation with a long history, but during the first millennium B.C. it embarked upon a path of imperial expansion which knew no limitations of human decency and kindness. And among the many nations that experienced Assyria's cruelty, its invasion of territory and its ruthless military methods, the small state of Judah was but one.

In Nahum's time, Judah had already lived through almost a century of terror and oppression at the hands of Assyria. But for Assyria, as for all oppressive human states, the end was finally to come; when evil nations fall, few of their former victims can resist the urge to rejoice. In Judah, the focus of anti-Assyrian feelings was Nineveh, which had become the imperial capital of the Assyrian Empire in the 7th century B.C. And the focal point of the entire book of Nahum is Nineveh and the anticipated demise of that capital city. The passions and feelings given vent in the Book of Nahum are those of a man and a nation who have suffered terror and oppression. And if, from the comfort of study or pew, we complain that the sentiments of this book are neither noble nor uplifting, we need to remind ourselves that we have not suffered at Assyrian hands.

THE MAN

The author of this little book was Nahum; his name, ironically, means "comfort", but there is little by way of comfort in his words. Virtually nothing is known with any certainty concerning Nahum, for he is not referred to in any other biblical book. We are told that he came from Elkosh, but that is of little help, for the location of Elkosh is unknown. Some 20 miles north of the ruins of Nineveh there is a town called (in Arabic) Al-Kush; local tradition had it that the tomb of Nahum was located there, but the tradition has little historical probability. Jerome, one of the first Hebrew scholars in the early Christian Church, claimed that Elkosh was a village in the region of Gaililee, but that opinion, too, is improbable. Of the variety of hypotheses, the most likely is that Elkosh was a small town in the south of Judah, of which the precise identity and location have now been lost. In any case, though his home town remains elusive, Nahum was probably a citizen of Judah, and the sentiments he expresses would be those of a Judahite of the late 7th century B.C. Although we cannot pin down the exact date of his prophecy, it would have been delivered between the years 663 B.C and 612 B.C., in all probability just a few years before 612 B.C., which was the date of Nineveh's final collapse.

THE NATURE OF THE BOOK

The short Book of Nahum contains only three chapters; they comprise almost entirely poetry, with only a few brief fragments of prose. The Hebrew text, which in places is somewhat obscure and difficult to translate, is vigorous and dramatic in its poetic style: its author was a poet of considerable ability and originality. The Book of Nahum is thus a work of literary excellence and style, but it presents problems with respect both to detailed interpretation and theological meaning.

The initial difficulty lies in determining the overall framework within which the book should be interpreted; a variety of hypotheses have been proposed. Some scholars maintain that Nahum is a liturgy, or a part of a liturgy, in which thanksgiving was offered in Jerusalem following the final sack of Nineveh, but such a view does not do justice to the prophetic character of the work. It has also been suggested that the book is a kind of "Cantata on Nineveh", but if this hypothesis has any merit, it is more probable with respect to the later use of the work, rather than interpreting its author's intent. It is simplest just to take the book at face value as a collection of a few of the prophetic oracles of Nahum. They have been collected and preserved on the basis of their common theme, Nineveh, and are similar in principle to the "foreign nation" oracles which are found in other prophetic books (e.g. Ezek. 25–32). In this context, the title verse (1:1) is very important, for without its guidance as to substance, it would not be easy to establish the focus of some of the prophetic sayings, given their general substance.

It is no longer possible to determine the context in which these oracles were first proclaimed by the prophet. They could have been delivered in Jerusalem in some annual occasion of worship in the temple, but the text provides little by way of evidence. It is reasonable to suppose that what prompted the delivery of the oracles would have been the receipt of news in Jerusalem that Assyria's enemies were preparing an invasion force. The writing was on the wall for Assyria as early as 626 B.C., when its Babylonian colony asserted independence and later joined forces with the Medes to rebel against its old master. The end came in 612 B.C. The following words paraphrase a key portion of the *Babylonian Chronicle of Nabopolassar*, a text preserved in the British Museum:

> In the month of Abu, the city of Nineveh was finally seized; the armies inflicted a terrible defeat on the city, which was made into a hill of ruins and heaps of debris.

After its defeat in 612 B.C., Nineveh was reoccupied again on an intermittent basis for several centuries, but it never regained the splendour it had once possessed as the capital city of Assyria.

THE MESSAGE OF NAHUM

Some of the common and familiar themes of the prophets reappear in the words of Nahum. For this prophet, as for others, the God of Israel was not merely a national deity, but a universal God whose power extended over all nations. God's judgment for evil could fall as much on foreign nations as it could upon the chosen people. Despite the universal and international themes of this prophecy, nevertheless, the book is still thoroughly nationalistic in tone. The coming judgment of Assyria is of great interest in Judah precisely because the citizens of Judah had already suffered so much from the Assyrians. Nahum is thus not a disinterested work; it reflects upon the anticipated judgment of a nation which, within divine providence, had also been an instrument of judgment in Israel and Judah.

Numerous writers have noted that the book appears to be marred by the imperfections of vengeance and mockery that constantly appear in its verses. There is little charity in Nahum's words, little love for the citizens of Nineveh or concern for their fate. In this sense, it contrasts sharply with the Book of Jonah, in which a quite different attitude towards Nineveh is expressed (and which may be read alongside Nahum as a counter-balance). And yet to be offended by the shades of vengeance and cruelty in Nahum may result in missing its purpose. The writer is engaged in a kind of theodicy, the vindication of the providence of God in the light of human evil and cruelty. Earlier prophets, Micah and Isaiah among them, had proclaimed that Assyria was an instrument of God's judgment on his chosen people. In a sense, such theology was acceptable, for the faithful amongst the chosen people saw and accepted their failure and hence the legitimacy of their judgment. But the instrument of judgment, Assyria, was not only evil, but actually worse than those nations it judged.

Should Assyria go unpunished? Nahum said no: the judge would also be judged, for evil was repugnant to God, whether undertaken by gentile or chosen nation. Thus Nahum celebrates the full completion, as it were, of the divine justice; all nations that pursued evil and cruelty would reap the harvest they had sown for themselves. In a certain way, then, the Book of Nahum can be received as a triumph of faith in a time of faltering faith. It is still not a nice book, but it is concerned with a terrible world; none, it affirms, can permanently escape judgment if they continue in the pursuit and practice of evil.

The Book of Nahum, sadly, has not lost its pertinence down through the centuries. When the Dead Sea Scrolls were discovered in the vicinity of Qumran in the years following World War II, a commentary on Nahum was found among the ancient texts. The commentary interpreted Nahum with respect to the tragedies that happened in Jerusalem in the mid-2nd century B.C. at the instigation of Antiochus Epiphanes. In each age, it seems, atrocities are perpetrated by pagan powers and seem to go unpunished. And in each age, the age-old question must be raised again: is God really just if these atrocities take place and there is no response from God? Nahum provides no complex philosophical analysis of the problems of theodicy. Rather, he affirms with conviction that in the end, within the divine scheme of things, evil is punished. Atrocities and cruelty will return to haunt the nations that perpetrated such evil in the first place. It is thus a solemn and awful book because of the solemnity of its subject matter.

THE JUDGE OF NINEVEH

Nahum 1:1–15

[1]An oracle concerning Nineveh.
The book of the vision of Nahum of Elkosh.
[2]The Lord is a jealous God and avenging,
the Lord is avenging and wrathful;
the Lord takes vengeance on his adversaries
and keeps wrath for his enemies.

³The Lord is slow to anger and of great might,
    and the Lord will by no means clear the guilty.
His way is in whirlwind and storm,
    and the clouds are the dust of his feet.
⁴He rebukes the sea and makes it dry,
    he dries up all the rivers;
Bashan and Carmel wither,
    the bloom of Lebanon fades.
⁵The mountains quake before him,
    the hills melt;
the earth is laid waste before him,
    the world and all that dwell therein.

⁶Who can stand before his indignation?
    Who can endure the heat of his anger?
His wrath is poured out like fire,
    and the rocks are broken asunder by him.
⁷The Lord is good,
    a stronghold in the day of trouble;
    he knows those who take refuge in him.
⁸But with an overflowing flood
    he will make a full end of his adversaries,
    and will pursue his enemies into darkness.
⁹What do you plot against the Lord?
    He will make a full end;
    he will not take vengeance twice on his foes.
¹⁰Like entangled thorns they are consumed,
    like dry stubble.
¹¹Did one not come out from you,
    who plotted evil against the Lord,
    and counselled villainy?

¹²Thus says the Lord,
  "Though they be strong and many,
    they will be cut off and pass away.
Though I have afflicted you,
    I will afflict you no more.
¹³And now I will break his yoke from off you
    and will burst your bonds asunder."

¹⁴The Lord has given commandment about you:
  "No more shall your name be perpetuated;

from the house of your gods I will cut off
the graven image and the molten image.
I will make your grave, for you are vile."

¹⁵Behold, on the mountains the feet of him
who brings good tidings,
who proclaims peace!
Keep your feasts, O Judah,
fulfil your vows,
for never again shall the wicked come against you,
he is utterly cut off.

Most people, when they reflect upon the nature of God, tend to think first of the comforting and pleasant aspects of the deity. As children, we sang of "gentle Jesus, meek and mild". And, as we grow older, we like to think of the love and mercy of God. But then, as we reflect upon the nature of the world, its violence and perpetually evil character, we come to realize that our pleasant notion of a loving God is too small; for all its truth, it jars with the reality both of human experience and of life in an evil world. Nahum's world was a wicked one; his people had experienced decades of repression by a ruthless enemy. And though he knew of God's love, Nahum also realized that human evil invited divine judgment. Above all, Assyria's history of human atrocities demanded some divine righting of wrongs, some action by which justice would be seen to be done.

And so Nahum begins his short prophecy with a terrifying portrait of God: his words paint in that other visage of God, in which are reflected pure hatred of human violence, oppression, and exploitation. And those who heard Nahum's words and who saw his vision of God, despite the awesome nature of what was revealed, must have heaved a great sigh of relief: "At last, justice would be done. At last God would act, and the punishers would be punished!"

Thus, as we read the opening verses of this prophecy (verses 2–11), we glimpse a fearful vision that would nerverthelesses have evoked hope in Nahum's audience. In powerful poetic language, the prophet describes the anger and vengeance of God; the anger is the more frightening because God is "slow to anger" (verse 3), so that the eventual emergence of wrath presupposes some terrible human cause. The advent of the angry God is described in terms indicating the turmoil of the world of nature. The sea and rivers dry up; the rich pasture lands of Bashan and Carmel wither and the green slopes of Lebanon fade before the coming of the Warrior God. But in the midst of this portrait of an avenging power, Nahum inserts some words which serve to remind his audience of the purpose of God's approach in judgment: "the Lord is good" (verse 7). The goodness of God is manifest in the refuge he offers to those who trust in him, but that refuge in turn is to be secured by the judgment soon to be executed against Nineveh.

The prophecy contained in chapter 1 provides at its end three specific messages which pertain to the meaning of the whole book.

(i) *God is a liberator* (verses 12–13). Whereas the opening verses of the book (2–11) contained the prophet's description of the avenging God, now Nahum declares God's own words addressed to the people of Judah. The message has various components, each of which interrelates with the others. (a) Despite the apparently invincible nature of Judah's enemy, Assyria would nevertheless be defeated and pass off the stage of human history. (b) Although in the past God used Assyria as his instrument in the judgment of the chosen people, that affliction would soon come to an end. (c) God's destruction of Assyria would simultaneously be his liberation of Judah. The message Nahum proclaimed to his people was an ancient one, going back to the days of Hebrew slavery in Egypt: God would liberate his chosen people from human bondage. But although the message was an ancient one, proclaimed by numerous prophets over several centuries, Nahum declares it for his own age and his own generation. In every century, as the experience of bondage returns again to the people of God, the message of liberation must also be declared again.

Nahum thus stands squarely in one of the great traditions of biblical faith. He declares from God a word of liberation. God never ceases to hate cruelty, oppression, and the chains of bondage that human beings attach to their fellow humans. And though there are times when God may appear to be deaf to the cries of the oppressed, eventually his prophets stand again to declare that liberation is coming and that the oppressors must answer for their crimes. The tragedy of the message of liberation, which is intrinsically a word of hope, is that it must be repeated again and again from one generation to another. And today, no less than in Nahum's time, the message of God's liberation must be declared, for still there are multitudes of the oppressed in this world.

(ii) *God is a judge* (verse 14). The words of verse 14, once again expressed as direct divine speech, are addressed to Nineveh, the capital city of Assyria; they are in the form of a sentence of death. The name of Nineveh would no more continue; its gods, the symbol of its power and might, would no longer be worshipped, for the great temple would be destroyed. "I will make your grave, for you are vile": the Giver of all human life thus announces death for the city in which violence had slain compassion, in which evil had conquered the good. There is no uncertainty in the divine speech concerning for whom the bell tolls; Nineveh, identified at the very beginning of the prophecy (1:1), must die.

The two complementary faces of God are thus set side by side in the prophet's opening words. One part of the divine countenance reflects the compassion of the liberator; the other part glows with the hatred of those who oppress and make liberation a constant necessity of God's participation in human experience. Nahum's is a sturdy theology, not for the weak and squeamish; we may all affirm heartily God's role as liberator, but we are hesitant also to affirm that liberation involves judgment. And that judgment, in turn, reveals the anger of a righteous God against the ruthlessness of human beings who think they can act with impunity.

(iii) *God is the hope for peace* (verse 15). Rounding out the opening portion of Nahum's prophecy are words reminiscent of Isaiah (40:9). A messenger would come to Judah with good tidings: the times of war would be followed by peace, for the ancient enemy was soon to be defeated. The feasts and festivals of the faith would be celebrated once again, for the pagan nation that had suspended them would cease to be Judah's ruler. Thus, although Nahum spoke of Nineveh's defeat before the event had happened, his faith here outstrips the contemporary realities of his time. A messenger would indeed come one day soon, and his message would be one of peace.

Nahum, despite the gloom of this oracle and the terror of its substance, here anticipates the Gospel. He speaks to a profoundly depressed people, who have known too long the tyranny of oppression; he tells them to lift up their heads, now hanging in despair, and to look for the messenger that would bring news of freedom, of a new life and a new celebration of the faith. And in the same way, the message of the glad tidings of the Gospel comes to those who are oppressed and in despair. The message is one of peace, a peace from external oppression and a new kind of peace with the God who is the giver of all life.

THE SIEGE OF NINEVEH

Nahum 2:1–13

[1]The shatterer has come up against you.
    Man the ramparts;
    watch the road;
gird your loins;
    collect all your strength.

[2](For the Lord is restoring the majesty of Jacob
    as the majesty of Israel,
for plunderers have stripped them
    and ruined their branches.)

[3]The shield of his mighty men is red,
    his soldiers are clothed in scarlet.
The chariots flash like flame
    when mustered in array;
    the chargers prance.
[4]The chariots rage in the streets,
    they rush to and fro through the squares;
they gleam like torches,
    they dart like lightning.
[5]The officers are summoned,

    they stumble as they go,
  they hasten to the wall,
    the mantelet is set up.
6The river gates are opened,
  the palace is in dismay;
7its mistress is stripped, she is carried off,
  her maidens lamenting,
moaning like doves,
  and beating their breasts.
8Nineveh is like a pool
  whose waters run away.
"Halt! Halt!" they cry;
  but none turns back.
9Plunder the silver,
  plunder the gold!
There is no end of treasure,
  or wealth of every precious thing.

10Desolate! Desolation and ruin!
  Hearts faint and knees tremble,
anguish is on all loins,
  all faces grow pale!
11Where is the lions' den,
  the cave of the young lions,
where the lion brought his prey,
  where his cubs were, with none to disturb?
12The lion tore enough for his whelps
  and strangled prey for his lionesses;
he filled his caves with prey
  and his dens with torn flesh.

    13Behold, I am against you, says the Lord of hosts, and I will burn your chariots in smoke, and the sword shall devour your young lions; I will cut off your prey from the earth, and the voice of your messengers shall no more be heard.

So dramatic is Nahum's poetic account of the siege of Nineveh, that it reads as if the siege had already taken place, as if the great city was already being reduced to ruins. But despite the air of realism running through the poetic lines, Nahum's poem is anticipatory; though the siege has yet to take place on the real stage of history, he can see it as clearly in the mind's eye as if the battle were being waged in front of him. One of the tragic aspects of this poem is that, although the battle was yet to be fought, the poet had experienced all the terrors of which he wrote. He described the siege of the perennial besiegers; he recounted the fighting in the streets of Nineveh which he already knew from the fighting of the Assyrians in the streets of Judean towns. And it is probable, too, that Nahum knew something of the nature of Nineveh; whether he had visited that great city, or whether he had merely learned of it from the accounts of others who had been there, his words betray knowledge of the city, its defences, and its vulnerability at certain points to attack.

The city of Nineveh, in the 7th century B.C., was one of the most extraordinary cities in the ancient world. Some of the ruins can still be seen, just east of modern Mosul across the River Tigris, and some 250 miles north of Baghdad. The inner city, built on the eastern banks of the Tigris, was surrounded by a great defensive wall, almost 8 miles in its circumference. The wall, ranging in height from 25 to 60 feet, was further protected by a great moat, set off some distance from the wall itself. And a number of heavily fortified gates gave access to the city through the great defensive walls. The western approach to the city, beyond the western wall, was defended by the River Tigris; to the east, beyond the city wall proper, lay a further system of ramparts and ditches, protecting an approach by an enemy from the east.

Within the city walls, on a hill in the western sector of the city, there was an enormous royal palace; some of it has survived, and within the ruins one can still see the immense stone reliefs depicting the military victories of Assyria. Near the palace was the ancient temple of the goddess Ishtar, one of the patron deities of the city. And further to the south, a few remains may still be seen of the once formidable Assyrian arsenal. Even now, the remains of Nineveh convey to its visitor the sense of its impregnability; in its days of glory, it must have seemed to be an eternal city, totally secure in its massive fortifications.

But Nineveh was not impregnable; from a military perspective, there were a number of vulnerable points. At the northeast corner of the city walls, where the road from Khorsabad approaches the city, there is high ground overlooking the city's centre. And running through the centre of the city was the River Khosr; it flowed through gates in the city walls, entering in the east wall and exiting through the west wall to flow into the Tigris. From the River Khosr, waters were drawn to fill the moats, but the waters could be controlled and directed from outside the city. Tradition has it that Nineveh's defeat was brought about in part by the manipulation of this water system. And parts of Nahum's account indicate that he anticipated its fall to be associated with its water system (verses 6, 8).

It is against this background of a powerful and well-defended city that one must read the dramatic poem of Nahum in chapter 2. His poetry has short staccato lines, conveying in sense and sound the chaos and conflict of the scene. He begins with a call to arms: "Man the ramparts; watch the road; gird your loins . . . " (verse 1), but no guardians can defend against the coming judgment of God. The enemy chariots and infantry breach the city walls; soon they are raging through the city streets, administering to the citizens of Nineveh the terrible medicine they in turn had administered to other cities. The river gates are opened (verse 6), letting in the devastating flood waters; the once proud palace is reduced to a shambles. And the city which was a treasure-house of loot stolen from the cities of Western Asia is now itself plundered, its great stores of silver and gold seized by the successful invaders (verse 9). The city of Nineveh, once as secure from enemies as the lion's den, has been breached by beasts of prey (verses 11–12); Nahum's metaphor mocks the symbolic lion with which Ishtar, goddess of Nineveh, was traditionally associated.

This poem of Nahum's evokes various reactions from those who read its words. It is a powerful poem, even in translation, but will there be no end to wars and siege? The sack of Nineveh, so vividly anticipated by Nahum, has been repeated hundreds of times in multitudes of cities down through the centuries of human history. Of wars, it seems, there will be no end. But there are, nevertheless, some instructive themes in the prophet's poem.

(i) The sack of Nineveh is concurrently the defeat of evil; it is not just another war, but the punishment of an empire's atrocities whose stench still survives down through the centuries. The knowledge that the sack of Nineveh was a direct consequence of that city's evil does not make it any more palatable, nor does it give grounds for celebration. But Nahum points to the heart of the matter in declaring the divine words: "Behold, I am against you, says the Lord of hosts" (verse 13). The practice and perpetuation of human atrocities inevitably invites the opposition of God. And Nahum declares, in his own distinctive way, that the fruits of violence and evil eventually must return to haunt their perpetrators.

(ii) The sheer splendour of Nineveh before its fall is a reminder of the impermanence and frailty of all the greatest human symbols of strength and confidence. Other cities had weaknesses, but Nineveh's system of national and civic defence seemed foolproof; even if the land were to be invaded, surely Nineveh could not fall! But it could; any fortress can fold under pressure, especially when its inner strength has been sapped by the corruption of violence. And the greater the glory before the fall, the hollower it seems after the collapse. Rudyard Kipling wrote:

> Lo, all our pomp of yesterday
>   is one with Nineveh and Tyre!

Nahum reminds us of the frailty of human pride and strength; he implies that we must seek a more enduring city in this world than that of Nineveh.

NINEVEH AND THEBES

Nahum 3:1–19

> [1]Woe to the bloody city,
>   all full of lies and booty—
>   no end to the plunder!
> [2]The crack of whip, and rumble of wheel,
>   galloping horse and bounding chariot!
> [3]Horsemen charging,
>   flashing sword and glittering spear,

hosts of slain,
    heaps of corpses,
dead bodies without end—
    they stumble over the bodies!
[4]And all for the countless harlotries of the harlot,
    graceful and of deadly charms,
who betrays nations with her harlotries,
    and peoples with her charms.

[5]Behold, I am against you,
    says the Lord of hosts,
    and will lift up your skirts over your face;
and I will let nations look on your nakedness
    and kingdoms on your shame.
[6]I will throw filth at you
    and treat you with contempt,
    and make you a gazingstock.
[7]And all who look on you will shrink from you and say,
Wasted is Nineveh; who will bemoan her?
    whence shall I seek comforters for her?

[8]Are you better than Thebes
    that sat by the Nile,
with water around her,
    her rampart a sea,
    and water her wall?
[9]Ethiopia was her strength,
    Egypt too, and that without limit;
    Put and the Libyans were her helpers.

[10]Yet she was carried away,
    she went into captivity;
her little ones were dashed in pieces
    at the head of every street;
for her honoured men lots were cast,
    and all her great men were bound in chains.
[11]You also will be drunken,
    you will be dazed;
you will seek
    a refuge from the enemy.
[12]All your fortresses are like fig trees
    with first-ripe figs—

if shaken they fall
    into the mouth of the eater.
13Behold, your troops
    are women in your midst.
The gates of your land
    are wide open to your foes;
    fire has devoured your bars.

14Draw water for the siege,
    strengthen your forts;
go into the clay,
    tread the mortar,
    take hold of the brick mould!
15There will the fire devour you,
    the sword will cut you off.
    It will devour you like the locust.

Multiply yourselves like the locust,
    multiply like the grasshopper!
16You increased your merchants
    more than the stars of the heavens.
    The locust spreads its wings and flies away.
17Your princes are like grasshoppers,
    your scribes like clouds of locusts
settling on the fences
    in a day of cold—
when the sun rises, they fly away;
    no one knows where they are.

18Your shepherds are asleep,
    O king of Assyria;
    your nobles slumber.
Your people are scattered on the mountains
    with none to gather them.
19There is no assuaging your hurt,
    your wound is grievous.
All who hear the news of you
    clap their hands over you.
For upon whom has not come
    your unceasing evil?

The dramatic poetry of battle in chapter 2 is now followed by a song in which taunt and mockery are interwoven with further scenes of conflict. Nahum is not merely describing Nineveh's coming end; he is also revealing his feelings, and those of his God, concerning the capital city's destruction. The "bloody city" (verse 1) will be strewn with heaps of corpses, so numerous that the cavalry stumble over the piled bodies of the slain. And the awful refrain of chapter 2 is repeated: "Behold, I am against you, says the Lord of hosts" (verse 5). God's contempt was such that Nineveh would become the focus of shame and derision amongst the world's nations.

In verses 8–10, Nahum compares the coming fate of Nineveh with the accomplished fate of Thebes. As Thebes had fallen, so too would Nineveh, for it was no better than the great Egyptian city. Thebes (or No-Amon) was one of the most splendid of ancient Egyptian cities; the remains of its great buildings may still be seen at the site, some 300 miles south of the modern city of Cairo. Like Nineveh, it was built beside a river. On the eastern bank of the Nile, at Karnak and Luxor, was one part of the city, whose great palaces and temples, though now partially in ruins, still suggest the permanence of some human achievements. To the west of the Nile, clustered along the foot of the steep cliffs and slopes of the Nile Valley, were the great temples of many generations of pharaohs. And further west, penetrating into the cliffs and foothills, there lay the Valley of the Kings, where the Royal Tombs of the New Kingdom were carefully guarded.

As the capital city of southern Egypt, Thebes was second only to Memphis in its glory and strength. And its location in the Nile Valley, where the steep cliffs come close to the river on either bank, together with its distance from the Egyptian border with Western Asia, had contributed to its citizens that familiar sense of invincibility. But the invincible Thebes had been conquered, and it was the Assyrians who had brought the ancient city to its knees. The Assyrian Emperor, Ashurbanipal, had proceeded with his armies into southern Egypt and in 663 B.C. had conquered Thebes. They had taken with them as loot from the city the massive wealth which Egypt had acquired from its own pursuit of imperial expansion.

Nahum's comparison of Nineveh and Thebes is a subtle one; at one level, it is simply an illustration of his theme that an impregnable city can be breached. But he is also conveying a deeper message, one having to do with evil and its eventual judgment. The deeper meaning is illustrated for us from the discoveries of archaeology. Among the texts that have survived from ancient Assyria is an inscribed cyclinder (the so-called Rassam Cylinder) on which are recounted some of the military adventures of Ashurbanipal. The Assyrian Chronicles contain the following passage, here in paraphrase, expressed as Ashurbanipal's own words.

> I went south in Egypt as far as Thebes and I conquered the city completely. I carried away it treasures, heavy and too numerous to count: silver, gold, precious stones, and the like.

As one continues to read Ashurbanipal's chronicles of his military campaigns, and supplements them with the illustrations from Assyrian art, one gains an impression of the total ruthlessness of Assyrian military power. Not only were atrocities performed, but they are described with apparent delight and pride. There was indiscriminate killing, human bodies were flailed and impaled on spikes, conquered kings had dog-collars placed around their necks and were treated as beasts deserving no mercy. Assyria did not simply boast an army; its soldiers and officers were the willing servants of violence, taking pleasure in the abuse of human life, and extolling the very acts which degraded their humanity. Thus we see that Nineveh and Thebes are not merely compared. The utter evil of the Assyrian sack of Thebes and countless other cities could not go unpunished; as they had done evil to others, so would evil be done to them. Nahum cries out not so much for vengeance as for justice, for the rampant evil of Assyria made a mockery out of all human existence.

As we perceive these fundamental themes of justice and the punishment of evil that penetrate Nahum's book, we can understand why his work does not conclude with a happy postscript; rather, it ends with a rhetorical question: "upon whom has not come your unceasing evil?" (verse 19). The question is addressed to Assyria, but its echoes address all human states that have exercised and abused their power. Nahum affirms that which is rarely self-evident from history as such, either ancient or modern. The atrocities of nations against other nations demand some response of justice; the prophet affirms that ultimately justice will be done. He cannot dress up the balancing of the scales of justice in pleasant words and pretty scenes. The eventual execution of justice brings its own horrors, though with them comes some relief for those who have for so long suffered injustice.

But we must, at the end, be careful not to oversimplify Nahum's message. He is not a political scientist, but a visionary theologian, or better, a poet. He presents not so much a doctrine of justice, which can be converted into political theory or liberation theology, but an affirmation of divine justice. He speaks as one who believes that God will act, not as one who is God's self-proclaimed lieutenant, thirsting for the battlefield so that he can engage in the slaughter of which he speaks. If we have grasped Nahum's message, we will not volunteer to join the ranks of Nineveh's attackers; rather, we shall seek to transform the evil within the nation to which we belong.

INTRODUCTION TO THE BOOK OF HABAKKUK

Habakkuk is one of several characters in the Old Testament who are named, but who remain virtually anonymous. Apart from the two occurrences of his name in the book named after him, Habakkuk is not referred to in any other Old Testament book. Indeed, even the pronunciation of his name is the subject of uncertainty. *Habakkuk* seems to be a Hebrew form of an Assyrian word for a certain kind of plant; but in the Septuagint, the earliest Greek translation of the Old Testament, the prophet is called *Hambakoum*. It would thus be unwise to draw any weighty conclusions from the prophet's name! He is referred to later on in Jewish literature, where he appears as a character in the apocryphal story of Bel and the Dragon, but there is little of historical value that can be drawn from this later reference.

Thus, what can be learned of the prophet Habakkuk must be drawn from the three chapters of his short book. He is called a *prophet* (1:1), and perhaps it may be inferred from this that he was a professional prophet who pursued his ministry in the temple in Jerusalem. From the substance of his writings, we can determine that he lived in the latter half of the 7th century B.C.; the precise date of his work is the source of much debate, but it might tentatively be set somewhere between the years 610–605 B.C. Habakkuk would thus be a contemporary of the better known prophet Jeremiah, and also of Nahum, whose book immediately precedes that of Habakkuk. As a prophet serving in the temple, his ministry would have involved the communication of God's "oracles" to the people; indeed, the substance of this book is referred to as an oracle which Habakkuk received in a vision (1:1), though this descriptive statement applies principally to chapters 1–2.

The poetry of this short book provides a further limited glimpse of the prophet's character: he was a man who had a way with words. Although the Hebrew text is somewhat obscure and difficult to translate in places, the power and vitality of the prophet's poetry have survived even in translation. And the poetry in turn breathes with Habakkuk's sense of the awesomeness and purity of the Almighty. But beyond such inferences as these, there is little that can be learned of the life and work of the prophet Habakkuk. To Voltaire has been attributed the saying: "Habakkuk was capable of anything", but all that we really know is that he was capable of communicating something of the vision and message of his God.

THE PROBLEM OF INTERPRETATION

There are various problems associated with the interpretation of this short book; they do not seriously deflect from its principal message, but they make difficult the detailed interpretation of the component parts of the book. There appear to be two principal parts to the work: the first part comprises chapters 1–2, which may be a collection of the prophet's oracles, while the second part (chapter 3) appears to be a hymn or prayer, having certain similarities to the substance of the Psalter. Both parts have been prefaced by the prophet's name (1:1 and 3:1), and although the authorship of chapter 3 in particular has been questioned, there are not many persuasive arguments against holding the view that the entire book may be attributed to Habakkuk.

But the problem of perspective remains: how should we approach the reading of this short work? To approach it merely as a collection of the prophet's sayings, analogous to other prophetic collections, may be too simple and may blind the reader to the continuity that holds together the whole. A number of scholars have proposed that the book must be interpreted from a liturgical perspective: if Habakkuk was a temple prophet, perhaps this composition was prepared for use in the temple. The more liturgical aspect of the ceremony, with alternation between speakers, would be traced in chapters 1–2; the hymn or prayer in chapter 3 would have been for congregational use. There are aspects of this hypothesis which are persuasive, but in the last resort it is not sufficiently precise to account for the sense of intimacy that pervades the dialogue between God and his prophet in the two opening chapters. It may be better to view the book as a whole as a written account of a religious, indeed visionary, experience of Habakkuk. But parts of the book, and especially chapter 3, would later have been employed in the worship of the temple.

There are further problems of interpretation for which, likewise, there are no simple solutions. The reference to the Chaldeans (1:6) indicates no doubt the powerful peoples who restored to strength the Babylonian Empire in the last quarter of the 7th century B.C. But who are the "wicked" persons referred to in 1:4? Are they, as some would argue, Judah's Assyrian enemies, who were soon to be conquered by the Babylonians (or Chaldeans)? Or are they Hebrews, citizens of Judah whose evil acts oppressed their fellow citizens? Once again, we cannot be sure, but the latter solution is more likely. It is therefore reasonable to suppose that the issues addressed by Habakkuk begin at home, but from there extend abroad to raise fundamental questions about the nature and acts of God. And it is in this larger context that the prophet's enduring message comes down to us.

THE MESSAGE OF HABAKKUK

The prophet's message emerges initially from the dialogue in which he is engaged with God. He asks God, from the setting of the evil times in which he lives in Judah, how much longer injustice and violence will triumph. God responds that he will use the Chaldeans as his instrument of judgment on the perpetrators of injustice and violence in Judah, but the divine response raises for Habakkuk more problems than it solves. Granted that the chosen people were evil, the Chaldeans were even worse; how could a good God employ an evil nation to judge a less evil nation? The answer he receives only partly resolves the prophet's dilemma: the foreign nation would also be judged after it had fulfilled its role, while in Judah the righteous remnant would hold on and survive through their exercise of steadfast faith. The themes of the dialogue are then brought together in the final words of prayer and praise (chapter 3).

Habakkuk's message was addressed initially to a particular age and a particular set of circumstances, but it is addressed in addition to the kind of questions that human beings raise in every age and in a multitude of circumstances. The prophet offers no simple answers; he provides some general perspectives within which we must seek to understand, and some advice as to how to hold on through times of trial. Like Habakkuk, we may raise the question: how long must evil and violence continue, not only in other places, but also in ourselves and in our own community? And if, in response, we are told that injustice and violence must be judged, we can accept that. But can we accept that the means by which the judgment may be executed is even more evil than that which is judged? There seems to be a fundamental contradiction in such a notion. This little book does not resolve the contradiction, but sets it in perspective.

First, God's actions in this world are not, as it were, miraculous: without the use of human agents. He works through people and nations. To judge an evil nation, he may employ another evil nation; to human eyes, this may appear unjust, but ultimately, Habakkuk affirms, all evil must be judged. Second, God's actions in the world reveal partially his sovereignty over human beings and nations. Sovereign actions are rarely easy to understand, but steadfast faith in the God who acts will carry us through the clouds of unknowing to an understanding that may come to us on the further side of darkness. Third, what makes it possible to accept the often mysterious acts of God is the fundamental conviction that the Lord is a moral being (1:13). While we may not be able to understand the manner in which God's moral being moves, its direction is always towards human deliverance and its consequence must always be the worship of God (3:18–19).

THE PRAYER OF HABAKKUK

Habakkuk 1:1–4

¹The oracle of God which Habakkuk the prophet saw.
²O Lord, how long shall I cry for help,
   and thou wilt not hear?
Or cry to thee "Violence!"
   and thou wilt not save?
³Why dost thou make me see wrongs
   and look upon trouble?
Destruction and violence are before me;
   strife and contention arise.
⁴So the law is slacked
   and justice never goes forth.
For the wicked surround the righteous,
   so justice goes forth perverted.

The book begins with Habakkuk engaged in prayer. His concerns are his own but as he expresses his particular concerns, in words, it is immediately evident that they are also those of any thinking human being. His prayer takes the form of a series of questions addressed to God: they are the kinds of questions to which there is no evident answer and thus they are put to God as a last resort. And the substance of the questions gives the prayer the character of a psalm of lament. In part, Habakkuk is questioning God; in part, he is despairing of making any sense out of the nature of God's world.

In literary terms, Habakkuk's prayer has an intensely individual form, as do the psalms of lament upon which it is modelled. And the structure of the book as a whole, with the divine response following the human questions, suggests that its origin lies in deeply personal religious experience. Whether that experience was gained in the temple, in the context of the prophet's formal ministry, or whether it arose in the seclusion of his own private life, we cannot know with any certainty. But the eventual writing down of the divine dialogue makes what was once private public.

The reader is enabled, as it were, to overhear this desperate dialogue with God. And as the prophet's opening questions strike a chord of familiarity in our own minds, we begin to perceive the perpetual relevance of Habakkuk's little book.

The prophet's opening questions develop two fundamental areas of difficulty in human and religious experience.

(i) *God does not seem to answer prayer*. The particular words that Habakkuk now prays presuppose a long history of the prophet's praying to which there had been no apparent response. The preceding and unanswered prayers had no doubt been partly personal, but primarily on behalf of the nation and community. Habakkuk was very conscious of the violence both within and beyond his nation; he was aware, too, of the evil of the violence that characterized his society. And so he prayed for help and for deliverance, both for himself and for his people. But for all his praying, nothing seemed to happen. He asked for help, but God did not seem to hear. He pleaded for deliverance from violence, but God did not deliver. And so now he prays about prayer itself, by implication questioning the capacity of the One to whom the prayer is addressed. How long should he pray, when none appears to be listening? Or why should he continue to plead, when there appears to be no interest on God's part in acting?

Habakkuk's concern is thus partly related to the apparent ineffectiveness of prayer as such, and partly related to God's lack of action. That for which he prays ought to be a matter of concern to God; the prophet indeed might expect divine action in his society, given its evil, without the need of any praying on his part. But nothing was happening. Prayer seemed to be the activity of a deluded mind; God appeared to be otiose.

Thus, the scene is set at the beginning of the book by the open expression of a common difficulty in *religious experience*, though it is a difficulty which many persons prefer not to vocalize. Scripture seems replete with promises implying we need only ask, and God will answer prayer. But theory and reality diverge in experience: many times, it seems, we ask and there is no answer. And when that for which we ask, namely deliverance from evil and violence, seems to be so clearly within the divine purview, the lack of an answer is even more difficult to understand. And there is even reticence on many people's part to raise such a matter in the form of a question to God. Is it not a little presumptuous to question God's ability? Is it not a little cheeky to imply that the divine promises concerning prayer are ineffective?

Habakkuk, though, is a man of integrity and courage. His integrity is such that he is genuinely perplexed by the silence and inaction of God. His courage is such that he does not hesitate to approach God and raise the question: "Why?" And the reader of the book is invited to join in the prophet's questioning at the beginning; we may bring our own similar problems and give expression to them in Habakkuk's words, hoping that the response to the prophet may also be a response to us. Why is it that God frequently does not seem to respond to human prayer?

(ii) *God does not seem to control human evil.* The prophet's world is marred by evil and violence, destruction and strife. The existence of evil is not the prophet's problem, but its unbridled character is hard to understand. In the nation of the chosen people, evil-doers should be controlled by the law; the natural human tendency toward injustice should be controlled by legally established forces of justice. Yet something was fundamentally wrong, for the force of law was slack and justice never seemed to prevail (verse 4). Again the prophet raises the question "Why?" Why do the wicked outnumber the righteous? Why does justice so quickly become perverted in the function of a human society?

Habakkuk's problem was particularly acute given the special status of his nation. With a God-given law and a divinely ordained system of justice, one might expect a society to function properly. But the problem was not peculiar to ancient Israel. In our modern world, too, most nations have a fine legal system and are supposed to function according to the norms of justice. But reality is normally otherwise: law and order rarely prevail and it seems that, from one generation to the next, violence and injustice are the principal characteristics of most human societies. Why? Why do not justice and righteousness prevail in human society? Why does God, the creator of all mankind, permit things to become the way they are? This too is a part of the prophet's problem which he brings to God in prayer; he seeks not only an intellectual solution to his problem, but a return of law and justice to the nation in which he lives.

It is said that the Book of Habakkuk marks the beginning of speculation in Israel. The prophet is baffled by the discrepancy between theology, on the one hand, and human experience on the other hand. Yet the book does not contain pure speculation, in any philosophical sense. Rather, it is that kind of speculation which emerges from a profound faith that finds difficulty in squaring what is believed with the practice of daily living. And therein lies the value of the book to the continuing community of faith: it raises openly the kind of questions that any thinking and believing person ought to ask. And insofar as the book contains answers, although they are couched in language specific to the prophet's time and place, they may nevertheless be understood as pointing to solutions not limited to their immediate context.

GOD'S FIRST RESPONSE

Habakkuk 1:5–11

> [5]Look among the nations, and see;
> wonder and be astounded.
> For I am doing a work in your days
> that you would not believe if told.
> [6]For lo, I am rousing the Chaldeans,
> that bitter and hasty nation,
> who march through the breadth of the earth,
> to seize habitations not their own.
> [7]Dread and terrible are they;
> their justice and dignity proceed from themselves.
> [8]Their horses are swifter than leopards,
> more fierce than the evening wolves;
> their horsemen press proudly on.
> Yea, their horsemen come from afar;
> they fly like an eagle swift to devour.
> [9]They all come for violence;
> terror of them goes before them.
> They gather captives like sand.

¹⁰At kings they scoff,
  and of rulers they make sport.
They laugh at every fortress,
  for they heap up earth and take it.
¹¹Then they sweep by like the wind and go on,
  guilty men, whose own might is their god!

Habakkuk, in his opening words of prayer, had raised some questions to God for which he desperately wanted an answer. Now God responds to his prophet and provides an answer of sorts, though it remains to be seen whether the divine response really deals with the prophetic query. These verses contain a speech with two focal points: one point is the fact that God is about to act, the other concerns the nation through whom he will act. The answer, though, is not at first sight tailor-made for the question.

The speech begins with an invitation to "Look"; though the speech describes what the prophet is to look for, the implication is that he will soon be able to see what is happening with his own eyes. Indeed, the events described in the divine speech may already have been set in motion. The prophet will now understand, however, that what is happening is an act of God, not an accident of history. And it is intimated clearly that the perception of current history as an act of God would be the source of considerable surprise to the prophet; indeed, it would be at first unbelievable!

There follows a description of one of the new super-powers that was in the process of emerging on the stage of human history, the Neo-Babylonian Empire, which had powerful armies and ambitions for expansion. The foreign state is referred to by the expression *Chaldeans* (verse 6), namely the tribes in southern Babylon who took control of the state in 627 B.C. and engineered its return to strength and freedom from Assyrian control. The newly powerful Babylon sacked and destroyed the great cities of Asshur (614 B.C.) and Nineveh (612 B.C.) and eventually took on the Egyptians in conflict at the Battle of Carchemish (605 B.C.). At some stage in this process of imperial revival, Habakkuk received the message from God contained in these verses. Although he certainly knew something of what was happening in world affairs, it is now made clear to him that these momentous historical events of his time were a part of the action of God.

The strength and might of the Babylonian armies are captured in powerful lines of poetry (verses 6–11). Their forces can move with great speed and their armies act ruthlessly, without any scruples of mercy and charity. Violence is their way of life; terror precedes their advance like a shock-wave, yet they themselves know no fear of enemies, so formidable is their power. The great fortresses that stand in their path offer no threat; they merely pile up dirt against the fortifications and capture them, then pass on for the next challenge to their imperial expansion. Violence has become the god of the Babylonians, that for which they live and that which they worship. Such is the substance of the divine speech to the prophet; it is hardly a theological speech in response to Habakkuk's troubled theological questions. There are elements of an answer here for Habakkuk, though there is not yet enough to remove the confusion from his mind.

(i) *God does respond to the prophet's prayer.* A part of the thrust of Habakkuk's initial complaint was that God did not seem to respond to his prayers. But he does respond directly to the prayer of inquiry; the prophet is not cut off from God, even though he cannot understand fully, as yet, the substance of the divine reply. Thus Habakkuk's courage in asking God why he did not seem to answer prayer was not misplaced; it was permissible, indeed responsible to raise the question, for the prophet's earlier prayers had been honestly prayed.

Habakkuk offers a limited paradigm of attitudes and actions in prayer. He prayed about the terrible state of his nation, but his prayers appeared to have no effect. But apparent failure did not reduce him to silence, nor did it cause him to doubt God. Rather, it raised a problem to be solved, and the only solution could come from God to whom his prayers had been addressed. So Habakkuk asked, needing an answer, and God answered.

(ii) *God is at work, even though his action may not be evident.* The focus of Habakkuk's prayer had been local, the evil and trouble within his own nation; to those local issues, he had been able to discern no local response that could be traced to God. But the divine speech addressed to Habakkuk indicates that he had not had sufficient vision. The apparently otiose deity was in fact at work, if only Habakkuk had had the eyes to perceive it. Far away in Babylon, events were taking place which would change the course of human history; they were not random events, nor merely the independent actions of a human state. Rather, in the larger scheme of things, they were a part of God's participation in human history which eventually would have their impact on the prophet's nation.

What is becoming clear is that Habakkuk's understanding was too limited. He believed that God was doing nothing; in reality, he simply could not see what God was doing. He made the mistake of assuming divine inaction simply because he could not see any sign of action. And even when he heard the divine speech, its implication must have been difficult to grasp. It was hard to believe that such distant events and such an alien people as the Chaldeans could have been part of the divine plan. But the message to the prophet was clear: he was wrong in thinking God was not at work. God was in action, if only he had the eyes to perceive it.

(iii) *God's response to prayer may be totally different from what is expected.* Habakkuk's immediate problem was his own nation, the evil and violence which characterized its life. And he phrased his questions to God in such a way as to presuppose a response that was as localized as the questions. Almost unconsciously, he knew the kind of answer that he wanted to get from God, and so he was quite unprepared for the kind of answer he actually got. He had real difficulties with the state of affairs that existed in his own nation, but he was not sufficiently flexible in his understanding to think that the resolution might be found in the actions of an alien and foreign power.

Again, Habakkuk's prayer and God's response teach us something about the very nature of prayer. It is a very natural and human thing to ask questions to which we genuinely want an answer, but to which we also know the kind of answer we want!

We perceive the problem in a limited way, and so we also presuppose the answer in a limited way. And because our understanding of the initial problem is so limited, we cannot possibly anticipate the scope of the unanticipated answer. There is no simple answer to the first part of this difficulty, namely our inability to see the larger picture. All we can hope for is flexibility and wisdom in understanding the divine response to prayer. If God responds to prayer in a way that appears initially incomprehensible, perhaps the question was inadequately expressed in the first place.

HABAKKUK'S ARGUMENT

Habakkuk 1:12–2:1

[12]Art thou not from everlasting,
　　O Lord my God, my Holy One?
　　We shall not die.
　　O Lord, thou hast ordained them as a judgment;
　　　and thou, O Rock, hast established them for chastisement.
[13]Thou who art of purer eyes than to behold evil
　　and canst not look on wrong,
　　why dost thou look on faithless men,
　　and art silent when the wicked swallows up
　　the man more righteous than he?
[14]For thou makest men like the fish of the sea,
　　like crawling things that have no ruler.
[15]He brings all of them up with a hook,
　　he drags them out with his net,
　　he gathers them in his seine;
　　　so he rejoices and exults.
[16]Therefore he sacrifices to his net
　　and burns incense to his seine;
　　for by them he lives in luxury,
　　　and his food is rich.
[17]Is he then to keep on emptying his net,
　　and mercilessly slaying nations for ever?

[1]I will take my stand to watch,
　　and station myself on the tower,
　　and look forth to see what he will say to me,
　　and what I will answer concerning my complaint.

The prophet is profoundly disturbed by the answer he has received to his initial questions. While he understands the essential substance of the divine response, he cannot fit it easily into his theological perspectives. He has a view of how he thinks God ought to act, but God's intimation of coming action is not in harmony with his presuppositions. Habakkuk has discovered, in other words, that the divine response to his initial questions has raised more difficulty than it has solved. And so now the new problems must be resolved, yet the approach of the prophet must be delicate. He does not want to imply that God's "theology" is unsound! And yet, if he is honest with himself, Habakkuk has to admit that what God has said seems to be out of harmony with all that he knows of God. And so he proceeds cautiously with an argument; in a sense, its purpose is to change God's mind, to alter the direction of God's previous statement. But he cannot phrase it quite so bluntly, and so he begins his argument with what seem to be solid theological foundations.

In a theoretical fashion, Habakkuk raises the question as to God's very nature, and he provides his own responses, drawing on the ancient hymns and traditions of the Hebrew faith. God is from everlasting, the Holy One (verse 12). God may certainly ordain a foreign nation to act as an instrument of judgment and chastisement on his own people because of their evil. But the fundamental characteristic of God raises a serious difficulty for Habakkuk. God's very essence is such that surely he cannot observe evil and wrong-doing, and allow it to flourish unchecked? Hence, how can he permit the Babylonians to act, with licence as it were, in the oppression of the chosen people (verse 13)? That is the fundamental problem. Granted that the Hebrews were evil, the Babylonians were surely worse. There seemed to be neither consistency nor moral integrity in the use of an extremely evil nation to punish a moderately evil nation!

The prophet then presses home his argument, to the point of exaggeration, in the extended metaphor of verses 14–17. His fellow countrymen are like fish of the sea; they swim about haphazardly, but have no sense of direction, for that is the way that God appears to have made them. On the other hand, the

Babylonian emperor is like the captain of a fishing boat. With hooks and nets, he hauls the hapless fish aboard his boat and rejoices in the size of his catch. His fishing net has become his god; it provides him with all he needs, and the poor fish upon whom he preys are helpless against his power. The metaphor concludes with a question from the prophet: is the fisherman to keep on emptying his net for ever? Is there to be no control over the merciless fisher of nations, for whom other peoples are merely fish to be caught in the endless drive towards the gratification of his desires?

The prophet makes a good argument, though, as often happens in the rhetoric of argumentation, the facts become slightly blurred. At the beginning of his dialogue with God, Habakkuk had been very aware of the sins and shortcomings of his own people and of the violence that was perpetrated in his nation. But when he perceived that the "Chaldeans" were to serve as God's instrument of judgment, the prophet changes his thrust. His own people were evil, but the Babylonians were worse, and so now he portrays the Hebrews as feckless fish and the foreign agent as a ruthless fisherman. Lying behind all the rhetoric is the prophet's perception of a serious problem. He has not forgotten that his own people are evil, but cannot accept their judgment at the hands of an even more evil people. And so, although he accepts the need of judgment, he tries to change God's mind as to the manner of judgment, and in so doing, he almost whitewashes his own people whom he had so recently condemned!

The prophet is maintaining his integrity in his dialogue with God, though now he is moving onto dangerous ground. His proper anxiety about the instrument of God's judgment will blind him to the continuing need for judgment, if he is not careful. He is almost at the point of saying: "Better not to be judged, than to be judged by a people more evil than we are!" But he is losing his sense of justice. The justice in divine judgment lies not in its instrument, but in the evil actions which called for judgment in the first place. If a murderer is condemned to death, the justice of his execution does not depend upon the moral integrity of the hangman! The evil of the executioner is a separate issue which requires its own judgment. That is something that will become more clear to Habakkuk as the dialogue continues.

Habakkuk's honest development of the argument is in danger of blinding him to the initial foundations from which he began. He had talked of violence and evil and nothing being done about it (1:2–3); now those evil-doers are like the fish of the sea, aimless and without a ruler (verse 14). Human responsibility for evil has been exchanged for a view of human nature in which human beings are merely creatures who cannot be held responsible for their actions. Habakkuk is being persuaded by his own thin rhetoric and risks losing sight of the truth!

The passage concludes with Habakkuk taking his stand and waiting for the next response from God (2:1). He speaks with the satisfaction of one who is well pleased with his argument. It is as if he says to God: "Now there's an argument for you! Let's see what you'll do with that one!" The prophet, for all his honesty and decency, still has a lot to learn about God!

GOD'S RESPONSE: THE VISION

Habakkuk 2:2–4

> ²And the Lord answered me
> "Write the vision;
>   make it plain upon tablets,
>   so he may run who reads it.
> ³For still the vision awaits its time;
>   it hastens to the end—it will not lie.
> If it seem slow, wait for it;
>   it will surely come, it will not delay.
> ⁴Behold, he whose soul is not upright in him shall fail,
>   but the righteous shall live by his faith."

God responds once again to the prophet's question, though on this occasion he does not give an answer as such, but merely indicates that a full answer is coming. When it comes, the prophet is instructed to write down the substance of the vision that he receives upon tablets; in this manner, the message that he receives will be preserved and may be read aloud to the present and to future generations. The vision, it is clear, will be pertinent not only to Habakkuk's immediate questions, but also to the questions that the chosen people will perpetually raise in response to the difficult experience of living in an evil world.

The prophet is also warned that the vision may take some time in coming. For Habakkuk, the delay may naturally evoke impatience and he must learn to wait for it, but he is assured that in God's good time the vision will come. And there is more than a suggestion in these verses that the vision and its fulfilment in historical reality are intimately related: not only will the vision come with certainty, but its fulfilment in time and place will be equally certain. But the delay in the vision's coming will be a source of considerable trial to Habakkuk. He must learn not only patience, but also faithfulness to the God who grants not only vision, but fulfilment.

Although at first sight this short passage may seem to be only an interlude in the larger context of the prophet's dialogue with God, it is nevertheless a critical passage for understanding the message of the book as a whole.

(i) It is taking time, but Habakkuk is gradually learning that *God's time is not man's time*. He had begun the dialogue by praying to God: "How long?" (1:2). God's apparent inaction in response to evil was a source of difficulty to the prophet, but he had made the mistake of measuring God on the human scale of time. He had thought that God does not act, but he was coming to realize that God had simply not yet acted. He knew that God ought to act in response to evil, and in this he was correct; he thought he knew *when* God ought to act, and in this he was wrong. And so now he was learning the difficult lesson of waiting in patience.

Just as, in human life, the timing of certain actions and events is of crucial importance, so it is also in the divine scheme of things. But human beings do not have either the knowledge or wisdom to know when God should act. It is easier to grasp that fact than its implications, for there are times when every scrap of theology we possess suggests God ought to act. The apparent lack of divine action, which may cause faith to falter, is in reality only our inability to perceive the timing of divine action. We must try to learn Habakkuk's lesson: "If it seem slow, wait for it; it will surely come, it will not delay" (verse 3).

(ii) *Faithfulness is the key to righteous living* (verse 4). The text of verse 4 is difficult to translate with certainty, but the general thrust seems to be clear. The person who is not upright will not have the courage and tenacity to succeed in life. The righteous person, that is the one whose life is penetrated by God's right-eousness, shall live successfully. The key to the life of the righteous is *faithfulness* (as the Hebrew text states literally; the RSV translation, *faith*, is influenced by the use made of the text in the New Testament: see below). The word *faithfulness*, in turn, points to the integrity of the relationship between a person and God which is central to the meaning of human existence. For Habakkuk, faithfulness meant continuing to cling to God, even when he could not understand God's actions, even when God's timing appeared to the prophet to be a lack of any kind of action at all.

Faithfulness requires a continuation in the relationship with God, even when experience outstrips faith and the purpose in continuing to believe is called into question. The life of faith does not require reason and knowledge to be abandoned, as Habakkuk's persistent questioning makes clear. But the life of faith may require continuing belief, even though reason and knowledge have long since been exhausted. We cannot always understand either God's action or his seeming lack of action. Nevertheless, if the relationship is secure, we can continue in the path of faith even when the road of knowledge has become a cul-de-sac.

(iii) *Righteousness and faith are directly related.* In the New Testament, the meaning of verse 4 is developed beyond the initial horizons of Habakkuk, in the context of the Christian Gospel. It is there cited, like all Old Testament texts, as it appears in the Septuagint (Greek) translation. St Paul wrote to the Church in Rome: "For in it [the Gospel] the righteousness of God is revealed through faith for faith; as it is written, 'He who through faith is righteous shall live' [quoting Hab. 2:4]" (Rom. 1:17). And to the Galatian Church he wrote: "Now it is evident that no man is justified before God by the law; for 'He who through faith is righteous shall live'" (Gal. 3:11). The theme is taken up again by the writer of the Epistle to the Hebrews (10:38) and, through Martin Luther's writing and preaching, became one of the key themes of the Protestant Reformation. A person is not acceptable by God on the basis of human works, but rather is justified on the grounds of faith.

Although the New Testament writers and the theologians of the Christian centuries have moved a long way from the initial kernel of thought expressed in Habakkuk, they stand nevertheless in the same tradition. What is central to the meaning of human existence? It is, in the ancient Jewish perspective, the faithful relationship with God, not the human capacity to know, to understand, or to act. From the perspective of the Christian Gospel, that same relationship to God is equally central. It is offered to us Gentiles in Jesus Christ; it cannot be bought or worked for by the recipient, but can be received from God in faith and with thanksgiving. But Habakkuk said it clearly: the meaning of our life and the possibility of righteousness flow from a commitment to God, in faith and in continuing faithfulness.

FIVE WOES TO THE WICKED

Habakkuk 2:5-20

⁵"Moreover, wine is treacherous;
    the arrogant man shall not abide.
His greed is as wide as Sheol;
    like death he has never enough.
He gathers for himself all nations,
    and collects as his own all peoples."

⁶Shall not all these take up their taunt against him, in scoffing derision of him, and say,
    "Woe to him who heaps up what is not his own—
        for how long?—
    and loads himself with pledges!"

⁷Will not your debtors suddenly arise,
  and those awake who will make you tremble?
  Then you will be booty for them.
⁸Because you have plundered many nations,
  all the remnant of the peoples shall plunder you,
 for the blood of men and violence to the earth,
  to cities and all who dwell therein.

⁹Woe to him who gets evil gain for his house,
  to set his nest on high,
  to be safe from the reach of harm!
¹⁰You have devised shame to your house
  by cutting off many peoples;
  you have forfeited your life.
¹¹For the stone will cry out from the wall,
  and the beam from the woodwork respond.

¹²Woe to him who builds a town with blood,
  and founds a city on iniquity!
¹³Behold, is it not from the Lord of hosts
  that peoples labour only for fire,
  and nations weary themselves for naught?
¹⁴For the earth will be filled
  with the knowledge of the glory of the Lord,
  as the waters cover the sea.

¹⁵Woe to him who makes his neighbours drink
  of the cup of his wrath, and makes them drunk,
  to gaze on their shame!
¹⁶You will be sated with contempt instead of glory.
  Drink, yourself, and stagger!
 The cup in the Lord's right hand will come around to you,
  and shame will come upon your glory!
¹⁷The violence done to Lebanon will overwhelm you;
  the destruction of the beasts will terrify you,
 for the blood of men and violence to the earth,
  to cities and all who dwell therein.

¹⁸What profit is an idol
  when its maker has shaped it,
  a metal image, a teacher of lies?
 For the workman trusts in his own creation
  when he makes dumb idols!

¹⁹Woe to him who says to a wooden thing, Awake;
　　to a dumb stone, Arise!
　　Can this give revelation?
　Behold, it is overlaid with gold and silver,
　　and there is no breath at all in it.

²⁰But the Lord is in his holy temple;
　　let all the earth keep silence before him.

The tone and style of this passage suggest that we are no longer
dealing with a private narrative recounting the dialogue between
Habakkuk and God. The passage contains an oracle, or series of
oracles; the words are addressed rhetorically to the "arrogant
man" (verse 5), presumably the Babylonian emperor, but the
context of their declaration would have been in some temple
setting (verse 20). Habakkuk is back at work, engaged in the
public proclamation of God's word which was his prophetic calling. But as we read his public words, we see that they contain
answers to some of his private questions, particularly those raised
in 1:12–13. The prophet had wondered how a holy God could use
an unholy nation to judge a less evil people. As we listen to him
speak, we perceive that he now knows the answer to that problem, but still the vision that he had been promised (2:2–3) has not
come.

The prophetic oracle is introduced in verses 5–6*a*; the introductory words are difficult to interpret, partly because of the uncertainty as to how to translate them (as noted in the RSV footnote),
and partly because they probably contain a riddle, as a literal
translation of verse 6*a* indicates ("Shall not all these take up a
riddle against him, and a taunt-song against him?"). The address
concerns the arrogant foreign ruler whose military activities
threaten Judah; it comprises five taunt-songs, each introduced by
the word "Woe", each indicating both crime and consequence.

(i) *The first message of woe* (verses 6*b*–8). The foreign ruler is
likened to a thieving money lender. He steals from some; from
others, he takes valuable items in pledge for tiny loans, making
himself wealthy by exploiting the needs and importunities of

others. Sooner or later, the prophet affirms, the oppressed will rebel. And then Habakkuk translates his metaphor: the plundered nations will eventually turn and plunder the Babylonian nation. Earlier, Habakkuk had wondered how a more evil nation could act as God's instrument in the judgment of a less evil nation. Now he understands very clearly that the instrument of judgment will eventually become the object of judgment; God's justice will be done.

What is intriguing about the oracle is the manner in which the Babylonian emperor's coming fall is expressed. It is not explicitly stated to be the consequence of a direct act of God. Rather, it is said to be a necessary and inevitable consequence of evil acts that had been perpetrated. Habakkuk, in other words, is beginning to perceive a moral order in the course of human history. He could not see it earlier, his mind being too constricted by time and place. But now he perceives it, as a consequence of receiving God's word. The tyranny of human empires may seem to succeed in the short run. But in the larger perspective, it becomes clear that all human tyranny has within it the seeds of its own destruction.

(ii) *The second message of woe* (verses 9–11). In metaphorical language, the prophet proclaims woe to the person who would build his house in a high and protected place, employing for his purpose the profits of unjust gain. The goal of security is undermined by the very means by which it is sought. And in translating the metaphor, the prophet indicates that the Babylonian royal house, or dynasty (the metaphor involves a word play), in its search for security has forfeited the safety it sought.

Again we can see the broader message emerging from the prophet's words. Tyranny has within it the seeds of its destruction; likewise, the evil pursuit of security brings about only the increased risk of danger. There is no security to be found in this world in the pursuit of exploitation and evil; it is in the very nature of the world's moral order that such longing for safety cannot be satisfied by immoral means.

(iii) *The third message of woe* (verses 12–14). The focus shifts now from the building of the royal house to the building of a city.

The city that is built on a foundation of iniquity and constructed at the expense of bloodshed cannot flourish; all will be for nought. Although the prophet refers to the construction of a city, his language is probably metaphorical for the construction of an empire. The Babylonians, through their military exploits, were attempting to construct an empire that would cover the face of the earth as it was known at that time. But their goals of world dominion were rooted in evil and nourished in blood; even as they built, they undermined their own construction.

In contrast to the futility of trying to build a human empire that covered the world, Habakkuk suddenly provides a glimpse of a different vision: "the earth will be filled with the knowledge of the glory of the Lord, as the waters cover the sea" (verse 14). The prophet has the noblest vision, but it is one that is shared by few human beings. Empires have come and gone since Habakkuk's time, each trying to fill the world with their own dominion and power. And, in the 20th century, empires are still with us whose goal is world-dominion and who would build their vision with oppression and bloodshed. Despite their apparent success, they cannot ultimately succeed; the ancient prophet offers a nobler goal to which to aspire.

(iv) *The fourth message of woe* (verses 15–17). The prophet now narrows his focus from the imperial goals of the enemy to their abominable practices. He alludes to drunken orgies by which the enemies bring upon themselves and their neighbours shame and degradation. But perhaps, fundamentally, it is to the drunkenness of power that the prophet alludes; in that drunken orgy of the exercise of power, terrible and wanton destruction are wrought. But, as before, the prophet indicates that the wanton use of violence against both the human world and the world of nature will return to haunt the perpetrators (verse 17). The violent persons will eventually be overwhelmed; the terrorists will be terrified—that too is a part of the world's moral order, established by God the Creator.

(v) *The fifth message of woe* (verses 18–19). The fifth message is concerned with idolatry, and a number of interpreters consider it to be out of harmony with the four preceding messages; they suggest it may be an addition from another and later hand. There cannot be certainty as to the origin of the passage. Nevertheless, although a message of this kind could be addressed to any of the practitioners of idolatry, it is not out of keeping with the preceding words addressed to the ruler of the Babylonians. We know from the survival of ancient inscriptions that Babylonian emperors ascribed their successes to their gods.

It is the futility of idols and the folly of idolaters that are highlighted in this brief message. There is something profoundly stupid in constructing an idol and then worshipping the work of one's own hands. And to address the idol as if it could answer only compounds the folly. To persons who place their trust in objects of wood or stone, the prophet can only proclaim yet another message of woe.

Idolatry, and its condemnation, are amongst the most common themes in the Old Testament. At a superficial level, the sin of idolatry seems peculiarly remote from our 20th century. Who among us has ever felt a sneaking and tempting urge to creep into the workshop, there to carve an idol! Indeed, few of us would have the ability, even if the urge should come. Yet the sin of idolatry is not so superficial, and its real temptation is already revealed in the preceding messages of woe. Idolatry is essentially the worship of that which we make, rather than of our Maker. And that which we make may be found in possessions, a home, a career, an ambition, a family, or a multitude of other people or things. We "worship" them when they become the focal point of our lives, that for which we live. And as the goal and centre of human existence, they are as foolish as any wooden idol or metal image. But what we can perceive so clearly in the words of a prophet from centuries long passed, we cannot always see so clearly in our immediate life and existence. As we reflect on Habakkuk's words, we should reflect also on the nature and direction of our own lives.

HABAKKUK'S PSALM

Habakkuk 3:1–19

¹A prayer of Habakkuk the prophet, according to Shigionoth.
²O Lord, I have heard the report of thee,
  and thy work, O Lord, do I fear.
 In the midst of the years renew it;
   in the midst of the years make it known;
   in wrath remember mercy.
³God came from Teman,
  and the Holy One from Mount Paran.
 His glory covered the heavens,
   and the earth was full of his praise.   *Selah*
⁴His brightness was like the light,
  rays flashed from his hand;
  and there he veiled his power.
⁵Before him went pestilence,
  and plague followed close behind.
⁶He stood and measured the earth;
  he looked and shook the nations;
 then the eternal mountains were scattered,
   the everlasting hills sank low.
   His ways were as of old.
⁷I saw the tents of Cushan in affliction;
   the curtains of the land of Midian did tremble.
⁸Was thy wrath against the rivers, O Lord?
  Was thy anger against the rivers,
  or thy indignation against the sea,
 when thou didst ride upon thy horses,
   upon thy chariot of victory?
⁹Thou didst strip the sheath from thy bow,
  and put the arrows to the string.   *Selah*
  Thou didst cleave the earth with rivers.
¹⁰The mountains saw thee, and writhed;
  the raging waters swept on;
 the deep gave forth its voice,
   it lifted its hands on high.

¹¹The sun and moon stood still in their habitation
   at the light of thine arrows as they sped,
   at the flash of thy glittering spear.
¹²Thou didst bestride the earth in fury,
   thou didst trample the nations in anger.
¹³Thou wentest forth for the salvation of thy people,
   for the salvation of thy anointed.
  Thou didst crush the head of the wicked,
   laying him bare from thigh to neck.   *Selah*
¹⁴Thou didst pierce with thy shafts the head of his warriors,
   who came like a whirlwind to scatter me,
   rejoicing as if to devour the poor in secret.
¹⁵Thou didst trample the sea with thy horses,
   the surging of mighty waters.

¹⁶I hear, and my body trembles,
   my lips quiver at the sound;
  rottenness enters into my bones,
   my steps totter beneath me.
  I will quietly wait for the day of trouble
   to come upon people who invade us.

¹⁷Though the fig tree do not blossom,
   nor fruit be on the vines,
  the produce of the olive fail
   and the fields yield no food,
  the flock be cut off from the fold
   and there be no herd in the stalls,
¹⁸yet I will rejoice in the Lord,
   I will joy in the God of my salvation.
¹⁹God, the Lord, is my strength;
   he makes my feet like hinds' feet,
   he makes me tread upon my high places.

  To the choirmaster: with stringed instruments.

The Book of Habakkuk concludes with a prayer (verse 1; the word could be translated more appropriately *psalm*, for it is used as the title of the Book of Psalms). The passage has many similarities to the biblical psalms. It begins with a title verse (3:1) and ends with similar musical notations (3:19*b*). The word *Selah* is used three times; although it is of uncertain meaning, its occurrence indicates the use of these poetic lines in the public worship of the temple.

The substance of the psalm contains many points of similarity to other passages of Hebrew poetry, some of them much more ancient than the time of Habakkuk. The poet has drawn on the old poetic traditions of the Hebrew faith to give expression to his vision of God's glory. There is some debate as to whether or not Habakkuk is the author of this passage, and the nature of the evidence is such that a firm conclusion is difficult to reach. But it is quite probable that we should interpret the psalm as an authentic composition of the prophet. He served as a professional prophet in the temple, and from such persons the temple hymns could have come. But this hymn is more appropriately placed in the prophet's book than in the Book of Psalms; though its substance makes it suitable for usage in Israel's worship in general, it is also tied intimately to Habakkuk's particular experience of God which has dominated the first two chapters of the book.

The prophet, in response to the questions he posed to God, had been told to await a vision and to record it when it came (2:2–3). In this psalm, we find not so much an account of the vision as a poetic response to the vision. The vision clearly took the form of theophany, the appearance of God to his prophet. And the psalm celebrates the theophany, describing in vivid poetry the effect of God's presence in both the world of nature and of nations.

The description of the theophany is penetrated by reminiscences of God's former appearances on behalf of his people. The principal substance of the psalm (verses 3–15) alludes to the Hebrew experience of God in the Exodus, at Mount Sinai, and during the period of wilderness wandering. In those ancient days, God had been with his people; the forces of nature had been the allies of God in bringing to nought all human opposition to the chosen people. God had acted for the salvation of his people (verse 14) in defeating all their foes. But the allusions to the past are celebrated not merely in memory, but also in anticipation; what God had done, he would do again. And thus we begin to perceive how this remarkable psalm brings the book not only to conclusion, but to climax.

(i) *There would be salvation for Israel*. The vision of God reinforced the faith that there would once again be salvation for Israel as there had been in the past. In the early years, God had constantly delivered his people from trouble and enemies; Habakkuk prays that in his own time, "in the midst of years" (verse 2), that ancient deliverance would become a present reality. And the prayer at the beginning of the psalm is converted to confidence at its end: "I will quietly wait for the day of trouble to come upon people who invade us" (verse 16). What had converted prayer to confidence was the substance of the vision. The God who had acted in the past was the same God who would act again.

We begin to perceive the effect of vision in a time when faith sags and vision is rare. Habakkuk and his people lived "in the midst of years", in the drab flatness of time that seems never to be punctuated by the splendid acts of God. The "midst of years" seems always to be a time characterized by the divine absence. Faith is replaced by nostalgia, hope by despair. But in the prophet's experience, the years of barren hopelessness were transformed by the vision of God's salvation; that was Habakkuk's gift to his own and to subsequent generations.

(ii) *There were solutions to the prophet's problems*. The opening chapters of Habakkuk indicate that the prophet has certain similarities to Job. Both had fundamental problems about life and faith; though the essence of their problems differed, both sought a solution from God. And, in the last resort, both found that their problems were resolved more by vision than by rational explanation. Job came to terms with God following an extraordinary confrontation with the Almighty (Job 38–41). Habakkuk, though he did achieve a degree of intellectual understanding, came to terms with God in the experience of theophany. Though he began this encounter in dialogue and rational argument, the real turning point in his relationship with God was the result of a vision of the Living God.

The Book of Habakkuk provides us with a happy balance with respect to the problems we encounter in both experience and theology. Problems and doubts inevitably come and, whatever their source, they challenge and trouble the mind. It is a false form of piety that refuses to question God, that refuses to exercise the mind in the attempt to resolve such problems. Neither Job nor Habakkuk refused to question, and both in a limited sense were able to resolve their intellectual dilemmas. Yet both remind us of the importance of religious experience, of the significance of the encounter with God that goes beyond the rational exercise of the mind. Religious experience is not an alternative to rational inquiry, but it may supplement it and contribute a degree of faith in God beyond that which the mind can achieve in its own right.

(iii) *The conclusion is joy*. A book that began with tortured questions from one tormented by experience concludes with a statement of rejoicing and joy (verses 17–19). The expression of joy is notable for the context in which it is set; it is described not as a consequence of happy circumstances, but despite the failure of all those things that might normally be a source of joy (verse 17). In the midst of disappointment and in the absence of every standard sign of God's blessing, Habakkuk can rejoice, for God "makes my feet like hinds' feet, he makes me tread upon my high places" (verse 19). Again, it is the vision of God that has enabled the prophet to transcend his circumstances and give voice to praise. Where there is no vision, the people perish, but Habakkuk affirms that where there is vision, the people may flourish.

INTRODUCTION TO THE BOOK OF ZEPHANIAH

THE MAN AND HIS WORLD

Zephaniah is today one of the least known of the Old Testament prophets, but in his own time and place he would have had a high profile. At the end of the 8th century B.C., the prophetic tradition had reached a kind of peak in the distinguished ministries of men like Isaiah, Micah, Amos and Hosea. But this early climax was followed by a gap; little is known of any active prophetic ministry in the early part of the 7th century B.C. until, like a phoenix, Zephaniah arose from the ashes of the ancient tradition towards the end of the century. To those who had thought the prophetic movement dead, his appearance must have been a sign of hope, though his message contained little that was cheerful. And the ministry of Zephaniah, concerning which we know so little, was to inaugurate another great era in Hebrew prophecy: he was to be followed closely in Judah by Jeremiah, Obadiah, Nahum and others.

All that is known of Zephaniah is the scant information concerning him in 1:1, for he is not referred to in other biblical books. His ministry is said to have occurred "in the days of Josiah", the king of Judah who reigned from 640 to 609 B.C. The precise point at which the prophet was active in Josiah's long reign is not specified, but a number of scraps of evidence conspire to suggest that it was in the earlier period. In particular, the conditions in Judah as described in Zephaniah's words imply that the time was before Josiah's major reform (622 B.C.). Thus, although there can be no certainty as to how long Zephaniah functioned as a prophet, his ministry can be dated tentatively to the years around 630 B.C.

In the opening verse of the book, a brief genealogy of Zephaniah is provided. It is unusual in specifying four generations, when normally one would be sufficient. Hosea, for example, is called simply "the son of Beeri", and Joel is the "son of Pethuel". So why is Zephaniah described as the "son of Cushi, son of Gedaliah, son of Amariah, son of Hezekiah"? There have been various suggestions, none of them entirely satisfactory. Some have supposed that the normal designation, "son of Cushi", would be misleading: the word *Cushi* means "Ethiopian" (or perhaps "African") and it might therefore be taken to imply that Zephaniah was a foreigner, not a true Hebrew. The longer pedigree, on the other hand, suggests solid Hebrew roots (though it does not remove the possibility of his grandfather's foreign marriage). Another possibility is that the purpose of the genealogy was to trace Zephaniah's lineage back to Hezekiah, the king of Judah (715–686 B.C.), but if such were the case, it is surprising that the word *king* is not added to make the link crystal clear. Indeed, it is possible that Zephaniah was simply a man with a sense of roots and tradition; his family tree may be of little significance to the modern reader, but it could have been important to him and to his contemporaries. In summary, we know the names of four generations of the prophet's ancestors, but are not much the wiser for the knowledge.

Finally, we are told in the opening verse that the book contains the "word of the Lord" as it came to Zephaniah; in this description, the book stands in the mainstream of the prophetic tradition. Zephaniah received a word, or divine oracles, which in turn he was responsible for communicating to his people.

The period during which the prophet ministered was not a happy one in the history of the Kingdom of Judah. For almost half a century, Judah had been ruled by a corrupt king, Manasseh (687–642 B.C.), and more briefly by his son Amon (642–640 B.C.). Under Manasseh, Judah had become little more than a colony of the Assyrian Empire, ruled by Esarhaddon (680–669 B.C.) and then by Ashurbanipal (668–627 B.C.). But it was not simply colonial status which brought such unhappy times to Judah; in addition there was extensive penetration of national religion and culture by alien elements. The relative spiritual health of King Hezekiah's reign had been squandered by his successor, Manasseh, and the ancient faith had been all but lost, absorbed into the invading paganism from Assyria. When Josiah succeeded to the throne at the age of eight in 640 B.C., he was hardly in a position to do anything, or even to see that anything must be done! Thus, although Josiah is best remembered for his extraordinary reformation in around 622 B.C., it must be supposed that conditions in the early part of his reign remained much as they had been in the time of Manasseh and Amon.

It was in this decadent society, politically servile and religiously corrupt, that Zephaniah ministered as a prophet. The ancient faith of Judah was in serious danger of demise, and it was no time for half measures or cautious steps. The prophet, though we know so little of his total message and ministry, spoke plainly and forcefully. And though insufficient evidence has survived from ancient history to determine the cause of each effect, it is not too rash to suppose that Zephaniah's work was in part responsible for the reformation which, later on, Josiah was to carry out in Judah.

THE BOOK

We have only three chapters of the collected sayings of Zephaniah, although (as with the other short prophetic books) we may reasonably suppose for the prophet a much more extensive ministry than is indicated by the paucity of his extant oracles. The prophet's sayings have been arranged by an editor to give a generally coherent framework to the book as a whole. (a) Words of judgment are expressed against Judah and Jerusalem (1:2–2:3). (b) The prophet declares God's oracles against various groups of foreigners (2:4–3:8), including Jerusalem once again. (c) The book concludes with some words promising hope in the distant future (3:9–20).

Although the editorial arrangement is reasonably clear, it is less certain that the arrangement of the messages in the book reflects the sequence or the time in which they were first delivered by the prophet. There are several clues, however, to suggest that the prophet delivered his messages in the context of some major religious festival in the temple of Jerusalem. The frequent references to the "Day of the Lord", the association of that day with *sacrifice* (1:7, 8), and the indication of a national assembly (2:1), might be taken to imply a setting for the prophet's ministry in a great festival celebrated in the temple in the nation's capital. Whereas normally such a festival would be a celebration of faith and hope, Zephaniah employs the occasion to indicate just how bleak the Day of the Lord, when it came, would actually be. Such, tentatively at least, is the setting in which to interpret the prophet's words.

Zephaniah's oracles, like those of the other prophets, are in poetic form. The poetry, while not the finest from a strictly literary perspective, is powerful and dramatic in its imagery. And one of the prophet's verses has left its mark indelibly on the tradition of western religious literature. Jerome's translation of Zeph. 1:15 (*dies irae, dies illa*) caught the imagination of Thomas of Celano, a 13th-century Italian friar who was companion and biographer of St Francis. Three significant lines in the friar's famous hymn are based on Zephaniah's vision of the Day of the Lord:

> Dies irae, dies illa,
> Solvet sacclum in favilla,
> Teste David cum Sibylla.

The ancient hymn is loosely rendered in *The English Hymnal*:

> Days of wrath and doom impending,
> David's word with Sibyl's blending,
> Heaven and earth in ashes ending.

Sung in plainsong, the hymn continued to be used over several centuries as a part of the Requiem Mass, being both a reflection of the judgment day and a prayer for mercy; and though plainsong was the medieval setting, the hymn has lost little of its power in the newer settings of Mozart, Berlioz, Verdi, and others. The *dies irae* of Zephaniah's ancient oracle continues to speak to us through this ancient tradition, a reminder of judgment tinged with apocalypse.

THE MESSAGE OF ZEPHANIAH

The message of Zephaniah has two distinct parts to it, though the parts are intimately interrelated.

(a) His message, on the one hand, is one of total and devastating divine judgment, which would be universal in scope. He sees the world itself as ordained for judgment, and human nations (including Judah) incorporated within this coming cataclysm of cosmic proportions. Although his primary concern and ministry is in Judah and Jerusalem, he cannot restrict his message to the immediate environment. Close neighbours, including Philistia, Moab and Ammon, would be caught up in the storm of judgment, just as would the more distant superpowers in Asia (Assyria) and Africa (Ethiopia). Presupposed by this vision of international judgment is the prophet's vision of God; the divine power is universal and the divine concern is always for righteousness, so that, in a world as thoroughly corrupted as that of Zephaniah, none could hope to escape the coming holocaust. Although the prophet issues one brief call for repentance and return (2:3), that concern cannot be seen as the main focus of his ministry. Zephaniah is not so much a reformer as a visionary; indeed, in a limited sense, he might be seen as one of the first prophets in the apocalyptic tradition in ancient Judah.

(b) The prophet's vision of judgment is balanced by a more distant vision of hope. From the ruins of Judah's destruction, he expects a remnant of the chosen people to survive. And beyond the dark pall suspended above his message of judgment, there is a brighter, though distant, horizon. The divine judgment could never be the last word, for despite God's wrath against evil, the divine mercy would ultimately triumph. God would eventually renew and restore his people "in his love" (3:17).

It is not easy to convert this sometimes bleak and sometimes remote message of Zephaniah into contemporary terms of current relevance. We would do the prophet little justice by reducing him to the role of *predictor*, though much of the judgment of which he spoke came to pass within half a century of the time of his ministry. We must see him in his setting to perceive his stature. After half a century of prophetic silence, Zephaniah stood up to declare once again the divine word. It was not a novel message in its substance; the novelty lay principally in the presence of one with the courage to speak the message. And in a time when the ancient faith had been corrupted for so long that few could remember its pristine purity, the prophet described the times and their consequences in clear and forceful language. It is a truism to state that generally people would rather not listen to the likes of Zephaniah. To put it another way, it is easier to think of his words addressing the corruption of an ancient world than to let them disturb the unruffled waters of our modern world. But we will fail to grasp the urgency of the prophet's message if we do not let it penetrate the complacency of our own century. When we hear the words addressed to Judah or Philistia, Ammon or Ethiopia, we should reflect on their pertinence to our own nation and our own world.

THE JUDGMENT OF JUDAH

Zephaniah 1:1–13

1The word of the Lord which came to Zephaniah the son of Cushi, son of Gedaliah, son of Amariah, son of Hezekiah, in the days of Josiah the son of Amon, king of Judah.

2"I will utterly sweep away everything
   from the face of the earth," says the Lord.
3"I will sweep away man and beast;
   I will sweep away the birds of the air
   and the fish of the sea.
I will overthrow the wicked;
   I will cut off mankind
   from the face of the earth," says the Lord.
4"I will stretch out my hand against Judah,
   and against all the inhabitants of Jerusalem;
and I will cut off from this place the remnant of Baal
   and the name of the idolatrous priests;
5those who bow down on the roofs
   to the host of the heavens;
those who bow down and swear to the Lord
   and yet swear by Milcom;

⁶those who have turned back from following the Lord,
    who do not seek the Lord or inquire of him."

⁷Be silent before the Lord God!
    For the day of the Lord is at hand;
the Lord has prepared a sacrifice
    and consecrated his guests.
⁸And on the day of the Lord's sacrifice—
    "I will punish the officials and the king's sons
    and all who array themselves in foreign attire.
⁹On that day I will punish
    every one who leaps over the threshold,
and those who fill their master's house
    with violence and fraud."

¹⁰"On that day," says the Lord,
    "a cry will be heard from the Fish Gate,
a wail from the Second Quarter,
    a loud crash from the hills.
¹¹Wail, O inhabitants of the Mortar!
    For all the traders are no more;
    all who weigh out silver are cut off.
¹²At that time I will search Jerusalem with lamps,
    and I will punish the men
who are thickening upon their lees,
    those who say in their hearts,
'The Lord will not do good,
    nor will he do ill.'
¹³Their goods shall be plundered,
    and their houses laid waste.
Though they build houses,
    they shall not inhabit them;
though they plant vineyards,
    they shall not drink wine from them."

Some orators will woo their audience with pleasantries before getting down to the hard substance of their speech, but Zephaniah will have none of this. He launches immediately into a speech, expressed as the words of God, in which the devastation of the natural world is proclaimed. Everything, man and beast, fish and fowl, would be destroyed when the divine action commenced. The promise implicit in creation would be abolished, along with the hope of survival delivered after the Deluge, and all life as we know it would be wiped out. Certainly the prophet would catch attention with his opening words, though only a few may have taken him seriously. The scope of coming devastation was so vast and comprehensive in Zephaniah's message, that most of his listeners would have branded him a religious crackpot.

The prophet's approach to his theme, like that of Isaiah and Amos before him, was to take a common and timely conception and convert it from its joyous tone to one of foreboding doom. If it is correct (especially on the basis of verses 7–8) to interpret this speech as being delivered in the temple, then we perceive more clearly the prophet's technique. He speaks to an audience busy in the celebration of creation and insinuates its return to chaos. He addresses those who are happily engaged in the activities of sacrifice and worship, and denounces those activities for the corruption and perversion which they embody. He calls to a city whose streets and suburbs are filled with festive crowds, and indicates that soon cries of despair will be uttered in the Fish Gate, the Second Quarter, the suburb of Mortar, and other areas of the Holy City (verses 10–11). Every joyous sound and sight, whether in the natural world, in the temple, or in the city, is but a hollow symbol of its opposite, the irresistible advance of misery and divine judgment.

The prophet's address, to this point, is simply a declaration of coming judgment, with no call to repentance and no programme of reform. But the reason for Zephaniah's terrible vision is clear enough: though it will impinge upon the world of nature as much as upon human society, the judgment is rooted in the actions and attitudes of men and women.

(i) *Religion was corrupt.* Although the immediate occasion was the cheerful celebration of one of Israel's great festivals, the participants by their character denied the very foundations of the festival. The priests had engaged in the repugnant worship of Baal, and on the roofs of houses in the twilight, the chosen people could be seen engaged in the star-struck phantasies of astral worship (verses 4–5). They made their solemn oaths by taking the Lord's name upon their lips, but also took out extra insurance in solemnly swearing by the pagan god Milcom (verse 5). They were engaged in the worship of God, oblivious to the fact that every facet of their lives was a denial of the activity in which they were involved.

The passage of time wonderfully dulls the senses and dims the powers of perception. The decades of Manasseh's reign had done their damage, leaving behind a nation that no longer knew true religion from false, that no longer perceived the insult and apostasy that its veneer of religiosity had become. Here was a nation that had not abandoned its religion, though it might have been better if it had; the ancient faith of Israel had been warped beyond recognition in Zephaniah's time. Although a situation such as this sometimes brings forth reformers, it may also produce these persons of vision who see that things are too far gone for reform. Shortly after Zephaniah's ministry, reforms were to be initiated, but for all their immediate benefits, they merely delayed the end which the prophet so clearly envisioned.

(ii) *Government had failed* (verse 8). Government officials and members of the royal household, upon whose shoulders the responsibility of leadership rested, had failed to fulfil their appointed tasks. They arrayed themselves "in foreign attire", an allusion no doubt to their participation in the rituals which Assyrian control had introduced to Jerusalem. Like modern western youth, attired in Hare Krishna garb, their gear was at odds with their heritage. And when the path of paganism is pursued by government officials, the people may be expected to follow.

(iii) *Apathy and indifference prevailed* (verse 12). The prophet describes the Lord diligently searching the dark corners of the city for those "who are thickening on their lees": the metaphor was a common one to describe laziness (see also Jer. 48:11), drawn from the vintner's trade. Wine was allowed to sit in the sun, to enrich the colour and add sweetness, but if left too long, it became turgid and undrinkable. Thus, a part of the reason for the coming judgment was to be found in that silent majority, not evil by any acts of heresy or horror, but culpable for having done nothing to arrest the slide into chaos occurring all around them in their nation's daily life.

Sometimes it is the apathetic and indifferent who are more responsible for a nation's moral collapse than those who are actively engaged in evil, or those who have failed in the responsibilities of leadership. Sir George Adam Smith expressed the situation with marvellous cogency:

> The great causes of God and Humanity are not defeated by the hot assaults of the Devil, but by the slow, crushing, glacier-like mass of thousands and thousands of indifferent nobodies. God's causes are never destroyed by being blown up, but by being sat upon.
>
> (*The Book of the Twelve Prophets*, II, 1899, p. 54)

Zephaniah's words on indifference touch the conscience of multitudes, those who are not guilty of unbelief, but are equally never overwhelmed by belief. They say: "The Lord will not do good, nor will he do ill" (verse 12). With the comfortable conviction that God is otiose, they pursue the same indolence in their own lives with the nearest that they can come to energy. Convinced that the world cannot be changed, they leave it be, allowing it to slip further down the slope toward disaster. Zephaniah, with his words, touches a chord in us all. The way things are is partly because that is the way we have allowed them to become. We can sit back, smug and somnolent in a desperate world, but we cannot at the same time absolve ourselves from all responsibility, and we shall eventually be caught in the very chaos we permit.

THE DAY OF WRATH

Zephaniah 1:14–2:3

¹⁴The great day of the Lord is near,
    near and hastening fast;
  the sound of the day of the Lord is bitter,

the mighty man cries aloud there.
[15]A day of wrath is that day,
   a day of distress and anguish,
a day of ruin and devastation,
   a day of darkness and gloom,
a day of clouds and thick darkness,
[16] a day of trumpet blast and battle cry
against the fortified cities
   and against the lofty battlements.

[17]I will bring distress on men,
   so that they shall walk like the blind,
   because they have sinned against the Lord;
their blood shall be poured out like dust,
   and their flesh like dung.
[18]Neither their silver nor their gold
   shall be able to deliver them
   on the day of the wrath of the Lord.
In the fire of his jealous wrath,
   all the earth shall be consumed;
for a full, yea, sudden end
   he will make of all the inhabitants of the earth.

[1]Come together and hold assembly,
   O shameless nation,
[2]before you are driven away
   like the drifting chaff,
before there comes upon you
   the fierce anger of the Lord,
before there comes upon you
   the day of the wrath of the Lord.
[3]Seek the Lord, all you humble of the land,
   who do his commands;
seek righteousness, seek humility;
   perhaps you may be hidden
   on the day of the wrath of the Lord.

As the prophet continues to develop the theme of the "Day of the Lord", he is grasped less by its causes and consequences, and more and more by the awesomeness of its character. The day has taken on apocalypic proportions, so that the nouns tumble forth from his mouth, unlinked by verbs (verses 15–16), as he tries to express in language the unspeakable horror which he has seen beyond the veil. Amos had spoken of the Day of the Lord to the festive crowds in northern Israel (Amos 5:18–20), setting his speech in the form of a funerary lament; Zephaniah's words take the form of the poetry of war, the staccato lines stammering out the chaos that would come, indicating its urgency. The day lay just beyond the immediate horizon of history, and its dawning was approaching quickly (verse 14).

The powerful poetry of verses 14–16 paints the picture of gruesome *son et lumière* pageant, the poet's words evoking the bitter sounds of tragedy and the dark shades of a doomed world. A warrior weeps, his strength of no avail and his cry adding desolation to the scene (verse 14). Distress and anguish, ruin and devastation, darkness and gloom, such are the dimensions of that day, but all are governed by the word *wrath* (verse 15), for it is the divine anger which will work such havoc. By the six references to the *day* (verses 15–16), the prophet's poetry anticipates the undoing of creation; whereas the days of creation had been capped by the divine praise, "It is good", the very goals of creation have been shrouded by gloom in this bleak panoply of judgment days.

The effect of the terrible days is one of distress for mankind (verse 17). Like the newly blind, they will stumble around devoid of any sense of direction, having abandoned in their evil the God-given gift of sight. The blood of the wounded runs freely, clotting in the very dust from which it originally came in the mysterious gift of life. The flesh of the dead lies stinking on the ground like the smelly cow-pats left by wandering cattle. And in this terrible time for human beings, all the traditional human defences would be futile. Silver and gold (verse 18), with which protection could normally be bought, would now be useless. The world, which had begun with such promise in creation, had gone too far; God would make an end of it all. Such was Zephaniah's vision of the *dies irae*.

"Come together and hold an assembly" (2:1): the prophet's words were in all probability addressed to such an assembly, but the assembled throng were rejoicing, not lamenting. Zephaniah would have them change the assembly from one of celebration to one of repentance, though he holds little hope that it would change the future. Soon enough, the people would be blown away like the drifting chaff they had become. Nevertheless, he holds out a modicum of hope, not that the Day of the Lord might be averted, but only that a few might be hidden from its horrors. "Seek the Lord," he calls, echoing no doubt the traditional festal invitations (see also Amos 5:6); perhaps, in the pursuit of right-eousness and humility, they might find a hiding place at the dawning of the apocalyptic day.

Zephaniah's dreadful vision can be sensed better by the poet than by the scholar or the literal interpreter of ancient texts. In a scholarly fashion, we may detect the elements of form and style in the ancient text, but if we do not share the vision, we have missed the prophet's point. Or again, if we search the details of this passage for literal clues as to the time and character of the end of the age, we are again missing the point of the prophet's vision. For what the prophet saw embraced both God and the world of human beings, and what he saw is still there to be seen by those with vision.

God is holy. He created the world and gave life to mankind, expressing thereby his love and righteousness. But the reality of the human world, as much in Zephaniah's time as our own, is a denial of every goal of creation. The human race as a whole, like the chosen people and their neighbours in the prophet's era, has undermined and polluted the very reasons for its existence. And Zephaniah saw very clearly that such a state of affairs could not continue unchecked for ever. His vision of apocalyptic wrath must in a sense always hang over this world, and each day that it does not dawn is but another extension on the world's lease on life. It may sound too dramatic, expressed in words, to imply that somehow the cosmos is out of control and the earth is tumbling helter-skelter to its doom. But Zephaniah, like the other proph-ets, did not perceive the Day of the Lord to be merely a cosmic event, beyond human control. Its roots lay in human lives and human actions. In the last resort, it is human beings who precipi-tate the dreadful Day of the Lord by working out in the world the corruption that festers within them.

THE DESOLATION OF FOREIGN NATIONS

Zephaniah 2:4–15

⁴For Gaza shall be deserted,
    and Ashkelon shall become a desolation;
Ashdod's people shall be driven out at noon,
    and Ekron shall be uprooted.

⁵Woe to you inhabitants of the seacoast,
    you nation of the Cherethites!
The word of the Lord is against you,
    O Canaan, land of the Philistines;
    and I will destroy you till no inhabitant is left.
⁶And you, O seacoast, shall be pastures,
    meadows for shepherds
    and folds for flocks.
⁷The seacoast shall become the possession
    of the remnant of the house of Judah,
    on which they shall pasture,
and in the houses of Ashkelon
    they shall lie down at evening.
For the Lord their God will be mindful of them
    and restore their fortunes.

⁸"I have heard the taunts of Moab
    and the revilings of the Ammonites,
how they have taunted my people
    and made boasts against their territory.
⁹Therefore, as I live," says the Lord of hosts,
    the God of Israel,
"Moab shall become like Sodom,
    and the Ammonites like Gomorrah,
a land possessed by nettles and salt pits,
    and a waste for ever.
The remnant of my people shall plunder them,
    and the survivors of my nation shall possess them."
¹⁰This shall be their lot in return for their pride,
    because they scoffed and boasted
    against the people of the Lord of hosts.

¹¹The Lord will be terrible against them;
  yea, he will famish all the gods of the earth,
and to him shall bow down,
  each in its place,
  all the lands of the nations.

¹²You also, O Ethiopians,
  shall be slain by my sword.

¹³And he will stretch out his hand against the north,
  and destroy Assyria;
and he will make Nineveh a desolation,
  a dry waste like the desert.
¹⁴Herds shall lie down in the midst of her,
  all the beasts of the field;
the vulture and the hedgehog
  shall lodge in her capitals;
the owl shall hoot in the window,
  the raven croak on the threshold;
  for her cedar work will be laid bare.
¹⁵This is the exultant city
  that dwelt secure,
that said to herself,
  "I am and there is none else."
What a desolation she has become,
  a lair for wild beasts!
Every one who passes by her
  hisses and shakes his fist.

The general and unfocused vision of the Day of the Lord is now brought into sharp relief as Zephaniah directs his words to particular nations and peoples of his age. This shift from the cosmos to particular nations was no doubt directed in part by the context in which the prophet delivered his oracles; it was traditional, in certain of the great festivals, to address words to foreign peoples and their rulers (see, for example, Psalm 2:1–3). The message falls into three parts, encompassing Judah's neighbours on all four points of the compass. (i) The Philistines are addressed first (verses 4–7), Judah's neighbours to the west. (ii) Ammon and Moab (verses 8–11) lay to the east of Judah, beyond the Jordan.

(iii) Ethiopia and Assyria (verses 12–15) lay to the south and north of the promised land respectively.

(i) *The Philistines* (verses 4–7). The Philistines (also called Cherethites, after *Crete*: verse 5) had settled along the south-eastern seaboard of the Mediterranean, west and south of the borders of Judah. Their cities (Gaza, Ashkelon, Ashdod and Ekron) were more or less independent city-states, though they functioned together in a loose federation. And from the time that the Hebrews had first settled in the promised land, the Philistines had been a perpetual thorn in the flesh, always a source of nagging anxiety on the south-western border of Judah.

The Philistine states would suffer, along with other nations, on the Day of the Lord. Their coastal cities would become desolate and deserted, because "the word of the Lord is against you" (verse 5). The coastal lands, once so densely inhabited by this warlike people, would become pasture lands for shepherds and their flocks. The pastoral scene here is not one of comfort, but rather a chilling intimation that people would be replaced by sheep in those pleasant coastal lands.

The prophet's message to the Philistines is curious in two ways. (a) Zephaniah does not indicate what crime the Philistines have committed to be thus judged by God, as (for example) Amos does in his oracles to the Philistines (Amos 1:6–8). The crime may be presupposed, but Philistia's judgment is simply incorporated within the general judgment that would engulf the world on the Day of the Lord. (b) The prophet refers to a "remnant of the house of Judah" (verse 7) taking possession of the land that once belonged to the Philistines. The reference to the remnant is an anticipation of the more positive message with which the book closes; it is significant, however, in indicating that Judah would no more escape judgment than Philistia, for the word *remnant* specifies that slender number who would survive the Day of the Lord.

(ii) *Moab and Ammon* (verses 8–11). In the case of Moab and Ammon, territories lying to the east of the Jordan River, crimes which demanded judgment are clearly specified. They had taunted the nation of Judah in its time of distress, delighting in the downfall of a neighbour. Therefore they would become like Sodom and Gomorrah, "a land possessed by nettles and salt pits, and a waste for ever" (verse 9). The simile is apt, for Sodom and Gomorrah, the archetypal cities of evil, were located at the south-east corner of the Dead Sea, not too far from Moab's southern frontier.

Once again, the prophet indicates that Judah's remnant would take possession of these Transjordanian territories, benefiting from the properties of those who had been their oppressors. And, as before, the source of the downfall of Moab and Ammon would be the Lord, against whom none could stand on the terrible day.

(iii) *Ethiopia and Assyria* (verses 12–15). The last section of this prophecy against foreign nations embraces the two great superpowers of the era. In Zephaniah's time, Assyria was still the world's dominant nation, with its capital city in Nineveh (verse 13). Ethiopia (or Cush) lay to the south of Egypt, though probably Ethiopia here is a poetic expression for Egypt, the second great superpower of that time (early in the 7th century B.C., Ethiopian pharaohs had ruled in Egypt). The citizens of both great nations would be destroyed. Nineveh, Assyria's phenomenal capital city, of which the ruins may still be seen in and around the modern city of Mosul in Iraq, would be reduced to a desert wasteland. Birds and beasts would haunt the ruins of a city that still, in Zephaniah's time, controlled the world.

This series of dreadful discourses addressed to foreign nations illuminates starkly two of the prophet's themes.

(a) The Middle Eastern world, in the latter half of the 7th century B.C., was in the process of change. Such change is always easier to see with the benefit of historical perspective, but it is exceptionally difficult for people who live in a particular era to understand the larger movements of history. Assyria's dominance in military and political affairs, for example, had been a part of the reality of life in Judah for more than a century; it would have been hard for the ordinary person to have conceived of a world without Assyria. But Zephaniah, speaking as a prophet on behalf of God, saw that nothing was permanent, not even the state that for so long had dominated his own country. All must change, and evil changes the tide of human history for the worse. But more than that, the prophet saw the hand of God behind the changing currents of his world, and that insight added urgency to the conviction of his message that his era was, in some sense, in its last days.

(b) There is an egotism in nations and capital cities that contributes to its citizens' terrible arrogance. They say, with Nineveh, "I am and there is none else" (verse 15). The great city, above all else, symbolizes mankind's puny attempts at permanence in a transitory and changing world. Nineveh and Jerusalem, London and New York, all of the great cities seem to offer in a subtle way the promise of enduring security that life itself denies. But the "I am" of the city is a hollow cry, for like all else in the world, the city too must pass away. We must not embrace the false sense of the city once championed by the citizens of Nineveh, whose great metropolis is now a tourist site; rather, with Abraham, we should look to the city "which has foundations, whose builder and maker is God" (Hebrews 11:10).

THE CORRUPTION OF JERUSALEM

Zephaniah 3:1–7

¹Woe to her that is rebellious and defiled,
　　the oppressing city!
²She listens to no voice,
　　she accepts no correction.
She does not trust in the Lord,
　　she does not draw near to her God.

³Her officials within her
　　are roaring lions;
her judges are evening wolves
　　that leave nothing till the morning.
⁴Her prophets are wanton,
　　faithless men;
her priests profane what is sacred,
　　they do violence to the law.

⁵The Lord within her is righteous,
    he does no wrong;
every morning he shows forth his justice,
    each dawn he does not fail;
    but the unjust knows no shame.

⁶"I have cut off nations;
    their battlements are in ruins;
I have laid waste their streets
    so that none walks in them;
their cities have been made desolate,
    without a man, without an inhabitant.
⁷I said, 'Surely she will fear me,
    she will accept correction;
she will not lose sight
    of all that I have enjoined upon her.'
But all the more they were eager
    to make all their deeds corrupt."

The city of Jerusalem, which from ancient times was supposed to be a symbol of peace to the world, is denounced by Zephaniah as "rebellious and defiled, the oppressing city!" (verse 1). It was rebellious against God, it was defiled in its character, and it oppressed those citizens who had sought within its walls a life of peace and righteousness. The city's arrogance was such that it would listen to no advice and accept no words of correction. It existed to be the spot on this bleak earth where God's presence could be symbolized, but it had abandoned trust in the very God that gave the city its *raison d'être*. Such is Zephaniah's dreary portrait of the so-called Holy City, and then as now the city's failure can only be a source of grief to the world's inhabitants. But the prophet goes further than merely describing the sad state of the city in his time; he also provides some of the reasons for its failure.

(i) *The failure of leadership* (verses 1–5). A city, like a ship, is vulnerable to the direction given by those at the helm. Zephaniah makes no reference to the king, presumably because Josiah was still a minor and not responsible for the state of affairs in

Jerusalem, but he singles out other key categories of persons upon whom blame must rest for the city's collapse.

(a) *Government officials:* rather than working for the people, the officials regarded the populace merely as potential victims. They behaved like "roaring lions", a simile portraying strength and ferocity, but at base it indicates that civil servants had become beasts of prey. They used the power of their positions to gain their own ends, wielding their government office to satisfy their perpetual craving for wealth and power.

Throughout human history, civil servants of all kinds have been faced with the temptation to abuse the power and authority entrusted to them. Without the delegation of power and authority, a city cannot function properly; but fallen into the wrong hands, they can become the instruments of a city's undoing. Jerusalem's officials had forgotten that they exercised their power and authority in trust, that they were the servants of the city of God. Their duty to God lay in serving the people; in failing to serve the people and seeking only to serve themselves, they had corrupted the Holy City.

(b) *Judges:* like evening wolves, they indulged their appetites with the crude viciousness of beasts that passed the daylight hours without food. Their hunger knew no bounds; the law was the tool which they would abuse to gain their greedy goals.

The maintenance of justice in any society depends upon the continuing integrity of the officers of the law. And when the senior officers of the law, the judges, have become corrupt, then the system of justice as a whole is on the verge of collapse. In Jerusalem, the vision of justice for all had been abandoned in the pursuit of profit for the few. The only interest the judges had in the law was in the profit it could be made to bring them. And having sold their souls to personal gain, the judges contributed further to the decline in the Holy City.

(c) *The prophets*, too, had failed in their calling. Zephaniah refers here to those professional prophets, a branch of the clergy, who served in the temple and were responsible for declaring the divine word to the assembled worshippers. But they had become "wanton" (verse 4), or reckless, abandoning the sanctity of their task and prostrating it to their personal ends. The services of false (but apparently true) prophets could be sold; the sweet words of the Lord could be declared, for a price, to hungry clients seeking direction or blessing. In a time when nothing was held sacred any longer, why should not the clergy cash in on the potential for profit that their office held? In Zephaniah's time, just as in our own, there were those persons engaged in the "ministry of the Word" who had seen and exploited its possibilities for personal gain.

(d) *The priests*, likewise, abused their office. They had two areas of responsibility: they undertook the rituals of temple worship and sacrifice, and they offered to the people instruction in the divine law. And although, as official clergy, they deserved to be recompensed for their work, they could not with integrity convert it into a capitalistic enterprise. But that is what they had done in Zephaniah's time, and in so doing, they profaned what was sacred and did violence to the law.

Thus, in part, the corruption of the city of Jerusalem could be placed at the feet of its leaders; laymen and clergy alike had set aside any sense of vocation and service to God and had pursued personal gratification instead. And in so doing, they had contributed to the corruption of an entire city. And though the names of these base individuals have not survived, the memory of their deeds has lived on for more than two millennia in the words of the prophet Zephaniah.

(ii) *The failure to learn from history and current events* (verses 6-7). A second source of Jerusalem's failure lay in the inability of the citizens as a whole to discern, either from past history or current affairs, the nature of God's actions in the world. There was a peculiar obtuseness in the city, a stubborn refusal to learn from all that was going on round about them what must eventually be Jerusalem's fate.

Other fortified cities, equally confident in their time of their impregnability, had been breached and their battlements left in ruins. Other city streets, once alive with the hustle and bustle of business life, now lay in ruins, like those of a ghost town. Other cities with vast populations now lay deserted, void of those inhabitants who once had given the metropolis vibrant life. But Jerusalem learned nothing from the fate of others. Only other cities can be destroyed, not ours! Only Gentile cities are judged by God, not the Holy City. We are safe and we can continue for ever in the sacred city, for no harm will ever touch us!

But Zephaniah's oracle punctures the arrogant delusion. What had happened to other cities was not simply the outcome of fate; it was in part judgment and in part sign for those with the wit to discern its meaning. Zephaniah, in his ministry, is eager to turn the Holy City from the folly of its path, but the citizens were "all the more eager to make all their deeds corrupt" (verse 7). The prophet's message to the city is always pertinent, and now as then we can learn from the fate of other cities. We need not think of the judgment of God as some thunderbolt streaking in from the far blue yonder; what the prophet describes as *judgment* is in a sense the natural culmination of corruption. The rigorous pursuit of evil in any human society, together with the steadfast refusal to learn from what is going on around us, constitute a recipe for disaster.

JUDGMENT AND SURVIVAL

Zephaniah 3:8–13

8"Therefore wait for me," says the Lord,
  "for the day when I arise as a witness.
For my decision is to gather nations,
  to assemble kingdoms,
to pour out upon them my indignation,
  all the heat of my anger;
for in the fire of my jealous wrath
  all the earth shall be consumed.

9"Yea, at that time I will change the speech of the peoples
  to a pure speech,
that all of them may call on the name of the Lord
  and serve him with one accord.

[10]From beyond the rivers of Ethiopia
    my suppliants, the daughter of my dispersed ones,
    shall bring my offering.

[11]"On that day you shall not be put to shame
    because of the deeds by which you have rebelled against me;
for then I will remove from your midst
    your proudly exultant ones,
and you shall no longer be haughty
    in my holy mountain.
[12]For I will leave in the midst of you
    a people humble and lowly.
They shall seek refuge in the name of the Lord,
[13]   those who are left in Israel;
they shall do no wrong
    and utter no lies,
nor shall there be found in their mouth
    a deceitful tongue.
For they shall pasture and lie down,
    and none shall make them afraid."

There is both good news and bad news in the prophet's continuing message to Jerusalem. The good news is that the destruction of the city which he had just proclaimed would not be the final end; beyond the judgment lay a day of restoration and new life. But the bad news is that the destruction must inevitably come; Zephaniah does not talk of repentance and reform. He considers things to have gone too far for that and sees the end as a tide that cannot be turned.

There is a visionary quality to this portion of the prophet's message; the shades of black and white mingle together, conveying an image that is both horrifying and hopeful at the same time. The purpose of the words was no doubt to impart courage and hope to the few that remained faithful, for there is no call here for a change of heart. But even to the faithful, the prophet's message must have inspired awe, for insofar as the prophet had something positive to say, it lay beyond the cataclysm.

Zephaniah envisages a day on which the nations of the earth as a whole would be judged. The outlines of that visionary day are not clear from his words, yet its judgmental character is plain enough: the accumulated wrath of God would be exposed in the destruction of those nations that had done evil. Yet there is an element to the visionary statement which appears at first contradictory. The "peoples" (verse 9) would learn a "pure speech" whereby they would be able to "call on the name of the Lord and serve him with one accord." If the word *peoples* refers to all human beings, then it seems that Zephaniah envisages, beyond the judgment day, a reversal of Babel. The multitudes of human language would be dissolved once again into the common tongue of worship and praise. Again, the reference to those from "beyond the rivers of Ethiopia" (verse 10) appears to refer, not to the Hebrew diaspora, but rather to the far-flung groups of the human race as a whole; all mankind would join together in bringing a new offering to God.

The focus in verses 11–13 seems to narrow once again to the chosen people and city of Jerusalem. The shame of the past, caused by the rebellious citizens of the Holy City, would no longer be remembered. The proud and the haughty would have been removed from the city in the preceding acts of judgment. Those who remained would be the "humble and the lowly" (verse 12), those who trusted in God and whose speech was pure. The remnant of the chosen people would find new and quiet pastures beyond the dark and inevitable day of judgment.

Language and imagery of the kind that Zephaniah employs here are not easy to interpret. But we begin to perceive why Sir George Adam Smith wrote of Zephaniah: "His book is the first tingeing of prophecy with apocalypse: that is the moment which it supplies in the history of Israel's religion." And the language of apocalypse seeks to break the normal constraints of human language. It has a message to convey, but the substance of that message cannot be communicated in normal speech, bound as it is by the limitations of human understanding and experience. With apocalyptic language, we need to read as much between the lines as in them and seek to grasp the essence of the prophet's vision. While we may never exhaust the richness of such language, we can at least grasp a few of its essential themes.

(i) *The judgment of the nations.* The sub-title may seem to be too other-wordly in its attempt to encapsulate the age-old problem with which the prophet grapples. In a nutshell, the problem is this: do the atrocities and horrors perpetrated by this world's nation states pass unpunished? Do the holocausts, the acts of genocide, the national oppressions, and the depravities of war perpetrated by a multitude of nations, our own included, never get called to the bar of justice? If we are to answer such questions simply from the annals of human history, the response would seem to be negative. It is true that nations rise and fall, but justice rarely seems to be done in proportion to the crimes committed. And yet if justice is not done, we must ask in what sense God is just, or in what manner there is justice in God's world. The prophetic language, here that of apocalypse, seeks to affirm ultimate justice. It cannot do so in cool and rational speech, for there is little evidence to back up its assertions. But above all, apocalyptic language and vision are deeply rooted in the notion of impartial justice. God is not blind, crime does not pass unpunished, and eventually the world's nations are summoned to answer for their deeds. Just how this will be, or what manner judgment will take, we cannot guess or understand; but we have grasped a part of the prophet's message if we have sensed his passion for international justice.

(ii) *The continuity of divine mercy.* The prophetic passion for justice could, if taken too literally, signal the end of the human race in the final judgment. But Zephaniah, and those who followed him, also had deep insight into the mercy of God. He refers to love and mercy only a few times, but his vision of the surviving remnant beyond the judgment provides a clue to his insight concerning the eternal compassion of God. The divine purpose in the creation of mankind would not be frustrated; whatever the cosmic climax of human evil, there would continue to be human life on earth.

The prophet Zephaniah thus gives us a view of the future which is part despair, part hope. He had no liberal vision of the human race at last perfecting itself through effort and education; human evil was too deep-seated for that. But nor was his future vision nihilistic, so filled with dark despair that there was no room for hope. Just as there would always be evil and the inevitability of judgment, so too there would always be hope, however distant its dawning might seem to be. The source of the prophet's despair was to be found in his understanding of human nature and human states; the source of his hope was to be found in God.

A POSTSCRIPT OF JOY

Zephaniah 3:14–20

¹⁴Sing aloud, O daughter of Zion;
    shout, O Israel!
Rejoice and exult with all your heart,
    O daughter of Jerusalem!
¹⁵The Lord has taken away the judgments against you,
    he has cast out your enemies.
The King of Israel, the Lord, is in your midst;
    you shall fear evil no more.
¹⁶On that day it shall be said to Jerusalem:
    "Do not fear, O Zion;
    let not your hands grow weak.
¹⁷The Lord, your God, is in your midst,
    a warrior who gives victory;
he will rejoice over you with gladness,
    he will renew you in his love;
he will exult over you with loud singing
¹⁸   as on a day of festival.
    "I will remove disaster from you,
    so that you will not bear reproach for it.
¹⁹Behold, at that time I will deal
    with all your oppressors.
And I will save the lame
    and gather the outcast,
and I will change their shame into praise
    and renown in all the earth.

²⁰At that time I will bring you home,
    at the time when I gather you together;
yea, I will make you renowned and praised
    among all the peoples of the earth,
when I restore your fortunes
    before your eyes," says the Lord.

The book which began so miserably ends with a proclamation of joyous praise. The change in tone is so remarkable and dramatic, that inevitably there are those that claim it must have been written by a different and later hand than that of Zephaniah; they may well be right, though it is always difficult to come to a firm conclusion on such matters. Nevertheless, the statement "I will bring you home" (verse 20) and similar expressions might certainly be taken to refer to the end of the exile. If such were the case, then the postscript would indicate that later interpreters identified Zephaniah's anticipated judgment with that which befell Jerusalem in 586 B.C., followed by the exile; this postscript would then reflect the joy of the end of exile.

On the other hand, the passage with which the book concludes has something of the character of a hymn or psalm, of the kind that might have been used in Israel's great festivals. And if, as has been suggested above, Zephaniah's prophecies were declared in the context of one of Jerusalem's festivals, it is possible that Zephaniah took one of the festival-hymns and adapted it to his purpose. In the adaptation, the song of praise so typical of the festival is still sung, but it has become a future song in the restored Holy City to which the prophet has already alluded (verses 8–13).

Whatever the origin of the passage, its substance is clearly the praise of the God of Israel. The bleak times in which Zephaniah actually lived have now receded from prominence, and this praise is addressed to the God who "is in your midst". Jerusalem has once again found its rightful place. And the people's God, notable for his wrath in the earlier prophetic statements, now reveals his face of love (verse 17); just as his people praise him, so too he exults in them in their newly-found role of righteousness. And to the prodigal nation there now comes the divine promise: "I will bring you home" (verse 20).

The conclusion of the book, whether or not it is the authentic work of Zephaniah, points nevertheless to a central theme in the words of the prophets as a whole. The religion of the Hebrews was concerned with the relationship between God and his people. The great majority of the prophetic pages are strewn with reminders that the chosen people constantly abandoned that privileged relationship, but occasionally a passage crops up in which a restored relationship is celebrated. Such is the case here. A renewed Israel celebrates its God; and a rejoicing God exults in his people. The narrative is packed with emotion and passion, and it opens the window a little so that those of us outside may share in a joy fulfilled in relationship. And as we overlook the scene, and overhear the words, we may grasp for ourselves some of the potential meaning of our existence. We do not truly live until we find life in relationship with God. And, mysterious though it must always be, God's life and joy are incomplete until he has sealed the relationship of love with all mankind.

INTRODUCTION TO THE BOOK OF HAGGAI

In the Book of Haggai, the passage of time has moved over more than a century from the situation that is reflected in the preceding Book of Zephaniah. Whereas the prophet Zephaniah lived approximately half a century before the great cataclysm of 586 B.C., when Jerusalem and its temple were destroyed, Haggai lived more than half a century after that great disaster. And while Zephaniah in his prophecies had anticipated doom, Haggai lived in the aftermath of doom, when a new page of history lay bare before the Jewish people.

Very little is known of Haggai beyond the precise dates during which one part of his ministry took place. Nothing is known of his father or family background. He is called a prophet, and the substance of his words makes it clear that he was engaged in the public proclamation of the divine word to the chosen people. The five dates in the book specify the time perspective of the prophet's ministry: the events took place between the months of August and December, 520 B.C. But it would probably be a mistake to confine Haggai's entire prophetic ministry to this four-month period. It is more probable that a record was kept of this short span of the prophet's life and ministry because of its considerable significance in the larger scheme of things. We do not even know the prophet's age at the time of this short spell in his life; the suggestion that he was an octogenarian (based on 2:3) is at best fragile, and not probable. But despite the lack of information on Haggai, a good deal is known of the time and circumstances in which he lived.

THE CONTEXT OF THE BOOK OF HAGGAI

The prophet lived and ministered during one of the lowest points in the experience of the Hebrew people throughout the whole biblical period. Some 66 years earlier, in 586 B.C., the city of Jerusalem had been defeated by the armies of Babylon and its temple had been desecrated. A large portion of Jerusalem's population had been exiled to live in the labour camps of Babylon; others had escaped the invaders and had settled in foreign countries, far from their homeland. Only a few had remained in the promised land; devoid of any leadership, they had survived, but they had neither the vision nor the will to retain the vitality of faith which used to be celebrated in Jerusalem.

The international situation began to change in 539 B.C. The newly powerful Persian Empire, under the leadership of Cyrus, defeated Babylon and thus became the new master of the fate of the exiled Jews who lived in the territories Persia now controlled. Cyrus made it possible, perhaps as early as 538 B.C., for exiles who lived in his newly acquired territories to return to their homelands. And so some of the Jews, after half a century of residence in Babylon, began to move back to their own country, a land which many of them (having been born in exile) had never visited.

Of those who returned home, in and after 538 B.C., a few seem to have set about the task of restoring the temple which had been destroyed in 586 B.C. Their efforts, however, were to little avail. Most of them would have been hard pressed to eke out a living in their new circumstances, and though the foundations for a restored temple were cleared and prepared, little progress seems to have been made with the reconstruction as such.

It is against this background that we are provided with a brief glimpse of the ministry of the prophet Haggai. Where the pre-exilic prophets had ministered to a violent and evil nation, Haggai was faced with the inertia of despair and sluggishness. Some of his people sought merely to survive; others survived in reasonable comfort, but had no vision for the people as a whole. And to cap it all, drought and various crop afflictions (arising, no doubt, from years of agricultural neglect) left the land poor and the people dispirited. This was no time, so it must have seemed to most people in the year 520 B.C., to start worrying about the state of the temple. It had been in ruins for decades; most would have thought that it should remain that way until such time as the economy improved.

Haggai was one of a small handful of men who perceived that, despite the sad state of the economy, something had to be done about the temple. Poverty and despair were no grounds for leaving Solomon's once splendid structure in such a sorry state of ruin. From a religious point of view, the temple was a symbol of God's presence amongst his people; while it remained a ruin, there was little hope for a revival of the faith. And from a strictly national point of view, the temple had once been the pride of Jerusalem and Israel; while it remained derelict, there could be no hope for the restoration of national pride, and therefore little hope of the people escaping from the despondency of their circumstances.

Thus Haggai was at once a man of vision and a man with a practical mission. His vision was rooted in his faith: he desired to see Jerusalem's temple restored to something of its former glory, so that in turn God's presence amongst his people could be clearly proclaimed. But his vision was wedded to practical realities. Unless he could persuade the people as a whole, and their rulers in particular, to set about the hard work of restoration, his vision would remain the stuff of dreams. Haggai's book provides a glimpse into some of the turning points from apathy to action. It does not, in itself, tell the complete story of the temple's restoration, but gives an extraordinary insight into the will and vision of one man who contributed to the realization of his own vision.

THE NATURE OF THE BOOK

This short work contains only two chapters and 38 verses. In the Revised Standard Version, the whole book is set out as if it were written in prose, in contrast to many of the prophetic books which are written principally in poetry. Despite the prose form of the English translation, many verses (especially of the prophet's words) have poetic form (see especially: 1:6, 9–11, etc.).

Despite the brevity of the book and the lack of background information, it is extremely precise with respect to dates. Five dates are provided (1:1, 15; 2:1, 10, 20), ranging from August to December, 520 B.C. The dates provide a framework for the book as a whole, dividing it into five sections (the commentary that follows treats the five dated sections separately), though it should be noted that some interpreters are suspicious of the incomplete date in 1:15, and thus divide the book into four units.

The book, in its present form, is apparently an edited collection of some of the prophetic oracles of Haggai, to which has been added a narrative account of the results of the prophet's ministry with respect to the reconstruction of the temple. Haggai himself is consistently described in the third person, and though he could have used such language of himself, it is more likely that his editor, or disciple, collected his sayings and arranged them in their present form.

THE MESSAGE OF HAGGAI

In seeking to delineate the prophet's message, it is important to recognize that we have in this book only a snapshot of what must have been a longer life and ministry. It is important to determine, therefore, why these particular verses and these particular incidents were preserved in writing for later generations. The details of the prophet's message will emerge from the commentary that follows, but the central theme is probably to be found in Haggai's capacity to hold together in his life and ministry both vision and practical application.

Haggai was both theoretician and practitioner. He had a vision of the temple and its religious significance for the chosen people; he also had the energy, drive, and political wisdom to convert the vision into physical reality. But more than that, he was able to hold a balance between current theology with its practical implications, and eschatological theology with its future implications. He affirms, in other words, the importance both of doing and of believing, of bringing about immediate change in the society without assuming that the eschaton, the end of the world, has concurrently come. The remarkable balance of faith in action and active faith has been revealed in part in the manner in which Haggai's work has been arranged by his editor (see further the commentary).

In summary, to grasp the true significance of this little book, we need to envisage the man in his age. Haggai has rarely been given the credit he is due. George Fohrer, a distinguished German Old Testament scholar, wrote: "Haggai is no more than an epigone of the prophets." It is unfortunate to suggest that he was no more than a pale reflection of his great predecessors, though it may have some validity with respect to the Book of Haggai from a strictly literary perspective. It is, perhaps, not a great book, though it is for the most part clear enough. But we should not let the mundane character of the book detract from the greatness of the man. Few people, in a single lifetime, can claim to have revitalized a dispirited nation. And few have found in such an experience so remarkable a balance between action and faith that was thought worthy of preservation for future generations.

AUGUST 29, 520 B.C.

Haggai 1:1–11

[1]In the second year of Darius the king, in the sixth month, on the first day of the month, the word of the Lord came by Haggai the prophet to Zerubbabel the son of Shealtiel, governor of Judah, and to Joshua the son of Jehozadak, the high priest, [2]"Thus says the Lord of hosts: This people say the time has not yet come to rebuild the house of the Lord." [3]Then the word of the Lord came by Haggai the prophet, [4]"Is it a time for you yourselves to dwell in your panelled houses, while this house lies in ruins? [5]Now therefore thus says the Lord of hosts: Consider how you have fared. [6]You have sown much, and harvested little; you eat, but you never have enough; you drink, but you never have your fill; you clothe yourselves, but no one is warm; and he who earns wages earns wages to put them into a bag with holes.

[7]"Thus says the Lord of hosts: Consider how you have fared. [8]Go up to the hills and bring wood and build the house, that I may take

pleasure in it and that I may appear in my glory, says the Lord. ⁹You have looked for much, and, lo, it came to little; and when you brought it home, I blew it away. Why? says the Lord of hosts. Because of my house that lies in ruins, while you busy yourselves each with his own house. ¹⁰Therefore the heavens above you have withheld the dew, and the earth has withheld its produce. ¹¹And I have called for a drought upon the land and the hills, upon the grain, the new wine, the oil, upon what the ground brings forth, upon men and cattle, and upon all their labours."

Dates are important in the Book of Haggai and so the book begins very precisely: what is about to be described took place in the second year of Darius the king (520 B.C.), on the first day of the sixth month. By correlating the study of ancient dating systems with the study of astronomical data on the phases of the moon, it is possible to convert ancient data of this kind into modern dates, with an accuracy factor of approximately plus/minus 24 hours. Thus, the scene is set towards the end of August in 520 B.C.

Jerusalem at that time was located in territory still controlled by the Persians, but within the empire there had been recent change. The Emperor Cambyses, son of Cyrus, had committed suicide in 522 B.C. and had been succeeded by Darius I; he, in turn, spent the first year or so of his reign coping with rebellions in various quarters of his far-flung empire. Change was in the air, and the events in Jerusalem may have been related in part to these larger currents of change. The governor of Jerusalem was Zerubbabel, a member of Judah's royal family; the extent of his authority, and its relationship to the governorship of Samaria to the north, remain uncertain. Zerubbabel's civic leadership was balanced by the religious authority of Joshua, the High Priest, a descendant of the ancient priestly line in Jerusalem. It was to these two men that Haggai addressed his message from God, for they were the ones who had sufficient authority to act, if they should respond to the prophet's words. But it is worth noting that the scene is set "on the first day of the month" (verse 1), presumably a holiday when many of the people would be gathered in the city. Although Haggai must address the established authorities, he has chosen a day when he will have the widest possible audience.

The prophet's speech is prefixed several times with the words and phrases which indicate that its source and authority were rooted in God (verses 2, 3, 5, 7, 9). The speech begins with a quotation of what the people say (verse 2), the words illuminating no doubt the typical attitude of the citizens of Jerusalem and the surrounding areas in Haggai's time. Their attitude was straight-forward: clearly the temple must be rebuilt sometime, but it was much too soon to start the job. There was still so much work to be done in completing the construction of family residences, in re-establishing agriculture, and in getting the economy onto a sound basis, that it would be folly to divert money and energy into the reconstruction of the temple. After all, it would contribute neither shelter to the homeless nor shekels to the economy.

The Lord's response, through the prophet, suggests that some-how the nation's priorities are wrong: is it proper for the people to devote all their attention to the construction and completion of their own homes, while the House of God lies in ruins? Then the prophet goes further, pointing out that the people's best efforts up to that point in time have not improved the economy or the community's well-being. They sowed plenty of seeds in spring, but there was no bumper crop. The necessities of life were there, but they were always insufficient.

The message is clear: the people had tried one policy, that of fending first for themselves, and it had not worked. They needed a change of policy: they should turn their attention from their own needs to that of the House of God, and immediately they should begin the task of reconstruction. And then the prophet goes further and explains the reason for their failure. Having put themselves first in their priorities of action, they had not experi-enced the blessing of God, but the curse of God. All the things that had gone wrong in their attempts to build a new life could be traced back directly to the ancient curses of the Covenant. Poor harvests, drought, lack of produce and other disasters had all been anticipated for a disobedient people in the curses described in Deuteronomy 28. The people, in other words, had brought failure upon themselves by adopting a policy which was in contravention of the ancient covenant faith.

From this opening day in the short episode from Haggai's ministry, a number of useful perspectives emerge.

(i) *Selfish policy*. Haggai addressed a community that had adopted a policy of fending first for themselves. From a practical perspective, it was an eminently sensible policy. Those who had returned from exile had found a land in ruins; not unreasonably, they had set about the task of retoring it to some semblance of economic health. But somehow things had got out of proportion. When the people had been exiled from their homeland, as Ezekiel and other prophets had made clear, they longed above all to be back on their native soil where it would be possible to worship in the temple. Yet once they returned, they quickly forgot the temple and devoted all their energies to their native soil! For a community that owed its existence and its restoration to the promised land to God, such a policy was selfish and doomed to failure.

It is a hard lesson to learn that practical policies are not always the best policies. But the real flaw in the policy that Haggai criticized was to be seen in its ordering of priorities; it was wrong, not because it was practical, but because it was selfish. A life devoted to one's own needs rarely brings fulfilment, whereas when the focus is shifted to an external need, the consequence is frequently satisfaction and fulfilment.

(ii) *Practical considerations*. Haggai says to the people: "Consider how you have fared" (verse 7). He addresses their common sense before he comes to theology. It would be evident to any who stood back and viewed the situation dispassionately that the current policy was not working. They put immense energy into agriculture, but the crops were no better. Wages increased, but in inflationary times they purchased nothing. The prophet is simply pointing out that, since the policy is ineffective, it would be best to abandon it.

Haggai's alternative policy, namely to set about rebuilding the temple, had its own practical wisdom, quite apart from any religious merit. Those who devoted their lives to building their own homes and working their own farms would have no time left for the temple. But, life being what it is, if they devoted their time and energy to the temple, they would somehow make the time and find the energy to fix up their homes and work the land. One of the remarkable aspects of numerous small communities in Western Canada, as elsewhere, is the manner in which a church was the first major structure in the community. The pioneers were faced with the needs of building shelter for themselves and then breaking up a virgin and hostile land. But they found the time and energy to build a church, despite the multitude of other tasks facing them, because the church symbolized and served the faith of the pioneers.

(iii) *Proper priorities*. Above all, Haggai communicates to his people the importance of getting their priorities right. The temple had to be rebuilt so that the glory of the Lord could again be present in Israel (verse 8). When the priorities were correct, other things would fall into place. And that message of Haggai, in August, 520 B.C., remains always pertinent: the fundamental priority in life should be God, not one's own desires.

SEPTEMBER 21, 520 B.C.

Haggai 1:12–15

[12]Then Zerubbabel the son of Shealtiel, and Joshua the son of Jehozadak, the high priest, with all the remnant of the people, obeyed the voice of the Lord their God, and the words of Haggai the prophet, as the Lord their God had sent him; and the people feared before the Lord. [13]Then Haggai, the messenger of the Lord, spoke to the people with the Lord's message, "I am with you, says the Lord." [14]And the Lord stirred up the spirit of Zerubbabel the son of Shealtiel, governor of Judah, and the spirit of Joshua the son of Jehozadak, the high priest, and the spirit of all the remnant of the people; and they came and worked on the house of the Lord of hosts, their God, [15]on the twenty-fourth day of the month, in the sixth month.

No doubt there were numerous committee meetings between the end of August and the third week of September, 520 B.C. Perhaps sub-committees were set up to examine the feasibility and an economic task force established to explore the costs of restoring the temple. But in a remarkably short period of time, when compared at least with modern progress in such matters, thought gave way to action. Zerubbabel and Joshua initiated the work of restoring to something of its former splendour the House of God. One can only guess at the actions and discussions of the preceding three weeks, but it is reasonable to suppose that there would have been considerable opposition to the initiation of this new policy. No progress is ever made without first overcoming the resistance of the nay-sayers. The fact that construction was started at all was a reflection on the civic and religious leadership in Jerusalem. Unless Zerubbabel and Joshua had given the project their support, it would probably never have got off the ground. But, against all odds, work began on the temple on September 21, 520 B.C. In various ways, it was a quite remarkable enterprise which was begun on that day.

(i) *The spirit of voluntarism.* The sheer size of Haggai's proposal is set in perspective when one recalls the nature of the original temple constructed in the time of Solomon. It had taken seven years to build and had been supported by heavy taxation and forced labour. In contrast, in Haggai's proposal, the temple was to be rebuilt by what amounted to voluntary labour.

The spirit of the volunteer, however, is illuminated in two ways in this portion of the narrative. (a) The people volunteered in a spirit of obedience to God (verse 12); such a statement has the appearance at first of contradiction for, as any soldier knows, to volunteer and to obey orders are quite different matters. But they did volunteer: there would be no recompense for their work, so far as we can tell, and their obedience to the divine word was rooted in their perception that the prophet spoke God's word. (b) They acted because they "feared before the Lord" (verse 12). The word *fear* here refers not to terror, but to *awe*, that reverence of God which is the beginning of wisdom (see Proverbs 1:7). Having returned to the true reverence for God, the people restored their priorities to the proper order and volunteered for work.

(ii) *The inspiration of leadership.* The voluntary spirit in the community was no doubt inspired in part by their leaders. The Lord "stirred up the spirit" (verse 14) of Zerubbabel and of Joshua, and through them the spirit of all the people. The language of "stirring the spirit" implies the restoration of vision and the renewal of energy. What had happened, in effect, was that there had been a complete change of heart in the community. Sluggishness had been replaced by the desire to work; despondency had been converted into enthusiasm. But the role of the leaders should not be underestimated. What Haggai had achieved, in human terms, was the transference of his own vision and enthusiasm to the community's leaders, Zerubbabel and Joshua, but unlike the prophet, these men were able to convert vision into action by virtue of the authority of the offices which they held. Haggai was engaged in what would be called nowadays "political action", and his engagement in turn had moved him into the leadership role among his people.

Many persons hold positions of leadership, though frequently they do not bring to their positions vision and enthusiasm, or the capacity to change the lethargy of others into constructive action. Without disparaging in any manner the gifts of the governor and the high priest, it was the contribution of the prophet that was the more instrumental in bringing the fresh air of constructive change to Jerusalem.

(iii) *The divine blessing.* In the midst of this narrative of action and planning, the prophet once again declares a divine oracle. This time, it is short and to the point: "I am with you, says the Lord" (verse 13). In the prophet's first message, there had been no such indication of divine presence; indeed, Haggai had intimated that the troubles in the land could largely be attributed to the divine absence. But now that the priorities were straight, now that action was about to begin, the prophet could bring to his people the word that would endorse their activity and encourage them as to its future success.

Haggai's proclamation of the word of divine encouragement echoes on in future scriptures and into our present world. In Jesus' final and great commission to his disciples, his final words to them were: "I am with you always, to the close of the age." Just as Haggai declared the words to those who were about to rebuild God's House, so too Jesus declared it to those who were about to build his Church. Indeed, to all who are engaged in the construction of the Kingdom of God, the promise of divine presence is repeated.

OCTOBER 17, 520 B.C.

Haggai 2:1–9

In the second year of Darius the king, [1]in the seventh month, on the twenty-first day of the month, the word of the Lord came by Haggai the prophet, [2]"Speak now to Zerubbabel the son of Shealtiel, governor of Judah, and to Joshua the son of Jehozadak, the high priest, and to all the remnant of the people, and say, [3]'Who is left among you that saw this house in its former glory? How do you see it now? Is it not in your sight as nothing? [4]Yet now take courage, O Zerubbabel, says the Lord; take courage, O Joshua, son of Jehozadak, the high priest; take courage, all you people of the land, says the Lord; work, for I am with you, says the Lord of hosts, [5]according to the promise that I made you when you came out of Egypt. My Spirit abides among you; fear not. [6]For thus says the Lord of hosts: Once again, in a little while, I will shake the heavens and the earth and the sea and the dry land; [7]and I will shake all nations, so that the treasures of all nations shall come in, and I will fill this house with splendour, says the Lord of hosts. [8]The silver is mine, and the gold is mine, says the Lord of hosts. [9]The latter splendour of this house shall be greater than the former, says the Lord of hosts; and in this place I will give prosperity, says the Lord of hosts.'"

Almost a month has passed now since the work of reconstruction began, and the timing is significant. The 21st day of the 7th month (viz. October 17, according to our modern calendar) was the last day of the Festival of Tabernacles. It would have been a public holiday, and people from the countryside would join the crowds from the city in the festivities of the day. And inevitably, on an occasion such as this, many of the folk must have gone over to the temple precincts to see what progress had been made in the restoration work. After all the ballyhoo about getting going again, the physical evidence of progress must have been slender. Only a month had passed since the work was initiated, and that single month had been disrupted, from the point of view of work, not only by the Festival of Tabernacles but also by the celebration of *Yom Kippur* (the Day of Atonement), which preceded the Festival.

Faced with the relative absence of progress, human nature reared its ugly head. Look what they are doing here! This will be a half-baked building compared with the old temple that Solomon built! And perhaps there were a few octogenarians present, people who had actually been familiar with the original temple before its destruction. Wistful recollections of the splendour of the past would have produced frustration in their audience drawn from the younger generation. And it would have been a fine day for those who had opposed the restoration project in the first place: better not to have started than to have produced this jerry-built structure!

In such a context Haggai once again addresses the governor, the high priest, and the assembled crowds. He takes note of the mumblings and discontent, but converts them to positive words of encouragement in his speech. Despite all criticisms, they are to take courage and get on with the job, for God is with them (verse 4). But the latter part of the prophet's message has a different tone to it and is not easy to interpret (verses 6–9). The expression "once again, in a little while" (verse 6) appears to be an idiomatic expression referring to the future. At some future point, God would cause an earthquake to occur (whether the sense is literal or metaphorical is not certain), as a result of which the wealth of nations would flow into Jerusalem. Again, just why an earthquake should result in such movement of wealth is unclear. The general intent of the oracle, nevertheless, is clear: the temple now under construction would one day be more splendid that its predecessor. And perhaps the prophet implies that this would be so because one day the Hebrews would once again have a wealthy empire as they did in the days of David and Solomon, drawing upon the wealth of other nations. In this portion of the message, we begin to see how the present and the future intertwine in the prophet's preaching.

The immediate task at hand was the restoration of the temple; one suspects that Haggai knew full well that it would not match Solomon's for splendour. The times had changed, and they must do what they could. But the prophet saw also a more distant age in a new world; he envisaged a future not unlike that of Ezekiel's, with its restored land and splendid temple (Ezekiel 40–48). The future, though, was always contingent upon the present; there would be no glorious future temple, if the present temple continued to lie in ruins. For the ruined temple had come to symbolize a ruined people. Only when the people were restored to faith would a restoration on a larger, world-wide scale become a possibility. And Haggai perceived, albeit dimly, that in the ultimate splendour of the temple, the Gentiles would have a role to play.

There is a fairly precise analogy between the situation which faced Haggai and that which constantly faces the Christian Church. The prophet had before him the task of building a temple; the Church has before it the task of building the Kingdom of God. But now, as then, there are those who are overcome by the power of negative thinking, who can see only problems and no possibilities. Look how long the Christian Church has been struggling at this business of the Kingdom of God, and where is it today? Frankly, the world does not seem to be a much better place than it was 2,000 years ago; if anything, in a nuclear century, it is worse. So is it not a waste of time to sweat and struggle with the Kingdom of God?

The trouble with negative thinkers, for ourselves as much as Haggai, is that they are usually correct, in part at least. If we are honest, not much progress has been made with the Kingdom over two millennia. And even the readers of Norman Vincent Peale would have to admit that our prospects for the future are not too bright. To counter such thinking, we need to remember Haggai's double focus. It may be true that we will not build such a splendid structure. But unless we set about the task, we will certainly fulfil the direst predictions of our opponents. It is only as we engage in the task of building the Kingdom that we leave open the door for a more marvellous work of God. That this is so is not always self-evident, but requires an act of faith. Nevertheless, we can perceive the truth in part. Over many centuries, people have searched for peace and the abolition of war. They have not succeeded, though they have perhaps improved the world a little. But if they had abandoned the pursuit of peace, many centuries ago, then even the hope and ideal of peace might have been lost to civilization. Likewise, the Church must continue to seek that peace of God for all the world, for if it is lost, there remains no hope.

DECEMBER 18, 520 B.C.

Haggai 2:10–19

[10]On the twenty-fourth day of the ninth month, in the second year of Darius, the word of the Lord came by Haggai the prophet, [11]"Thus says the Lord of hosts: Ask the priests to decide this question, [12]'If one carries holy flesh in the skirt of his garment, and touches with his skirt bread, or pottage, or wine, or oil, or any kind of food, does it become holy?'" The priests answered, "No." [13]Then said Haggai, "If one who is unclean by contact with a dead body touches any of these, does it become unclean?" The priests answered, "It does become unclean." [14]Then Haggai said, "So is it with this people, and with this nation before me, says the Lord; and so with every work of their hands; and what they offer there is unclean. [15]Pray now, consider what will come to pass from this day onward. Before a stone was placed upon a stone in the temple of the Lord, [16]how did you fare? When one came to a heap of twenty measures, there were but ten; when one came to the winevat to draw fifty measures, there were but twenty. [17]I smote you and all the products of your toil with blight and mildew and hail; yet you did not return to me, says the Lord. [18]Consider from this day onward, from the twenty-fourth day of the ninth month. Since the day that the foundation of the Lord's temple was laid, consider: [19]Is the seed yet in the barn? Do the vine, the fig tree, the pomegranate, and the olive tree still yield nothing? From this day on I will bless you."

December 18 (the 24th day of the 9th month) must have been a significant day in the early period of the temple's reconstruction, but the frustrating thing is that, from the evidence which has survived, we cannot be absolutely certain what it was that gave the day such significance. Haggai delivered three oracles on that December day, each dated: the first two were given together, and the third separately. (a) A warning oracle (verses 10–14), which is clearly dated. (b) An oracle of blessing (verses 15–19), in which the date is repeated (verse 18). (c) An oracle to the governor (verses 20–23), which was given on the same date, although the date formula (verse 20) suggests a different setting. But what was the significance of the day that prompted these oracles? There was not, to the best of our knowledge, a significant festival or holiday on December 18. Some have suggested that it was on this day that the foundation stone was laid (on the basis of verse 18), but that is improbable; a little bit of restoration work had been started in 538 B.C., and now in Haggai's time the work was resumed. But no foundation stone was required in a restoration project (the original presumably being still in place), and the sense of verse 18, in the Hebrew, has more to do with the resumption of construction.

Although it is speculation, it is possible that a specific agricultural day gave significance to the time, and hence gave rise to the oracles. The late autumn rains, which softened the hard ground, were followed by ploughing and seeding the land for a spring crop. By mid- to late-December, the seeding should have been completed, and perhaps an impromptu holiday was declared. In any case, we shall see that the second oracle, which emphasizes "this day" (verse 19), was closely related to the agricultural cycle of the year.

(1) *The message of warning* (verses 10–14). In the first oracle, the prophet is instructed to address two questions to the priests. The questions are to be asked for didactic reasons; that is, the priests, in answering the questions, would learn from their answers something more than they knew. Their answers to the questions, drawn from their professional knowledge, would prepare the ground for further illumination.

(a) The first question is straightforward. If a priest were carrying meat that had already been sanctified for offering in a sacrifice and if, while carrying that meat, his clothes happened to touch some other foodstuffs (for example, bread, wine, or oil), would those other foodstuffs become holy by virtue of their indirect contact with holy things? The answer was negative. Holiness, in a literal sense, was not contagious, and the priests would have had no difficulty in giving the correct answer.

(b) The second question was like the first question, but in reverse. If a person were ritually unclean, for example by virtue of having touched a corpse, and if he happened to touch any of the aforementioned foodstuffs, would they thereby become corrupt? Again, the priests would have had no difficulty in answering. The foodstuffs would become unclean by virtue of such contact, for ritual uncleanness was contagious. The answers to both questions were implied clearly enough in the priestly laws (see Lev. 6:27–30; 11:24–28; 22:4–7).

The question and answer period is followed by the prophet's teaching, but the sense of verse 14 is not immediately clear and several hypotheses have been proposed to explain it. Some interpreters, for example, have suggested that the prophet here alludes to the offer of help in the building work which came from the Samaritans (Ezra 4:1–3); the teaching implies that the help should be refused, for it would pollute the holy place under reconstruction. But a more probable interpretation is that the ritual questions were designed to evoke answers from which moral teaching might be drawn. The people were engaged in a holy task, the building of a temple, but the holiness of the task would not automatically rub off on them. They must still be concerned, despite the honour of their work, with their own moral integrity. On the other hand, if they themselves became degenerate, then their moral corruption could certainly undermine the integrity and holiness of the temple which they were erecting.

If the latter interpretation is correct, then Haggai is echoing, in his own distinctive fashion, the traditional prophetic concern for moral integrity to accompany ritual integrity. The people were engaged in a noble task, but that did not grant them a moral licence to behave as they pleased. Just because they were working for God did not mean they could abandon moral integrity; indeed, if they did so, they would undermine the very work in which they were engaged. Stated in such black and white terms, the teaching may seem obvious. Yet there is an aspect to human nature which makes it necessary: when we are engaged in any good work, it is all too easy to think that the merit of the work will somehow cover like a blanket the imperfections of our lives.

(ii) *The message of blessing* (verses 15–19). Again, a series of questions are asked, this time theoretical questions. They are addressed presumably to the people as a whole, not just the priests, as in the preceding oracle. And the prophet is anxious that his audience reflect very carefully on the questions he puts to them: three times, he urges them to "consider" (verses 15, 18).

Haggai asks the people to reflect on their situation before the temple reconstruction began. How did they fare then (verse 16)? Their supplies of grain and wine were far less than they should have been. For all their hard work, their agricultural efforts were ruined by diseased crops, mildew, and hail. And despite all the disasters, the people had never thought to relate them to their spiritual health; they had never thought of turning back to God in repentance. Then, with particular emphasis (verses 18–19), the prophet asks them to think on this particular day. Is the seed in the barn? No, it has just been planted in the earth. Do the fruit trees yield a harvest? Of course not: it is the middle of December! Nevertheless, Haggai affirms on behalf of God, "from this day on I will bless you."

The prophet, in other words, predicts a bumper harvest of crops and fruit at a time in the agricultural year when no sensible agronomist would risk his neck. A sensible man would wait a month or so to observe the weather conditions and the amount of precipitation. But Haggai's perspective was entirely different. The seed was now in the ground and the work of the temple reconstruction was now proceeding apace. Therefore, with absolute conviction and some courage, he firmly predicts a bountiful harvest, not because he has inside knowledge on future weather or special means of blight control, but because the conditions in his community are now appropriate for the experience of divine blessing.

In this prophetic prediction, we begin to see something of the prophet's strength of character and certainty of vocation. After all, the reconstruction work on the temple had only been under way for about three months at the time of his statement, and the whole task would take about four and a half years (it was completed in the 6th year of Darius: Ezra 6:15). If Haggai were wrong in this conviction, he could hardly expect the continuing voluntary support of his people in the coming years. But in this action, we see Haggai clearly in the role of prophet, as distinct from that of political activist. He had received a promise from God, he believed it and, knowing the risk involved, he proclaimed it in public. His career and reputation were now on the line!

THE MESSAGE TO ZERUBBABEL

Haggai 2:20–23

²⁰The word of the Lord came a second time to Haggai on the twenty-fourth day of the month, ²¹"Speak to Zerubbabel, governor of Judah, saying, I am about to shake the heavens and the earth, ²²and to overthrow the throne of kingdoms; I am about to destroy the strength of the kingdoms of the nations, and overthrow the chariots and their riders; and the horses and their riders shall go down, every one by the sword of his fellow. ²³On that day, says the Lord of hosts, I will take you, O Zerubbabel my servant, the son of Shealtiel, says the Lord, and make you like a signet ring; for I have chosen you, says the Lord of hosts."

The final prophecy in the Book of Haggai, also delivered on December 18, 520 B.C., ties the prophet's present world to a more distant and anticipated future. On the surface, the prophetic message is addressed directly to Zerubbabel, the governor of Judah and the descendant of the line of David. The prophet declares what God is about to do. In the future, no doubt the near future in the prophet's expectation, God would shake heaven and earth, overturning the world's nations and overwhelming their vast military might. And on that day, the prophet indicates (verse 23), God would establish Zerubbabel as his personal servant and "signet ring" (the symbol of divine authority); the language has distinctly messianic overtones. Zerubbabel, of the family of David, had been chosen by God.

Certainly the prophecy conveys the distinct impression that Haggai anticipated the dawning of the messianic age on the completion of the reconstruction of the temple, and he expected Zerubbabel to be the messianic prince. But, as is well known from subsequent history, such was certainly not the case, and some have written of Haggai's prophecy that it was "partially dishonoured by history". Nevertheless, while this perspective may well be correct with respect to Haggai the man, it misses the point of the book. By the time that Haggai's prophecies were collected and edited in their present form, it must have been clear enough that the messianic age, God's new world, had not come to pass. And the same truth must have been equally clear to those persons who preserved and treasured Haggai's book through future generations. So why was such an oracle inserted and preserved in this little book if it had missed the mark so wildly?

We need to stand back a little from the scene to perceive the wider significance of the message. Before the destruction of Jerusalem (587/586 B.C.) and the defeat of Judah, the future of the chosen people had been linked intimately to the continuity of the line of David. But the exile had changed many people's thinking, and the limited return to the promised land, to live as citizens in a territory now belonging to the Persian Empire, did little to disturb that new thinking. How could the future of the chosen people be tied to a royal family, when there was no independent king and no independent national status? In other words, the whole significance of the Davidic line was in danger of being lost among the chosen people.

Haggai preaches restoration, even though the circumstances of his age suggest that any restoration would be futile. He works for the restoration of the temple, even though he knows that, in human terms, it could not have quite the significance it had in

Solomon's time. And he also affirms the restoration of the line of David, even though he lives in an empire ruled by the Persian Darius. He knows that the line of David must continue, and naturally pins his hopes on its representative, Zerubbabel. But for Zerubbabel to assume a truly royal role, the nations of the world would have to be conquered (verse 22). Haggai has the principles right but, as in much futuristic language, he collapses time, and expects to see what must come to pass in his own age. But those who preserved his message saw in it a larger perspective. God's new world would indeed be brought about with a representative of the line of David, albeit not Zerubbabel. Nevertheless, the messianic age would be linked to one of the same lineage as Zerubbabel.

Haggai's "that day" (verse 23) thus takes on new significance with the passage of time. The timetable of God is more obscure than at first it appears, though it is no less certain. And, in addition, God's "day" is always contingent to some extent on the response of the people of God to the divine word: that is why Haggai was engaged in prophetic ministry. But we perceive, in this strange and final oracle, a fundamental principle with respect to the interpretation of the prophetic writings. Brevard Childs has expressed it well: "Thus the prophetic word became the criterion by which to judge history instead of the reverse move which has dominated historical critical scholarship" (*Introduction to the Old Testament as Scripture*, 1979, p. 471). In the last resort, Haggai's vision and final recorded message were neither disappointed nor disappointing!

INTRODUCTION TO THE BOOK OF ZECHARIAH

Zechariah and Haggai were contemporaries in Jerusalem and both were concerned with the rebuilding of the ruined temple. And yet, judging by the books named after them, they were very different types of men, Haggai being the more practical and Zechariah the more visionary. The brevity and clarity of Haggai's book are contrasted by the length and difficulty of Zechariah's work. Indeed Jerome, one of the great scholars of the early Christian Church, surely hit the nail on the head when he described Zechariah as "the most obscure of books". Its vision-accounts and oracles, its apocalyptic sayings and intimations of the future, are all of such a kind that render interpretation difficult. Yet the difficulty of the book should not intimidate the reader; it is worth recalling that this book is one of the most frequently quoted in the New Testament. Of more than 70 quotations from, and allusions to, Zechariah in the New Testament, approximately a third appear in the Gospels, and most of the rest are to be found in the Revelation of St John. The New Testament writers, in other words, were able to relate much of Zechariah's thought to their own time, and an understanding of this later perspective may help us to grasp the message of the book as a whole.

The prophet Zechariah is described as "son of Berechiah, son of Iddo" (1:1), though elsewhere he is referred to simply as "son of Iddo" (Ezra 5:1). There may be some confusion in the texts as to his lineage, although Ezra may provide simply the shortened form, for "son of" (in Hebrew) may equally be rendered "grandson of". There was a man called *Iddo*, of priestly descent, who accompanied Zerubbabel and Joshua in the return from exile; if this is the same person referred to here as Zechariah's grandfather, it would indicate the prophet's priestly background, but the identification is not certain. In summary, we know little of the prophet's biography beyond the scant and indirect information contained in the book named after him.

The dates provided in the book clearly link Zechariah's ministry to that of Haggai. His ministry is said to begin in the eighth month of the second year of Darius (1:1), or approximately November, 520 B.C. Zechariah's visions are specified as taking place (or starting) on the 24th day of the 11th month of Darius' second regnal year, approximately February 15, 519 B.C. (1:7). And the later date given in 7:1 may be rendered as December 7, 518 B.C. Thus, on the surface, Zechariah had a slightly longer ministry than did Haggai, though we cannot be certain in either case that the books provide anything like a full account of the ministries of the respective prophets. The context in which Zechariah ministered, however, was essentially the same as that of his contemporary: see further the Introduction to the Book of Haggai.

THE LITERARY FORM OF THE BOOK

Apart from the difficulties involved in the interpretation of visions and apocalyptic language, there are severe problems pertaining to the formal structure of the Book of Zechariah. The first eight chapters have a generally recognized unity of thought and substance. Zechariah himself is mentioned three times in conjunction with the various dates given, and the substance of the chapters, for all its difficulty, can be related to the prophet's time and the rebuilding of the temple. But the latter part of the book (chapters 9–14) is quite different in style and substance. The prophet is not explicitly named, nor are dates given. Poetry is employed, whereas in the first portion of the book prose dominates. And the apocalyptic substance of the latter part of the book distinguishes it from the visionary substance of the first part of the book.

Given the range of differences between chapters 1–8 and 9–14, it is not in the least surprising that many scholars have taken the latter chapters to be the work of a hand other than Zechariah's. Indeed, the alternative authorship of chapters 9–14 was raised at least as early as the 17th century and has never really been abandoned. But although there has been general agreement concerning the distinctive character of the latter half of the book, there has been no agreement as to its origin or date. Some would date it in the 5th century B.C., but some to the Greek period (late 4th century B.C. and after), and some would break it into numerous subsections and deal with each separately. In fact, now the pendulum is swinging in the other direction, and some scholars are arguing once again for the unity of the book, proposing that its latter section reflects a late period of the prophet's ministry, perhaps a decade or so after that reflected in chapters 1–8.

The debate over Zechariah which has been waged over several centuries is unlikely to be resolved in the immediate future, so it would be wise to adopt a cautious position with respect to the structure and possible unity of the book. (a) Whether or not the two parts of the book come to us from Zechariah, it is important to recognize the differences between them, both in theological and chronological perspective. (b) Chapters 1–8 contain clearly dated sections in which vision-accounts and prophetic oracles dominate. Chapters 9–14 fall into two sections, (i) 9–11 and (ii) 12–14, both introduced as an "oracle" or "burden", in a manner similar to the Book of Malachi. (c) If the book's two portions do come from separate persons, nevertheless the fact that an editor has bound them together must not be overlooked. That is to say, for all the differences between the parts, we must also look for the linking themes which are presupposed by their present literary arrangement. (d) Finally, for all the probability of hypotheses arguing for at least two sources for the book, the only manuscript evidence we have indicates that the Book of Zechariah achieved its present unity at an early date. The earliest surviving manuscript evidence, a Greek text of the Twelve Prophets found among the so-called Dead Sea Scrolls, shows no evidence of a break between chapters 8 and 9. This evidence proves nothing with respect to authorship, but it does indicate that from an early date the entire book, in its present form, was believed to have some unity of substance and thought.

THE MESSAGE OF ZECHARIAH

The 14 chapters of the Book of Zechariah convey a message that is at once rooted in its own time and at the same moment breaks out of the barriers of all concepts of finitude. In the opening chapters, at least, the same down-to-earth reality of rebuilding a temple that dominated Haggai's book can be seen behind Zechariah's visions. Like Haggai, he was a man with a practical mission, but more than Haggai he stressed the larger theological significance of the practical activities in which he was engaged. Zechariah and his contemporaries were engaged in the physical work of building, but what he could see, more than the others, was the significance of their physical activity on God's larger spiritual plans for his people. The temple was a symbol of God's presence among his people; the temple rebuilding, however, somehow symbolized, and perhaps even inaugurated in some mysterious fashion, God's renewal of his chosen people beyond that immediate time and place.

In the latter part of the book, the rooting in time and history gives way to a larger vision, inevitably one that stretches the capacity of human words and language. The chapters are filled with a sense of tension, capturing the eternal struggle between good and evil, but locating that struggle in the context of God's chosen people and their future. Although this section ends finally with a sense of God's triumph, it is a dark passage, penetrated as much by despair and violence as it is by hope. In some ways, it echoes with the dualism of Zoroastrian eschatology, the conflict between good and evil in the cosmos, though it has been shaped in a distinctly Jewish fashion. (The Jews were probably acquainted with Zoroastrianism through their contact with the Persians.)

The message of Zechariah tests our powers of interpretation, and it requires of us at least as much spiritual and artistic sensitivity as it does technical knowledge. We may grasp the problem through an analogy, albeit an imperfect one. Our ancestors in the 18th century would have found it impossible to anticipate the wonders of the 20th century, and even if they had glimpsed in a visionary sense our current reality, they could not have described it in the language of their time. Televisions and microwave ovens, personal computers and pocket calculators, jet aircraft and space travel, transatlantic telephones and digital wrist-watches—all these things would be not only foreign to the citizen of the 18th century, but could not even be adequately described in the language of that time. The 18th-century visionary, even in attempting to describe a reality two centuries beyond his own time, would be stymied. But the biblical visionaries have a vastly more difficult task. They have glimpsed a future in the divinely given vision, and somehow they must communicate its substance. As in the analogy, they face immediately the problem of the inadequacy of their language. One may see or sense certain realities, but to recount them inevitably involves stretching human language beyond its natural capacities. Likewise, in interpreting such language, we must take care not to reduce it to banal literalism, as if the human speech of a given time or place could ever capture the essence of God's future.

Having recognized the difficulties, however, we must also note the simplicities of such language as the prophet uses. Why does Zechariah speak of these things to his contemporaries? Why were such sayings preserved for future generations? The prophet was not a predictor, in any simple sense of that word. It is unlikely that he thought they would be better off by possessing a kind of timetable of future events that would come to pass long after their own funerals had been conducted. The prophetic message, rather, has a kind of perpetual contemporaneity to it, for it addresses the issues that trouble mankind in every generation. Must evil always triumph over good? Is God really almighty? Will the world get better, or only worse? Will the Kingdom of God, of peace and of righteousness, ever be established in this sad world? It is questions such as these that are addressed in the Book of Zechariah. They are answered from the perspective of faith in God and hope in God's future. But insofar as the book contains answers, they are addressed from faith and to faith. And insofar as those answers pertain in part to a future world, they are expressed in language which is difficult to interpret, but breathes nevertheless with an ultimate hope in God which cannot be destroyed.

Part I: Chapters 1–8

AN OLD MESSAGE FOR A NEW AGE

Zechariah 1:1–6

> ¹In the eighth month, in the second year of Darius, the word of the Lord came to Zechariah the son of Berechiah, son of Iddo, the prophet, saying, ²"The Lord was very angry with your fathers. ³Therefore say to them, Thus says the Lord of hosts: Return to me, says the Lord of hosts, and I will return to you, says the Lord of hosts. ⁴Be not like your fathers, to whom the former prophets cried out, 'Thus says the Lord of hosts, Return from your evil ways and from your evil deeds.' But they did not hear or heed me, says the Lord. ⁵Your fathers, where are they? And the prophets, do they live for ever? ⁶But my words and my statutes, which I commanded my servants the prophets, did they not overtake your fathers? So they repented and said, As the Lord of hosts purposed to deal with us for our ways and deeds, so has he dealt with us."

The first recorded sermon of the prophet Zechariah was delivered within a few weeks of the inauguration of the rebuilding of the temple in Jerusalem. Although the audience to whom these words were addressed is not clearly specified, the broad implication is that the prophet was addressing a general audience of citizens in Jerusalem. Among those who would hear him were the civic leaders, those engaged in the reconstruction project, and citizens in general. On the face of it, the prophet's message is not related directly to the major project now under way, though on reflection what he says has a great deal of relevance to the task at hand. And superficially, the prophet's message was a very old one, though the context in which he delivered it made it new and refreshing. Several important themes emerge from this opening sample of the prophet's preaching and they set the stage for what is to follow.

(i) *The central message.* Zechariah begins with a theme from the central message of the prophetic tradition that had been established long before his own time. "Return to me, says the Lord of hosts, and I will return to you" (verse 3). The prophet repeats the old, old story, claiming no originality for his central message; indeed, he quotes the substance of what earlier prophets had proclaimed (verse 4). But the lack of novelty in his message in no way diminished its importance. The heart of Israel's covenant faith had always been the relationship between God and his chosen people. And the prophets had always been the conscience of Israel: when the people had turned away from faith in God, the prophets had called them back, urging them to restore the relationship upon which their lives depended. In all this Zechariah stands firmly in the ancient prophetic tradition.

Nevertheless, the repetition of the old message in the post-exilic age must have seemed like the fresh wind of God to some in the audience. Many must have thought in those dark days that God's covenant with Israel was ended, buried in the exile and symbolized by the ruined state of Jerusalem. So many of the external signs of the covenant had gone, that it would have been hard to believe that God's offer of relationship still remained open. But the offer was still there, as Zechariah's confident preaching made clear; it was still possible to turn back to God, who was still waiting to turn to his people.

It is hard for us to recapture the thrill of the prophet's message. His people, struggling to survive in a ruined land that belonged now to a foreign power, would have all but lost the vision. Yet the prophetic message from God, "Return to me . . . and I will return to you", is repeated to every generation. For all the shambles of the world around us, one basic truth remains unchanged: in the relationship with God, life's meaning may be found.

(ii) *Learning from the past.* Few generations of the human race have been able to learn from their history; even historians are notoriously blind to the message emerging from the stuff of their trade. But Zechariah perceives the absolute importance of his own generation learning from the mistakes of those that had gone before. Earlier prophets had preached the same message of repentance to the ancestors of those who were now Zechariah's audience. They had preached faithfully, but the ancestors had not listened, and so had experienced the judgment of which the prophets had warned (verse 4). Only when the judgment had finally overtaken them, in defeat and exile, had their predecessors seen the light; then they repented (verse 6), but it was a little late.

It was largely the failure of previous generations that had culminated in the present disaster of Zechariah's time. And the prophet sees all too clearly that, unless past failures are remedied, there can be little hope of escaping from the present. And so he urges his people: "Be not like your fathers" (verse 4). It was a sad message to have to declare, but a true one. And the consequences of the disastrous course pursued by the fathers were physically evident to all those who heard Zechariah's sermon. Thus the prophet calls upon his people to reflect on the culmination of a walk in life separated from God, and to recall the first priority of the ancient faith, that of faithfulness to God. There was a lesson to be learned from past experiences and unless it was learned, the terrible experiences of the past would gradually fill the future.

(iii) *Faith and the temple.* The prophet was also concerned that the work on restoring the temple did not produce a falsely based confidence among his people. For several weeks the construction had been going on, but even as the restored structure began to take shape, perhaps Zechariah was haunted by the spectres of the past. Former generations had believed the holy city to be impregnable, because it was the home of God's temple. In 586 B.C., when the temple had been destroyed, the citizens had discovered just how vulnerable their capital city was. But the restored temple, for all its importance, could recreate among the unwary all the old false confidence which contributed to downfall.

And so Zechariah's sermon represents in a way a return to the basics. To paraphrase: the temple is being restored, and that is splendid, but never forget that first and foremost God requires of his people obedience and faithfulness. And where that is not present, it is more important to find it by turning back to God, than it is to devote money and energy to a house of worship. The prophet, in other words, seeks to counter a perennial human tendency, namely the inclination within religious communities to deal with external matters rather than internal matters. The community in Jerusalem was sick at heart, and there were those who thought that a restored temple would cure all society's ills. And, indeed, the restoration of the temple would have an important role to play. But the work on the temple would become a monument to folly, unless it was accompanied by spiritual reconstruction. Zechariah's call, "Return to me, says the Lord", was as essential to his community as Haggai's call to buckle down to hard work and building.

And what was true in the prophet's time is as true in our own. We are constantly faced with the need to rebuild, whether it be the local church, the national church, or the state of a nation. To set about the task of rebuilding, we need the vision and stimulus of a person like Haggai. But if the work of rebuilding is to be more than a veneer that covers an inner sickness, the message of Zechariah is equally important. No rebuilding project, no national fund-raising drive, no new constitution or new strategy for church growth, will do any good whatsoever, unless it is accompanied by a fundamental change of heart amongst the people as a whole. That is a part of the prophet's enduring message for future generations.

VISION IN THE NIGHT

Zechariah 1:7–17

7On the twenty-fourth day of the eleventh month which is the month of Shebat, in the second year of Darius, the word of the Lord came to Zechariah the son of Berechiah, son of Iddo, the prophet; and Zechariah said, 8"I saw in the night, and behold, a man riding upon a red horse! He was standing among the myrtle trees in the glen; and behind him were red, sorrel, and white horses. ⁹Then I said, 'What are these, my lord?' The angel who talked with me said to me, 'I will show you what they are.' ¹⁰So the man who was standing among the myrtle trees answered, 'These are they whom the Lord has sent to patrol the earth.' ¹¹And they answered the angel of the Lord who was standing among the myrtle trees, 'We have patrolled the earth, and behold, all the earth remains at rest.' ¹²Then the angel of the Lord said, 'O Lord of hosts, how long wilt thou have no mercy on Jerusalem and the cities of Judah, against which thou hast had indignation these seventy years?' ¹³And the Lord answered gracious and comforting words to the angel who talked with me. ¹⁴So the angel who talked with me said to me, 'Cry out, Thus says the Lord of hosts: I am exceedingly jealous for Jerusalem and for Zion. ¹⁵And I am very angry with the nations that are at ease; for while I was angry but a little they furthered the disaster. ¹⁶Therefore, thus says the Lord, I have returned to Jerusalem with compassion; my house shall be built in it, says the Lord of hosts, and the measuring line shall be stretched out over Jerusalem. ¹⁷Cry again, Thus says the Lord of hosts: My cities shall again overflow with prosperity, and the Lord will again comfort Zion and again choose Jerusalem.'"

A substantial portion of the first section of the Book of Zechariah is taken up by an account of eight visions experienced by the prophet (1:7–6:15). All the visions are introduced by a single date (1:7), approximately February 15, 519 B.C., a few months after the work had begun on the restoration of the temple. And all the visions, by implication, occurred "in the night" (1:8); they were not necessarily dreams, but rather visions received by a conscious prophet. Muhammad, in later centuries, was to experience night visions which were instrumental in launching his mission in Mecca. So too Zechariah, perhaps meditating upon his task in the hours of the night, received these visions as a form of communication from God. We cannot know precisely the form which such extraordinary experiences assumed, but visions were one of several means by which the prophets received the divine revelation. It is possible, judging from the substance of the first vision, that Zechariah's place of meditation, at the time when he saw the visions, was a quiet valley just outside the city of Jerusalem.

Vision frequently superimposes itself on some part of immediate reality: Zechariah, presumably in the glen close to a grove of myrtle trees (verse 8), suddenly saw a rider upon a red horse amongst the myrtle trees. Behind him were three other horses, perhaps also with riders, each horse a different colour (though the colour of the horses does not seem to have any symbolic meaning in the vision). In addition to the horses, an angelic being appeared alongside the prophet, and so he asked the angel: "What are these, my lord?" The angel redirected the question to the leader of the horsemen, who in turn informed Zechariah that the horsemen were the scouts of God, sent to patrol the earth. Then the leader of the scouting patrol informed the prophet's angelic companion that they had patrolled the earth and all was at peace. The angel, serving in the role of mediator, responded to the report by addressing a prayer to God, who is not specified as being present: he asked how long God would hold back his mercy from Jerusalem and the surrounding cities. The divine wrath against the cities of the chosen people had extended for 70 years (verse 12; see also Jeremiah 25:11); the period of time is presumably intended to be general rather than specific, 70 years being the expression used to designate a lifetime.

God's response to the angel was apparently comforting, for he in turn communicated instructions to Zechariah. The words "cry out" (verse 14) indicate the message which the prophet, in turn, was to proclaim to his people. God had in no way abandoned his concern for Jerusalem (Zion), and indeed he was angry with the world's nations which were, at that time, in peace and prosperity. God's former wrath with Jerusalem had been real, but the world's nations had taken the judgment of Jerusalem beyond all reasonable bounds in their own bid for power and profit. Hence the divine compassion would be extended once again to Jerusalem, its temple rebuilt, and the city restored. The time of poverty would be replaced by a new era of prosperity, and anguish calmed by new comfort and consolation. From this account of the first vision, some of the themes of Zechariah's ministry begin to emerge.

(i) *God had not abandoned his people.* There must have been times when Zechariah and his fellow citizens in Jerusalem wondered whether they were the followers of some otiose deity, distant, apparently sleeping, and having no concern for the plight of his people. But the vision discloses to the prophet that even in times when God seemed absent, the divine horsemen were still patrolling the world, and their rendezvous was close to the holy city. There is an eerie quality to the vision, the sense of a veil drawn back to reveal realities always present, but rarely visible. And to Zechariah a part of the meaning of the vision would have been crystal clear: despite the sense of abandonment in the cold light of day, the night vision revealed that God was still active in his world.

There are many people whose lives from time to time are like those of the citizens of Jerusalem. All around lies in ruins and the attempts to rebuild life do not seem to progress very fast. For all the efforts and attempts at faithfulness, God seems somehow uncaring, out of touch with the pain of his people. And to such there is comfort in the vision of Zechariah; without vision, we cannot always perceive God at work in the world, but the vision of faith reveals that he is never absent.

(ii) *The problem of peace.* For earlier prophets, it was the problem of war which dominated their preaching; the threat of invasion and attack was a portent of judgment. But in Zechariah's time, peace was a problem. The scouting of the world's nations indicated they were "at rest" (verse 11), normally a happy state of affairs, but not always. Darius, by 519 B.C., was bringing his vast empire under control, and for a while at least international conflict had died down. But the peace of the world was a puzzle to many in Jerusalem. They had experienced, through ruthless war and years of exile, the judgment they deserved, but the enemies of former times and many of those who had exploited Jerusalem's misfortunes lived now at peace, their conscience unbothered by former atrocities. It was one thing to believe that God could judge his own people for their evil, but it sorely taxed the faith to see that other nations, with darker histories, remained untouched by the hand of God. Peace, under such circumstances, not only tested the faith, but also raised the question as to God's justice. And in such an unsettling time, the prophet again perceived a larger truth: "I am very angry with the nations that are at ease" (verse 15).

The prophet clarifies how difficult it is to determine the will of God from the circumstances of our time. Peace in our world is never a sure indication that all is well. Nor should peace be a source of consolation to those who think that, after all, they have got away with evil, they have escaped the long arm of the divine law. There remains always, despite the appearance of circumstances, the work of divine justice to be done in the world. And Zechariah draws back the curtain briefly to let us see, in principle, the inexorable movement of God's justice.

(iii) *The continuity of compassion.* The most compelling part of the prophet's first vision is its assurance that God's compassion for Jerusalem and its people has not been exhausted (verse 17). It is easier for us simply to read such a word of assurance than it is to grasp its impact at a time when all the evidence seemed, to its first audience, to deny its truth. Jerusalem was still in a sorry state, its walls ruined and its great buildings in disrepair. The work on the restoration of the temple had progressed only a little, perhaps the apparent futility of it all being highlighted by the surrounding wreckage of a once great city. And the Jerusalem that had once been the splendid capital of a proud nation was now merely a ruined outpost in the further reaches of the Persian Empire. It could not have been easy to believe in such a time that God still had compassion on his city and chosen people.

But again we perceive how the prophet's vision may outstrip reality. There are times in human experience when every scrap of empirical evidence conspires to deny the compassion of God. There are occasions when the ruin of life, whether in health or other circumstances, seems to testify only to the absence of divine compassion. On such occasions we require the prophet's vision, which reaches out beyond the immediate reality to perceive a perpetual and continuing compassion from which God will not draw back.

THE SECOND VISION: FOUR HORNS

Zechariah 1:18–21

> [18]And I lifted my eyes and saw, and behold, four horns! [19]And I said to the angel who talked with me, "What are these?" And he answered me, "These are the horns which have scattered Judah, Israel, and Jerusalem." [20]Then the Lord showed me four smiths. [21]And I said, "What are these coming to do?" He answered, "These are the horns which scattered Judah, so that no man raised his head; and these have come to terrify them, to cast down the horns of the nations who lifted up their horns against the land of Judah to scatter it."

Four horns constitute the focus of the second vision. The description of the vision is extremely concise and not immediately clear, but perhaps in any case the vision as such was only in stark outline, so that the prophet must ask his interpreter: "What are these?" (verse 19). He sees four horns, but whether or not the horns are attached to animals is uncertain. The horn, for example that of a bull, was a symbol of strength throughout the biblical world, so that at least the general symbolism of the four horns would have been clear to the prophet and his audience. Although interpreters of this text have attempted from time to time to identify the four horns with specific nations, the sense of the passage is probably more general: the four horns represent all nations hostile to the chosen people from the four points of the compass.

In response to the prophet's question, the angelic companion replies that the horns represent the nations "which have scattered Judah, Israel, and Jerusalem" (verse 19). The prophet's vision at this point seems to span the centuries of history, incorporating not only his own nation and city, but also Israel, which had been defeated and dispersed some two centuries earlier. The prophet then enquires after the function of the smiths, four of whom have appeared following the horns. He is told that the role of the smiths is to destroy the horns. Just as the horns had terrified the men of Judah, so too the horns would be terrified by the smiths who carried, presumably, the hefty hammers of their trade. Just as a dangerous bull might have its horns removed to reduce its threat to passers-by, so too the great nations would be stripped of their strength by the divinely commissioned smiths.

The thrust of the second vision reinforces the message of the first. Despite the strength of Judah's enemies, and despite the fact that nothing in current history seemed to threaten their power, nevertheless there remained one who had the strength to crush the opposition symbolized by the four horns. God had not forgotten his people; he was preparing the agents of their deliverance, the four "smiths", who would terrorize the terrorist neighbours of the chosen people. And thus, although the message of comfort following the first vision (verse 17) is not repeated here, its prospect nevertheless is held out implicitly. God would act. Whether Zechariah anticipated this deliverance in the near or distant future cannot be determined, for the vision is not specific with respect to time, but it is full of hope and conviction.

What is striking about the substance of the prophet's visions is its unconditional character. Whereas prophets before the exile had spoken of future events principally in conditional terms, the future of the chosen people depending upon their response to the divine word, Zechariah envisions God's firm intervention in human history in the judgment of gentile nations. It is true that his language is concise, a kind of shorthand account of what he has seen, but he is describing here something inevitable. The arrogance of human nations, especially in the practice of injustice, cannot pass unnoticed and unjudged; it must be dealt with. Zechariah announces the coming of a day of reckoning, not to those about to be judged, but to those who have suffered so long at the hands of the mighty. And while there may seem to be little consolation in hearing the judgment of others announced, there is consolation in the affirmation that God has not abandoned justice.

THE THIRD VISION: A CITY WITHOUT WALLS

Zechariah 2:1–13

[1] And I lifted my eyes and saw, and behold, a man with a measuring line in his hand! [2] Then I said, "Where are you going?" And he said to me,

"To measure Jerusalem, to see what is its breadth and what is its length." ³And behold, the angel who talked with me came forward, and another angel came forward to meet him, ⁴and said to him, "Run, say to that young man, 'Jerusalem shall be inhabited as villages without walls, because of the multitude of men and cattle in it. ⁵For I will be to her a wall of fire round about, says the Lord, and I will be the glory within her.'"

⁶Ho! ho! Flee from the land of the north, says the Lord; for I have spread you abroad as the four winds of the heavens, says the Lord. ⁷Ho! Escape to Zion, you who dwell with the daughter of Babylon. ⁸For thus said the Lord of hosts, after his glory sent me to the nations who plundered you, for he who touches you touches the apple of his eye: ⁹"Behold, I will shake my hand over them, and they shall become plunder for those who served them. Then you will know that the Lord of hosts has sent me. ¹⁰Sing and rejoice, O daughter of Zion; for lo, I come and I will dwell in the midst of you, says the Lord. ¹¹And many nations shall join themselves to the Lord in that day, and shall be my people; and I will dwell in the midst of you, and you shall know that the Lord of hosts has sent me to you. ¹²And the Lord will inherit Judah as his portion in the holy land, and will again choose Jerusalem."

¹³Be silent, all flesh, before the Lord; for he has roused himself from his holy dwelling.

The prophet, still located outside the city at the scene of his visions, sees a surveyor passing by, with a measuring line in his hand. The scene no doubt evokes the substance of the first vision, in which God had said "the measuring line shall be stretched out over Jerusalem" (1:16). Zechariah asks the surveyor where he is going, and the man replies that he is about to measure Jerusalem and determine its dimensions. Then two angelic beings step onto the stage of the vision, one of them the prophet's companion and interpreter, the other a new figure in the visionary sequence. The new figure approaches the prophet's angelic companion and requests him to address the young surveyor. The message to the young man is that the city would have a vast population and that its protection would be provided by God rather than by the conventional city walls.

The description of the vision is followed by a more traditional prophetic oracle (verses 6–13), which is thoroughly poetic in form, despite the manner of its translation in the RSV. The oracle may originally have been quite separate from the vision, being delivered at another time or place in the prophet's ministry, but its location in this context is significant: it indicates the source of the city's larger population and emphasizes that God would be the city's protector. The growth in Jerusalem's population would be the result in part of the return to their homeland of many of those Jews still in exile, and also of growth from people coming out of Gentile nations (verse 11). And the city would be protected, not by its walls and military strongholds, but because "I dwell in the midst of you, says the Lord" (verses 10–11).

From this third vision and the accompanying oracle, we begin to see the breadth of the prophet's conception of the coming work of God.

(i) *The reformers were restricted in their vision.* Work was already proceeding, in Zechariah's time, with the restoration of the temple. Some complainers must have pointed out that it was futile to restore the temple while the city walls were still in ruins, offering no protection for the sacred building. Others, those engaged in the restoration work, must already have been thinking of repairing the city walls as soon as the temple project was completed. But both groups knew that sooner or later the walls around the city's perimeter must be restored. Walls were the conventional defences of all ancient cities against military attack. And the young man setting off to survey the city represents this conventional thinking. Jerusalem must have walls; they should be built where the old ones used to stand. But the thinking represented by the young surveyor's action is fundamentally flawed; it projects into the future the notions of the past. It sees a future population no different from that of former times. It stresses the importance of defensive walls, oblivious to the fact that walls had failed to hinder the Babylonian armies in 587 B.C.

Zechariah's vision emphasizes the fact that the future is different from the past, and that God's coming actions cannot be projected on the basis of what used to be. The criteria for growth of population and military defence would differ radically from former times, and so the prophet learns in this third vision to expand his horizons of the future. The implication of the vision is that the Holy City would belong to a different order of reality than that to which the old walled city had belonged. For Zechariah, as much as for his people, it was vital at that critical time in history to grasp the possibility of a future greater than they had imagined. Simply to project into the future the memory of past grandeur would ultimately be a restraint upon the work of God.

(ii) *God's future work would embrace varieties of people.* For most of the prophet's companions, their thinking about Jerusalem and the restoration of the temple would have been restricted largely to the city's current population, one which was considerably reduced from former times. Some citizens had stayed on in Jerusalem after 586 B.C., others had returned from exile, but in terms of numbers alone, there was no basis for a great city in Jerusalem, even with a restored population. But Zechariah anticipates a return of exiles not only from Mesopotamia, but also from the four corners of the world to which the Jews had fled (verses 6–7). And he further anticipates the citizens of Gentile nations joining the chosen people and becoming the people of God (verse 11).

The prophet envisages a kind of international homecoming in which many people, essentially aliens in their own lands, would find at last a home in the city of God. And the ancient message has, in a certain sense, many levels of fulfilment. In the generations following Zechariah's time, many Jews continued to return to Jerusalem from the distant lands in which they had taken up residence. And to this very day, in the modern state of Israel, the return continues: Jews from the new world and the old world return to their ancient home, there to take up residence once again. But from the Christian perspective, the prophet's anticipation of Gentiles joining the flood to the holy city is given substance in the birth and growth of the Christian Church. The proclamation of the Gospel to the Gentiles, as well as to Jews, opened up to many pilgrims in this troubled world the possibility of residence in the city of God, a city without walls, yet offering an enduring and secure home.

(iii) *The presence of God.* Vision and oracle combine to affirm that the transformation of the future city of Jerusalem would be a consequence of the divine presence in its midst. In the vision, the wall of fire without and the divine glory within would replace the required ramparts of a secure city. In the oracle, twice it is declared: "I will dwell in the midst of you" (verses 10, 11). Thus, to a populace busy restoring the physical structures of the city of Jerusalem, the prophet reminds them of certain absolute basics. Restored walls are no good without the surrounding "wall of fire" (verse 5). A restored temple, whatever its splendour, would be of no significance unless the Lord were in the city. But walls and temple, insofar as they symbolized reliance on divine protection and divine presence, were important features of the city.

And so Zechariah communicates through vision and speech a balanced message. There is important work at hand and he encourages it to continue, but he is concerned that no physical work on the city result in misplaced trust. When all is said and done, if the citizens of Jerusalem began gradually to trust in the work of their hands, then they would have laboured in vain.

THE FOURTH VISION: JOSHUA AND THE SATAN

Zechariah 3:1–10

[1]Then he showed me Joshua the high priest standing before the angel of the Lord, and Satan standing at his right hand to accuse him. [2]And the Lord said to Satan, "The Lord rebuke you, O Satan! The Lord who has chosen Jerusalem rebuke you! Is not this a brand plucked from the fire?" [3]Now Joshua was standing before the angel, clothed with filthy garments. [4]And the angel said to those who were standing before him, "Remove the filthy garments from him." And to him he said, "Behold, I have taken your iniquity away from you, and I will clothe you with rich apparel." [5]And I said, "Let them put a clean turban on his head." So they put a clean turban on his head and clothed him with garments; and the angel of the Lord was standing by.

[6]And the angel of the Lord enjoined Joshua, [7]"Thus says the Lord of hosts: If you will walk in my ways and keep my charge, then you shall rule my house and have charge of my courts, and I will give you the

right of access among those who are standing here. ⁸Hear now, O Joshua the high priest, you and your friends who sit before you, for they are men of good omen: behold, I will bring my servant the Branch. ⁹For behold, upon the stone which I have set before Joshua, upon a single stone with seven facets, I will engrave its inscription, says the Lord of hosts, and I will remove the guilt of this land in a single day. ¹⁰In that day, says the Lord of hosts, every one of you will invite his neighbour under his vine and under his fig tree."

Reality impinges upon vision, and some of the persons and issues uppermost in the prophet's mind now take on substance and shape in the visionary sequence. Zechariah perceives Joshua, his colleague who is high priest in Jerusalem, standing before God's angel. The scene is like that of a court: God is present, acting in the role of judge, with the Satan at his hand in the role of prosecuting attorney. (*Note: the Satan*, in Hebrew, means the "opposer," or "accuser". The word is not here a personal name, *Satan*, as it becomes in later Jewish and Christian history. The Satan, as in Job 1–2, is a servant of God whose only authority is God-given. But in this text, we begin to sense the malicious character of the Satan, which may have been part of a trend towards the later concept of the demonic being, *Satan*.)

The courtroom dialogue begins with some words of rebuke addressed by God to the accuser, though the substance of the words implies that the Satan has already been vocal in his charges against Judah and Jerusalem. The charges are abruptly halted: "Is not this a brand plucked from the fire?" (verse 2), words implying that Judah had already suffered severely for its sins. The high priest Joshua, who here seems to represent the people in their worship, is seen standing before the court in filthy garments, representing perhaps the sad state to which the people's sins had brought Judah, and the imperfection of their worship. The court scene is not elaborated in detail; indeed, the major part of the proceedings seems already to have taken place, when instructions are given to have the filthy garments removed from Joshua. The words following the removal of the garments indicate clearly the symbolism of the action: "I have taken your iniquity away from you" (verse 4). And as new high-priestly garments are put on, the implication is equally clear: a new righteousness is given to the high priest, who represents the people. And suddenly, Zechariah speaks spontaneously, becoming thereby a character in his own vision: "Let them put a clean turban on his head," he says, sensing the incompleteness of the high priest's garb.

The re-clothing ceremony is then followed by a divine address to Joshua. He is told that if he observes the law and all his priestly responsibilities, he will rule with authority in the temple and its precincts. The reference to the "Branch" (verse 8) is somewhat obscure; although the immediate reference may be to Prince Zerubbabel, Joshua's companion, the words have (or have come to have) messianic overtones. And the reference to the "stone" (verse 9) is equally obscure; it has been subject to numerous interpretations, none of them certain, although the symbolism clearly has to do with the removal of the land's guilt. As a consequence of forgiveness and the divine gift of a new character of righteousness, there would be a spirit of contentment and neighbourly charity in Judah (verse 10).

The vision speaks to Zechariah, and through him to his people, of both present and future.

(i) *Encouragement for the present.* It would have been difficult in Zechariah's time, with work proceeding apace on the temple, to believe that things could ever be as they used to be in temple worship. It was one thing to restore a crumbling house of worship, but the essence of true worship was to be found in the people and their spiritual leadership. And Joshua, standing in God's presence in his miserable rags, symbolized the sorry state of the nation's spirit. They were not the same people that they used to be: they had sinned too much and corrupted the priestly office for too long to hope that they could ever restore the pristine purity of the old forms of worship. And yet the vision of new clothes for Joshua imparted encouragement to their current activities in restoring the temple. What ruined all hope, humanly speaking, for the present, was the clear memory of a history of evil and a legacy of guilt. The gift of new clothes to Joshua indicated that the past could be removed and a new start could be made. Their task in restoring the temple was not in vain; within its walls, true worship could once again be offered to God.

This vision of the gift of new garments continues to hold out hope for subsequent generations. Like a person who arrives at a formal dinner party wearing tee-shirt and jeans, the awareness of the miserable rags of our past life creates unease in the divine presence. And yet Zechariah reminds us of one of the essential ingredients of all Christian life and worship: it is forgiveness. And forgiveness means that the dirty garments of the past life can be discarded, so that we may enjoy a relationship with God, not ill at ease in our own soiled garb, but dressed in the moral finery that God may grant to those who seek him in truth.

(ii) *Hope for the future.* The prophet's vision has overtones of a more distant age in which pure worship and peaceful living would become at last the norms of daily life for the people of God. And the tone is re-echoed in the vision of St John, at the beginning of Christian history, when he envisages a newly-clothed Church: "for the fine linen is the righteous deeds of the saints" (Revelation 19:8). The overtones of Zechariah's vision, and the explicit hope of that of St John, are that the Messiah would be the One through whom this transformation would come.

But we, no less than Zechariah, are caught in the tension between time and eternity. There is always the continuing struggle to cope with the past and live in the present. And occasionally in the midst of the struggle we glimpse a better future, usually of such a visionary quality that it seems unreal. The circumstances of Zechariah's time gave little grounds for confidence that a time would come when "every one of you will invite his neighbour under his vine and under his fig tree", nor does our world seem to be moving any closer toward such pastoral contentment. And yet this future vision, despite its distance and lack of focus, is essential for the present, because the future can never be divorced from the present. Just as Zechariah's words and actions were to shape the future of his own people and world, so too do ours. And it is our vision of the future which may enable us to impart something of its substance into the present world.

THE FIFTH VISION: THE LAMPSTAND

Zechariah 4:1–14

¹And the angel who talked with me came again, and waked me, like a man that is wakened out of his sleep. ²And he said to me, "What do you see?" I said, "I see, and behold, a lampstand all of gold, with a bowl on the top of it, and seven lamps on it, with seven lips on each of the lamps which are on the top of it. ³And there are two olive trees by it, one on the right of the bowl and the other on its left." ⁴And I said to the angel who talked with me, "What are these, my lord?" ⁵Then the angel who talked with me answered me, "Do you not know what these are?" I said, "No, my lord." ⁶Then he said to me, "This is the word of the Lord to Zerubbabel: Not by might, nor by power, but by my Spirit, says the Lord of hosts. ⁷What are you, O great mountain? Before Zerubbabel you shall become a plain; and he shall bring forward the top stone amid shouts of 'Grace, grace to it!' " ⁸Moreover the word of the Lord came to me, saying, ⁹"The hands of Zerubbabel have laid the foundation of this house; his hands shall also complete it. Then you will know that the Lord of hosts has sent me to you. ¹⁰For whoever has despised the day of small things shall rejoice, and shall see the plummet in the hand of Zerubbabel.

"These seven are the eyes of the Lord, which range through the whole earth." ¹¹Then I said to him, "What are these two olive trees on the right and the left of the lampstand?" ¹²And a second time I said to him, "What are these two branches of the olive trees, which are beside the two golden pipes from which the oil is poured out?" ¹³He said to me, "Do you not know what these are?" I said, "No, my lord." ¹⁴Then he said, "These are the two anointed who stand by the Lord of the whole earth."

Perhaps the spiritual intensity of the series of visions has reduced the prophet to a state of stupor. Prior to the fifth vision he must be shaken into wakefulness, and then he is asked once again what it is that he sees. The vision is of a golden lampstand: there is a stem surmounted by a bowl to contain the fuel oil, and there are seven lamps, or spouts, protruding from the bowl. (Visually, this may have been a quite different object from the seven-branched *menorah*, which became so familiar in later Jewish art.) On either side of the lampstand, the prophet saw two olive trees (and olive oil, it should be remembered, could be used as a lamp fuel). Zechariah asks his accompanying angel what is the meaning of this vision; he does not receive a direct reply to his question, though there is an implication that he should know the symbolism of what he sees. Rather than a reply to his question, the prophet is given a message to declare to the prince, Zerubbabel, though the message, as we shall see, paves the way towards an understanding of the vision.

God's message to the prince was that his task, namely the rebuilding of the temple, would be accomplished, "not by might, nor by power, but by my Spirit" (verse 6). The "great mountain" (verse 7) is a metaphorical allusion to the mountain of difficulties which lay in the path of the temple's completion. All obstacles to the task of restoration would be levelled into a plane, until at the last the top stone, marking the completion of the project, would be set in place amidst the jubilant shouts of the onlookers. Prince Zerubbabel, who had been instrumental in launching the work of temple restoration, would eventually be successful in its completion, so much so that even those who earlier had complained of "small things" would be compelled to join in the rejoicing.

The symbolism of the vision is taken up once again in the concluding verses. The seven lamps on the lampstand are the "eyes of the Lord", though it must be admitted that the interpretation at this point is as obscure as the vision. The number *seven* symbolizes perfection, though the sense in which lamps could symbolize *eyes* (or the Hebrew could be translated *wells*) is uncertain. Perhaps because of his continuing uncertainty, Zechariah continues to question his companion. What do the two olive trees represent? And what is the significance of the two pipes, apparently providing a supply of oil to the lamp's fuel tank? The prophet is told that the two trees represent the "anointed", that is, Joshua the priest and Prince Zerubbabel.

The principal purpose of the fifth vision appears to be that of balancing and supplementing the fourth. In the preceding vision the primary focus had been on Joshua, the spiritual leader of the people. Now it is clear that both Joshua and Zerubbabel, representing the civil government, have a role to play. And if the lampstand, representing the eyes of God, indicates the divine compassion for all the world flowing through the worship of Jerusalem's temple, then the vision as a whole emphasizes the importance both of the priestly family and the Davidic dynasty in carrying out the divine purpose. But in addition to this principal purpose, the fifth vision contains several valuable insights of permanent value.

(i) *God's work is achieved by God's strength:* "Not by might, nor by power, but by my Spirit, says the Lord of hosts" (verse 6). The words *might* and *power* refer respectively to military strength and physical activity. Thus, the prophet indicates, neither the power of armies nor the effort of sheer hard work could by themselves achieve the task God had set his people. And the prince, who was traditionally both the commander-in-chief of the nation's armed forces and the director of all national tasks, would have to learn that ultimately his success would depend upon the Spirit of God. It was the Spirit of God which in the last resort would make possible the completion of the temple's restoration.

It is important to retain a correct perspective in interpreting these words, for in no manner do they imply a *laissez-faire* attitude. The message was addressed to a man already active in the work of God, one indeed who was exercising all his power in the attempt to bring to completion God's house. The prophet did not imply that Zerubbabel could sit back and watch God complete his task for him. Rather, he indicated an essential ingredient of all work for God, namely the Spirit of God, which not only made the task possible, but would also enable its completion.

And in building the Kingdom of God, as much as the temple in Zechariah's time, the principle remains the same. We must of course be engaged actively in the work of the Kingdom; both might and power are required. But these things alone will not bring success. Our willingness to act, our health which makes action possible, our strength in work as such, all are in a sense the gifts of God and the vehicles through which God may act. We need to learn, as did Zechariah, to use all that we have and all that has been given to us, without in the last resort placing our dependence for success on those things. Success is finally possible only in the Spirit of God.

(ii) *The danger of despising small beginnings.* The work on the temple had had its opponents from the beginning and no doubt many were still around in 519 B.C. They were not bad persons as such, but they were devoid of vision. They knew how they thought a renewed temple should be, but they were, in their own minds, realists. They sensed that the nation's priorities should be to re-establish the economy, before embarking on a grand building scheme which would not benefit the gross national product. And in any case, the days of grand schemes were past; these were not the days of David and Solomon, when the wealth of nations flowed into the coffers of Jerusalem. These were not even days of national independence, when the future of a restored temple could be secured. It was a time of small things, a time when the wise men advocated caution, not courage, and when grand vision had succumbed to timid thought.

Zechariah, in his vision, despises the despisers, but anticipates nevertheless the time when the despisers would be transformed involuntarily into rejoicers. His spirit is an open one, looking not for final vindication over the small-minded people of his generation, but only for their conversion. But his warning is ever timely: the people who despise the day of small things are almost always people of sound common sense. Yet the valuable commodity of common sense can obliterate, if we are not careful, all capacity for vision. And we who live in an age of small things, at least in matters of faith, need to be stirred occasionally by those with vision. Our practical and hard-nosed realism needs to be leavened from time to time with the yeast of what God's future might be.

(iii) *People matter more than institutions.* The preoccupation in Zechariah's time with restoring the temple could easily have recreated that old and false confidence in the importance of the institution as such. But in the prophet's fifth vision, we are reminded of the importance of people. The temple was the home of the lampstand, symbolizing both God's window on the world and God as the light of the world. But it was the two olive trees, representing Joshua and Zerubbabel, which provided the fuel so that the lamp could burn brightly. The temple without the lamp would have been just a building, and the lamp without fuel would have been merely an ornament. But the burning lamp brought life and light to the temple and the world, and it was human beings who made the lamp burn.

The Church, as institution, is never enough; no anonymous organization will by itself transform the world. People are always needed, for through them the life and light of God may flow. And as both Joshua and Zerubbabel had a part to play, indicating the role of both clergy and laity, so too the Church depends for its vitality upon both the clergy and the laity. Through all the members of the Christian Church, without exception, the life and light of God must be made available to the world. And as the roles of both priest and prince were in part taken up and fulfilled in Jesus the Messiah, so too in Christ must we serve as fuel for God's lamp in a dark world.

THE SIXTH AND SEVENTH VISIONS

Zechariah 5:1–11

[1]Again I lifted my eyes and saw, and behold, a flying scroll! [2]And he said to me, "What do you see?" I answered, "I see a flying scroll; its length is twenty cubits, and its breadth ten cubits." [3]Then he said to me, "This is the curse that goes out over the face of the whole land; for every one who steals shall be cut off henceforth according to it, and every one who swears falsely shall be cut off henceforth according to it. [4]I will send it forth, says the Lord of hosts, and it shall enter the house of the thief, and the house of him who swears falsely by my name; and it shall abide in his house and consume it, both timber and stones."

[5]Then the angel who talked with me came forward and said to me, "Lift your eyes, and see what this is that goes forth." [6]And I said, "What is it?" He said, "This is the ephah that goes forth." And he said, "This is their iniquity in all the land." [7]And behold, the leaden cover was lifted, and there was a woman sitting in the ephah! [8]And he said, "This is Wickedness." And he thrust her back into the ephah, and thrust down the leaden weight upon its mouth. [9]Then I lifted my eyes and saw, and behold, two women coming forward! The wind was in their wings; they had wings like the wings of a stork, and they lifted up

the ephah between earth and heaven. ¹⁰Then I said to the angel who talked with me, "Where are they taking the ephah?" ¹¹He said to me, "To the land of Shinar, to build a house for it; and when this is prepared, they will set the ephah down there on its base."

(i) *The flying book* (verses 1–4). Again the prophet looks into his visionary landscape and this time sees a flying book, or more precisely a very large unrolled scroll. (The scroll antedated our modern form of book, being a long strip of papyrus, or parchment, on which the text was written; the scroll was simply rolled from one spindle to another in the course of reading.) The measurements are given, approximately 30 feet × 15 feet, to indicate that this was not a "normal" flying book, but one of unusually large proportions, for most scrolls would be considerably narrower. The book was flying over the land, trailing its message for all to see, in the fashion of those commercial messages towed by light aircraft over the crowds at fairs or football matches.

Zechariah is then told the significance of the flying scroll: it represents the divine curse and it flies back and forth, entering the homes of thieves and perjurers, creating destruction wherever it goes. The flying curse is longer than the arm of the law, for it is steered as if by automatic pilot, unerringly homing on those who by their actions have invited God's curse. And its victims are those who have broken two of the Ten Commandments which were so central to the life of Covenant; the curse was directed to those who had stolen, and those who had perverted justice by giving false testimony in court.

The focus of the visionary messages has now shifted from the temple and the leaders of the people to the moral fibre of the society as a whole, and the shift is significant for grasping Zechariah's message in its totality. All the work that was being done in the restoration of the temple presupposed that there remained a relationship of covenant between God and Israel and that therefore worship was still possible. And the visionary statements about Joshua and Zerubbabel also presupposed a continuing covenant; God, through his chosen leaders, would continue to direct his people. But all these affirmations of the continuity of the covenant raised certain basic questions. The original covenant of Sinai, as the prophet knew very well, contained not only the promise of blessing, but also the threat of the divine curse. And so it is to the curse that he turns in the sixth and seventh visions.

The problem behind the visions may be stated as follows. On the one hand, the nation's effort was being directed towards the restoration of the temple; on the other hand, it was clear that theft and perjury were common in the land. Might not the pervasiveness of crime cancel out the blessing implicit in the good work being done on the temple? The vision, and its antecedent problem, provide a small window overlooking the social conditions of the prophet's world. So far we have seen only the difficulties encountered with those who did not wish to participate in the work of the temple. But now we see, beyond the struggles at the centre of society, the sad state of affairs in the community as a whole. Law was only loosely enforced and the lack of strength in the judiciary was such that the process of law was easily perverted. Judah had sunk a long way from its grander days; it was now a petty colony in a greater empire, loosely administered, without national pride or moral fibre. Crimes flourished, in part because of poverty and in part because it was so easy to break the law in a community so laxly administered. But to those with a finger on the nation's pulse, like Zechariah, the crime was worrisome; from the perspective of the covenant faith, crime invited the curse that could undo all the other good work that was under way.

Thus the message of the prophet is that crime, despite the incompetence of police and the failure of the law courts, does not pay: it was under the judgment of God, and the curse of God would eventually find the criminals in their own homes. It is a vision of faith, affirming that, despite society's sorry state, a renewed life for the nation was possible. There would be, in the completion of the temple, blessing, despite the curse which might seem to be a natural consequence of so crime-ridden a society. But it is above all a vision of God's initiative in coping with his society's ills. There is little emphasis here on an active programme of social reform, perhaps because such a task seemed impossible. But there is enormous confidence in the blessing of God for the nation as a whole, and conviction that crime would eventually be rewarded by its own ends, rather than corrupting the society in which it was carried out.

(ii) *The genie in the jar* (verses 5–11). The focus of the seventh vision is an *ephah*, a word which designates both a measure of quantity (approximately five gallons) and also a container. It is the latter sense that is implicit here: the prophet sees a large pot or jar, no doubt considerably larger than normal as was the scroll, and the pot seems to be moving about the land (verses 5–6). Zechariah is told that the pot represents the "iniquity" of the people in the land as a whole, its movement symbolizing the widespread nature of such iniquity throughout the community. Then the prophet sees the lid of the pot lifted, and to his astonishment he notices a woman inside it, peeping through the mouth of the container. Like a genie in a jar, the woman is traversing the land, spreading her influence wherever she goes. The woman, Zechariah is told, represents "Wickedness".

Then the movement of the vision continues: the woman is thrust back into the pot, presumably by the prophet's accompanying angel, and the heavy lid is firmly secured. Two female angels now enter the scene, with wide wings like those of storks and, lifting the pot, they fly off with it. Zechariah asks where it is being taken and is told that its destiny is the land of Shinar, or Babylon. There a house (or temple) would be built for it, and it would remain in the remote place permanently.

Whereas in the preceding vision specific crimes had been mentioned, those of theft and perjury, in this vision it is the general spirit of wickedness that is personified as a woman in a pot. Presumably it is a *woman* that is employed in the vision because the Hebrew word for *wickedness* is feminine. But equally it is female angels who represent the good and dispose of wickedness. The imagery of the vision is multi-faceted. At one level, it takes up the age-old notion of the genie in the jar, of the power supposedly within our control that can be used for our own purposes. At another level, it hints at the hiddenness of wickedness, lurking in the household vessel, then peeping out to lure us with evil's possibilities. But suddenly the imagery is reversed: the vessel which suggests that evil may be mastered and which implies its subtleness becomes, in God's hands, the perpetual prison of wickedness. Those who would keep evil in the home, a kind of pet to be played with from time to time, may learn from the divine action. Wickedness must be removed as far as possible from the home, permanently sealed up, and left in a distant land.

In the seventh vision, the prophet reveals the depths of the divine concern for the moral state of the nation. It is not just evil acts that matter; the spirit of wickedness, ever threatening to break out in a plague of further evil, must also be mastered. And again the prophet anticipates divine initiative in the removal of wickedness from the land. But the vision is instructive with respect both to society in general and personal living in particular. (a) It reminds us that it is not only the surface that matters, but what lies beneath the surface. Crime can ruin a society's health, but the prevalence of a spirit of wickedness may be even more dangerous. And individually, we may think we are the masters of our own actions, but so long as we cherish and nourish the thoughts and desires of evil, we are never safe. (b) The only way to deal with evil is to remove it totally. We may think we have it in control, that we are masters of evil, not mastered by it. But there is no certainty in that approach; to be truly free, we must remove it entirely, and in that we must continually seek divine aid.

THE FINAL VISION: FOUR CHARIOTS

Zechariah 6:1-15

¹And again I lifted my eyes and saw, and behold, four chariots came out from between two mountains; and the mountains were mountains of bronze. ²The first chariot had red horses, the second black horses, ³the third white horses, and the fourth chariot dappled grey horses. ⁴Then I said to the angel who talked with me, "What are these, my lord?" ⁵And the angel answered me, "These are going forth to the four winds of heaven, after presenting themselves before the Lord of all the

earth. 6The chariot with the black horses goes toward the north country, the white ones go toward the west country, and the dappled ones go toward the south country." 7When the steeds came out, they were impatient to get off and patrol the earth. And he said, "Go, patrol the earth." So they patrolled the earth. 8Then he cried to me, "Behold, those who go toward the north country have set my spirit at rest in the north country."

9And the word of the Lord came to me: 10"Take from the exiles Heldai, Tobijah, and Jedaiah, who have arrived from Babylon; and go the same day to the house of Josiah, the son of Zephaniah. 11Take from them silver and gold, and make a crown, and set it upon the head of Joshua, the son of Jehozadak, the high priest; 12and say to him, 'Thus says the Lord of hosts, "Behold, the man whose name is the Branch: for he shall grow up in his place, and he shall build the temple of the Lord. 13It is he who shall build the temple of the Lord, and shall bear royal honour, and shall sit and rule upon his throne. And there shall be a priest by his throne, and peaceful understanding shall be between them both."' 14And the crown shall be in the temple of the Lord as a reminder to Heldai, Tobijah, Jedaiah, and Josiah the son of Zephaniah.

15"And those who are far off shall come and help to build the temple of the Lord; and you shall know that the Lord of hosts has sent me to you. And this shall come to pass, if you will diligently obey the voice of the Lord your God."

Just as the prophet's first vision was concerned with horses of various colours, so too is his last. The final vision (verses 1–8) rounds out the substance and sense of the entire sequence of visions, and it stresses their central message. It is followed by a prophetic oracle (verses 9–15) which seems to be closely related to the visions and requires specific actions which will clarify for the prophet's audience the meaning of his visions. The Hebrew text of chapter 6 is difficult to translate in several places and its somewhat opaque style contributes to the difficulty of interpretation.

(i) *The vision of horses and chariots* (verses 1–8). The horses of the first vision reappear in the last, but now chariots have been added to the scene. Whereas in the first vision, the horses were returning after scouting the world, here they are portrayed as

about to set off on a military campaign. They come out from the
valley between bronze mountains, the symbolic gate of heaven,
and set off into the four corners of the world to accomplish their
task. The horses and chariots have been given a mission by the
"Lord of all the earth" (verse 5) and must not rest until it is
accomplished. Emphasis is given to the chariot that goes "toward
the north country" (verse 9), for it is there that the centre of the
world's greatest power, the Persian Empire, was established. (In
a strictly geographical sense, Persia (Iran) was north-east, but the
road there led directly north from Jerusalem.) The mission would
"set my Spirit at rest in the north country", that is, it would
establish the power of God's spirit over the northern empire. And
the implication is that if the north could be conquered, so too
could all other foreign nations.

The vision of the departure of horses and chariots on world-
wide missions of military intervention establishes not only a central part of the meaning of all eight visions, but also a chronological perspective within which to interpret the prophet's words.
The restoration of the temple and of leadership in Judah presupposed a renewal of the Kingdom of God in the world; it intimated
that more lay in the future than simply a refurbished temple and a
rejuvenated government. Only when foreign nations were over-
thrown could the chosen people be truly free once again. But the
visionary language is also tinted with apocalyptic tones. Although
the words are concerned with Zechariah's immediate present,
with the temple and government in Jerusalem, time is collapsed
in the vision to join the present to what was a more remote future.
What was happening anticipated in a mysterious fashion what
was yet to happen. And though we may find the visionary words
as difficult to grasp in detail as did the prophet's first audience, we
may share with them the absolute conviction of the prophet's
central message. God was and is sovereign in human history. And
though the hand of God must always be difficult for the ordinary
mortal to discern, we can share the prophet's faith that the
passage of history is not a random process, but moves somehow
towards the fulfilment of God's purpose in the world.

(ii) *The prophecy of coronation* (verses 9–15). The prophetic oracle which follows the final vision includes both a set of instructions concerning certain actions to be taken by the prophet, and a message to be delivered to the people through him.

Zechariah was to visit the house of a certain Josiah, who had with him as his guests a delegation of dignitaries that was visiting Jerusalem from the exiled community in Babylon. This delegation from the diaspora had brought with them a contribution of "silver and gold", presumably intended as a gift to support the restoration work in the "old country". From this silver and gold, the prophet was to make a crown and then conduct a ceremony not unlike a coronation, but at this point the text becomes somewhat obscure.

Joshua the priest was to be the first recipient of the crown, but then the Lord says to him, through Zechariah: "Behold, the man whose name is the Branch" (verse 12), namely Zerubbabel. It looks, in other words, as if the crowned priest is then to crown the prince. And the description of responsibilities in verse 13 seems to encompass both priest and prince. Both have a share in government and "peaceful understanding shall be between them both" (verse 13). This dual coronation, however, is clearly to be a symbolic act, rather than an actual royal event. In part this is so because it would have been impossible, and illegal, to crown a king and priest in the Persian colony of Judah. But in part the symbolic nature of the action is made clear by the disposition of the crown following the ceremony: it was to be lodged in the temple as a perpetual memorial.

Thus the concluding oracle, with its requirement of symbolic action to replace the former symbolism of the visions, brings to overt conclusion the message implicit in the eighth vision. When all the world's nations were brought at last under the divine rule, then a new king could be established in Jerusalem, and the messianic character of this new king is indicated by the fact that he would incorporate both priestly and kingly roles. Some four centuries later, the Jewish community of Essenes, living at Qumran, expressed in their writings an anticipation of two messianic figures, king and priest. In the first century A.D., the early

Christians affirmed the fusion of both roles in Jesus Christ: he was both King in the Kingdom of God and Priest, representing his people before God.

One of the moving aspects of this concluding oracle is the introduction of three men who are otherwise anonymous in the annals of human history: Heldai, Tobijah, and Jedaiah. They had taken a long journey from their community in Babylon to visit Jerusalem, bearing with them greetings and gifts. But they could hardly have known when they set out on their journey the use to which their gifts would be put. A crown was fashioned from their silver and gold, and after its single use it was placed in the temple. Their gift would be a reminder to themselves and to future generations that a King was coming, that God had not forgotten his people. And, in another sense, the use of their silver and gold in the fashioning of a crown was a reminder to these pilgrims, so far from home, that although they remained in exile, they were still remembered. Cut off from the homeland by space and history, they still remained a part of the family of God. And though in human terms they had no central role to play in the restoration of the temple, their gift became a sign of the Messiah. Like the gifts the wise men brought to the newly-born Jesus, the gifts of the three men from Babylon symbolized an even greater gift of God to the world.

THE SERMONS OF ZECHARIAH—I

Zechariah 7:1–14

¹In the fourth year of King Darius, the word of the Lord came to Zechariah in the fourth day of the ninth month, which is Chislev. ²Now the people of Bethel had sent Sharezer and Regem-melech and their men, to entreat the favour of the Lord, ³and to ask the priests of the house of the Lord of hosts and the prophets, "Should I mourn and fast in the fifth month, as I have done for so many years?" ⁴Then the word of the Lord of hosts came to me; ⁵"Say to all the people of the land and the priests, When you fasted and mourned in the fifth month and in the seventh, for these seventy years, was it for me that you fasted? ⁶And

when you eat and when you drink, do you not eat for yourselves and drink for yourselves? [7]When Jerusalem was inhabited and in prosperity, with her cities round about her, and the South and the lowland were inhabited, were not these the words which the Lord proclaimed by the former prophets?"

[8]And the word of the Lord came to Zechariah, saying, [9]"Thus says the Lord of hosts, Render true judgments, show kindness and mercy each to his brother, [10]do not oppress the widow, the fatherless, the sojourner, or the poor; and let none of you devise evil against his brother in your heart." [11]But they refused to hearken, and turned a stubborn shoulder, and stopped their ears that they might not hear. [12]They made their hearts like adamant lest they should hear the law and the words which the Lord of hosts had sent by his Spirit through the former prophets. Therefore great wrath came from the Lord of hosts. [13]"As I called, and they would not hear, so they called, and I would not hear," says the Lord of hosts, [14]"and I scattered them with a whirlwind among all the nations which they had not known. Thus the land they left was desolate, so that no one went to and fro, and the pleasant land was made desolate."

The visions of the preceding chapters have provided us with only a partial insight into the ministry of the prophet and his role in the community of Jerusalem. Now, in chapters 7–8, we are given a short exposure to his sermons, or prophetic messages. The text of these two chapters does not contain in full the messages as they were originally given, but rather brief synopses, conveying to the reader a kind of patchwork quilt of Zechariah's thought and theology. The passage is introduced by a specific date (7:1: approximately December 7, 518 B.C.), setting it off from the previous "book of visions", but although the date introduces the two chapters as a whole, it appears to pertain primarily to the question and answer given in verses 2–7. Chapter 7 contains in condensed form two messages, whereas chapter 8 has more the character of an anthology of the prophet's sayings from different places and varying times.

(i) *The question concerning fasting* (verses 2–7). There is difficulty at the very beginning of this passage, stemming from the grammar of the Hebrew text, as to who sent whom. In the RSV, the people of Bethel sent two persons to Jerusalem, Sharezer and

Regem-melech; Bethel, only a dozen miles north of Jerusalem, had originally been a great centre of worship in the northern kingdom of Israel, and had not belonged to Judah. But why a delegation from Bethel should come to Jerusalem for advice is not entirely clear. The New English Bible has the more probable translation of verse 2: "Bethel-sharezer sent Regem-melech with his men to seek the favour of the Lord." Bethel-sharezer was presumably an official in the exiled community in Babylon; Regem-melech was the spokesman whom he sent in order to secure an answer to a troubling question of religious practice.

There is more to the question than meets the eye. Should the fast in the fifth month, which had been observed for so many years, still be observed? It was not a general question about fasting, but referred specifically to ceremonies involving mourning and fasting in memory of the original destruction of the temple, which had occurred many years earlier in the fifth month (2 Kings 25:8–9). The question presupposes a certain sense of futility in remembering the destruction of the temple, when the work of restoration was almost complete. The prophet's answer (verses 5–8) concerns fasting, though it is not a precise answer to the question raised; that is given later in 8:18–19. And the prophet's response in verses 5–8, though stimulated by a specific question, is addressed to "all the people of the land and the priests" (verse 5); it has relevance to the life of the community in Jerusalem, as well as to those in exile.

Zechariah responds to the question with three questions of his own, each of which requires thought on the part of his audience, and each of which should illuminate the significance of fasting. (a) The first question is, "Was it for me that you fasted?" Or were you really fasting out of a sense of self-pity? Are you genuinely sorry that the temple, the symbol of God's presence, was destroyed, or has the ritual simply become a symbol of lamenting that things are not as they used to be? The prophet pinpoints the manner in which any ritual may be perverted from its true purpose. And self-pity, with its laceration of the soul and its manufactured grief, is a form of indulgence, not an offering to God. (b) The second question (verse 6) points to the opposite of fasting, eating and drinking, indicating that they were in effect no different from abstinence. Eating and drinking satisfy human needs, just as fasting may, but fasting should be directed to some external goal, not to the satisfaction of the self. (c) The third question (verse 7) is unclear in the present editorial arrangement of the book, but the "words which the prophets proclaimed" may refer to the summary of verses 9–14 (discussed below), which has been separated from its original context by the insertion of an editorial comment in verse 8.

(ii) *The disaster antedating the fast* (verses 8–14). Verses 9–10 contain a summary of prophetic preaching prior to the destruction of Jerusalem in 587/586 B.C. The requirements of God, in moral terms, had been clear enough prior to the destruction of the first temple. (a) "Render true judgments": the expression refers both to the proper conduct of the law courts, and also to the general promulgation and practice of justice throughout the community. (b) "Show kindness and mercy": the kindness and mercy of God toward his people should have been reflected in all their dealings with one another. (c) "Do not oppress . . . ": the oppression of weaker persons, to advance one's own power and wealth, corrupted a society and undermined its integrity. (d) "Let none of you devise evil . . . in your heart": not only overt actions, but also internal schemings, penetrated the life of society like a deadly disease.

These fundamental requirements of God had been clear enough before the destruction of the temple, having been established in the law (*Torah*) and repeated over and over again by the prophets (verse 12). But the people had diligently refused to hear the word of God through his servants, and so when disaster threatened to destroy them, and their temple, the citizens of an earlier generation had found God equally deaf. They had been scattered, in judgment, to live in exile in foreign places, and their once pleasant land had become a desolate place.

The prophet's point becomes very clear. The temple had been destroyed because of the fundamental moral and religious failure of a former generation. Having abandoned the foundation of God's revealed truth (verse 12), they could expect neither his protection of the temple nor his presence in the temple. But with respect to the fast, what was the point in lamenting a ruined temple unless one also remembered why it was ruined? And, for that matter, what was the point in restoring a temple unless one remembered what it was that led to its destruction in the first place? The prophet emphasizes the folly of remembering an event, if that remembrance is divorced from an understanding of the event. And an understanding of the event, in turn, would involve a community-wide renewal of the moral foundations of the faith. It would be hypocritical to fast in commemoration of a ruined temple, unless one also practised justice and mercy, and avoided oppression and evil thinking. Likewise, in our own time, it is pointless to commemorate wars, unless we also recall what led to wars. And, in more general terms, it is fruitless to participate in the memorial festivals of the Church, such as Good Friday, unless we recall in addition their meaning and their implication for faith and morality.

THE SERMONS OF ZECHARIAH—II

Zechariah 8:1–23

[1]And the word of the Lord of hosts came to me, saying, [2]"Thus says the Lord of hosts: I am jealous for Zion with great jealousy, and I am jealous for her with great wrath. [3]Thus says the Lord: I will return to Zion, and will dwell in the midst of Jerusalem, and Jerusalem shall be called the faithful city, and the mountain of the Lord of hosts, the holy mountain. [4]Thus says the Lord of hosts: Old men and old women shall again sit in the streets of Jerusalem, each with staff in hand for very age. [5]And the streets of the city shall be full of boys and girls playing in the streets. [6]Thus says the Lord of hosts: If it is marvellous in the sight of the remnant of this people in these days, should it also be marvellous in my sight, says the Lord of hosts? Thus says the Lord of hosts: Behold, I will save my people from the east country and from the west country; [8]and I will bring them to dwell in the midst of Jerusalem; and they shall be my people and I will be their God, in faithfulness and in righteousness."

⁹Thus says the Lord of hosts: "Let your hands be strong, you who in these days have been hearing these words from the mouth of the prophets, since the day that the foundation of the house of the Lord of hosts was laid, that the temple might be built. ¹⁰For before those days there was no wage for man or any wage for beast, neither was there any safety from the foe for him who went out or came in; for I set every man against his fellow. ¹¹But now I will not deal with the remnant of this people as in the former days, says the Lord of hosts. ¹²For there shall be a sowing of peace; the vine shall yield its fruit, and the ground shall give its increase, and the heavens shall give their dew; and I will cause the remnant of this people to possess all these things. ¹³And as you have been a byword of cursing among the nations, O house of Judah and house of Israel, so will I save you and you shall be a blessing. Fear not, but let your hands be strong."

¹⁴For thus says the Lord of hosts: "As I purposed to do evil to you, when your fathers provoked me to wrath, and I did not relent, says the Lord of hosts, ¹⁵so again have I purposed in these days to do good to Jerusalem and to the house of Judah; fear not. ¹⁶These are the things that you shall do: Speak the truth to one another, render in your gates judgments that are true and make for peace, ¹⁷do not devise evil in your hearts against one another, and love no false oath, for all these things I hate, says the Lord."

¹⁸And the word of the Lord of hosts came to me, saying, ¹⁹"Thus says the Lord of hosts: The fast of the fourth month, and the fast of the fifth, and the fast of the seventh, and the fast of the tenth, shall be to the house of Judah seasons of joy and gladness, and cheerful feasts; therefore love truth and peace.

²⁰"Thus says the Lord of hosts: Peoples shall yet come, even the inhabitants of many cities; ²¹the inhabitants of one city shall go to another, saying, 'Let us go at once to entreat the favour of the Lord, and to seek the Lord of hosts; I am going.' ²²Many peoples and strong nations shall come to seek the Lord of hosts in Jerusalem, and to entreat the favour of the Lord. ²³Thus says the Lord of hosts: In those days ten men from the nations of every tongue shall take hold of the robe of a Jew, saying, 'Let us go with you, for we have heard that God is with you.'"

The remembrance of things past turns gradually, in these ser-monic verses, to anticipation of things to come. And in his words, Zechariah reveals something of the irenic nature of his personality. Though he refers to judgment, he is overwhelmed by a powerful conviction of God's coming goodness to his people. Though he has experienced war, his vision is dominated rather by peace. Beyond the jaded Jerusalem in which he lives, he can sense the sparkle of the city as it would be in the future. He speaks to encourage his people, to evoke confidence, not fear, to advocate truth, not falsity, and to paint such a picture of the City of God as would strengthen the hands of all who laboured to build it.

The prophet shares with God a vision of the new Jerusalem which is in stark contrast to the reality of the time. The miserable estate of the city as it was in 518 B.C. would once again be transformed, so that Jerusalem would be called the "faithful city" (verse 3). There were few senior citizens in the city of Zechariah's time; too many of the people had died in youth or middle age, and of those elderly in exile, few would have taken the long and tiring trip back to the promised land. But a community without its senior members is less than a full community; it lacks the experience and wisdom, the familial ties and sense of tradition, that only the old can contribute. And thus an essential ingredient of Zechariah's vision of a restored community was the presence of older folks. Old men and old women would sit in the streets (verse 4), enjoying the sun and contributing by their very presence to the rich fabric of city life.

Children, too, would be part of the vibrant life in the new Jerusalem, though there would have been few youngsters in the streets in Zechariah's time. Many families with young children would not have risked the arduous journey from Babylonian exile to make a new start in the shambles that was Jerusalem. And among the families that had remained in Jerusalem, sickness and poverty would have taken their toll in the lives of the young. But the prophet foresees a city with children playing in the streets, evincing that carefree joy that only the young possess. His words about boys and girls (verse 5) are not those of a demographic planner, anticipating the impact of a young population on the future workforce and the gross national product. It is their joy he foresees, and it is the effect of that childish happiness in enriching the entire community which he seeks to communicate to his audience.

But beyond the presence of the elderly and of children, Zechariah anticipates the restoration of the entire community. It was a difficult vision to communicate in a decimated city, its population poor and struggling, with most people having their relatives still living in exile in far-off lands. But those in exile would return, the population would grow, and the ancient covenant with God would be restored once again: "they shall be my people and I will be their God" (verse 8).

This vision of a rejuvenated and enriched city was to be a source of strength and encouragement to those who, with the prophet, struggled in the doldrums of Jerusalem as it actually was (verses 9–17). They were to continue valiantly with their work on the temple, confident that the completion of their work would inaugurate a new age of peace. The vineyards would bear once again a heavy harvest of grapes, with their promise of joyful celebration, and the dew on the ground would offer promise of plentiful crops (verses 12). The city, sneered at among the nations as a faded shadow of past glory, would once again be splendid, for this transformation was a part of the divine purpose. But in these words of Zechariah, as in his earlier prophecies, we can see how his immediate future and the world's more distant future are fused into one. They worked for immediate blessing and a speedy change of fortune, but in a mysterious fashion their labour foreshadowed and moved towards the dawning of a messianic age.

Zechariah's vision of a new world beyond the horizon of the immediate future culminates in two specific and important messages.

(i) *Fasting* (verses 18–19). At last the prophet returns to the original question concerning fasting which introduced this series of oracles (7:2–3), and he expands the question to include fast days celebrated in the fourth, seventh, and tenth months, all days commemorating one or another aspect of the fall of Jerusalem and the destruction of its temple. But the original question now took on an entirely different light, following the substance of the preceding verses. The essence of the fast days was to remember those tragic events in the past, which in turn had culminated in the misery of the present. But Zechariah has a quite different approach to the present. It was possible to interpret the present in the light of the past, as did those who observed the fast. But it was equally possible, and much more fruitful, to interpret the present in the light of the future, and this was the prophet's fundamental perspective. To read the present in the light of the past tended towards introspection and self-pity, but it was relatively easy; there can be a certain comfort in self-induced misery. But to read the present in the light of the future required both strong faith and hard work, and that would be too challenging for many folk.

Zechariah therefore advocates that the fasts be transformed into festivals, that the days of mourning be replaced by "seasons of joy and gladness" (verse 19). And he adds his own encouragement: "love truth and peace." A love of the truth would free his people from those past lies which culminated in disaster for Jerusalem and its temple. A love of peace would bring about that wholeness and integration of the chosen people which God had always desired for his nation.

(ii) *Gentiles* (verses 20–23). Again, the prophet returns to the theme of the Gentiles, the citizens of foreign nations (see also 2:11). He pictures a situation in which the well-being and success of Jerusalem have become international news. Just as, in recent centuries, citizens of Britain and Europe heard glowing tales of the grand new world beyond the Atlantic and set out to discover a new life, so too people would long to go to the new Jerusalem. They would encourage one another to go, and if they met a Jew, they would beg to be allowed to accompany him to Jerusalem. At last the ancient vision of Abraham would begin to take substance: through God's chosen people, all the nations of the world would be blessed.

But alas, neither the Jerusalem of Zechariah's time nor the same city at the end of the 20th century is a city towards which the multitudes flock in search of peace. Now, as then, the Holy City is scarred by turmoil and strife. And yet still we can perceive the vitality and permanence of the prophet's message. There is within us all a longing for citizenship in that city of which he spoke, blessed with the laughter of children and the grace of the elderly, characterized by satisfying work and happy homes. And Jew and

Gentile alike may share in the vision: God plans still for all his people an enduring city in which it may be said: "God is with you" (verse 23).

Part II: Chapter 9–14

THE COMING KING

Zechariah 9:1–17

An Oracle

¹The word of the Lord is against the land of Hadrach
    and will rest upon Damascus.
For to the Lord belong the cities of Aram,
    even as all the tribes of Israel;
²Hamath also, which borders thereon,
    Tyre and Sidon, though they are very wise.
³Tyre has built herself a rampart,
    and heaped up silver like dust,
    and gold like the dirt of the streets.
⁴But lo, the Lord will strip her of her possessions
    and hurl her wealth into the sea,
    and she shall be devoured by fire.

⁵Ashkelon shall see it, and be afraid;
    Gaza too, and shall writhe in anguish;
    Ekron also, because its hopes are confounded.
The king shall perish from Gaza;
    Ashkelon shall be uninhabited;
⁶a mongrel people shall dwell in Ashdod;
    and I will make an end of the pride of Philistia.
⁷I will take away its blood from its mouth,
    and its abominations from between its teeth;
it too shall be a remnant for our God;
    it shall be like a clan in Judah,
    and Ekron shall be like the Jebusites.

⁸Then I will encamp at my house as a guard,
 so that none shall march to and fro;
no oppressor shall again overrun them,
 for now I see with my own eyes.

⁹Rejoice greatly, O daughter of Zion!
 Shout aloud, O daughter of Jerusalem!
Lo, your king comes to you;
 triumphant and victorious is he,
humble and riding on an ass,
 on a colt the foal of an ass.
¹⁰I will cut off the chariot from Ephraim
 and the war horse from Jerusalem;
and the battle bow shall be cut off,
 and he shall command peace to the nations;
his dominion shall be from sea to sea,
 and from the River to the ends of the earth.

¹¹As for you also, because of the blood of my covenant with you,
 I will set your captives free from the waterless pit.
¹²Return to your stronghold, O prisoners of hope;
 today I declare that I will restore to you double.
¹³For I have bent Judah as my bow;
 I have made Ephraim its arrow.
I will brandish your sons, O Zion,
 over your sons, O Greece,
 and wield you like a warrior's sword.

¹⁴Then the Lord will appear over them,
 and his arrow go forth like lightning;
the Lord God will sound the trumpet,
 and march forth in the whirlwinds of the south.
¹⁵The Lord of hosts will protect them,
 and they shall devour and tread down the slingers;
and they shall drink their blood like wine,
 and be full like a bowl,
 drenched like the corners of the altar.

¹⁶On that day the Lord their God will save them
 for they are the flock of his people;
for like the jewels of a crown
 they shall shine on his land.

17Yea, how good and how fair it shall be!
Grain shall make the young men flourish,
and new wine the maidens.

The second part of Zechariah breathes a different air from that of
the first eight chapters. The tone is different, there are no explicit
references to the prophet, and as we noted in the introductory
remarks to the book as a whole, these chapters may either come
from a later period in the prophet's life, or from a different hand
in a later age. But the chapters are not unrelated to the first half of
the book. Zechariah's intimations of a future world are here
taken up and elaborated in greater detail, and there is a similar
breadth of concern which incorporates the Gentiles, along with
the Jews.

Part II falls into two separate sections, chapters 9–11 and
chapters 12–14, each introduced by the title "An Oracle" (in the
RSV), though the Hebrew word might be better translated
burden. But the two subsections are themselves a mosaic of
smaller units, fitted carefully into the present whole, and it is not
easy to determine the dividing lines between the smaller sections
which have been used in the compilation of chapters 9–14; the
commentary simply follows the chapter divisions of the English
Bible. The difficulty of interpreting these chapters is aggravated
further by the complexity of their substance. On the one hand,
they are filled with historical allusions, though few of the allusions
can be pinned down precisely in time. On the other hand, the
focus of the chapters lies clearly in the future, and apocalyptic
allusions are even more difficult to elucidate than historical ones.
We must suppose, from the manner of writing, that the spirit and
vision of this portion of the book are more important than the
historical background upon which the author has drawn. And we
will sense in the words of these concluding chapters conflicting
visions, the intermingling of war and peace, and both the promise
and the threat of God's coming day.

The passage begins with the declaration of the prophetic word
of God against various foreign nations, the declaration indicating
the passage of divine judgment from the north to the south.
God's judgment is proclaimed against Hadrach, Damascus, and

Hamath, all cities in Syria, and from there it travels south to the great coastal cities of Tyre and Sidon. The enormous wealth and military defences of those maritime ports would be powerless on the judgment day; stripped of the accoutrements of power, Tyre would be devastated by fire. Moving still further south along the Mediterranean coast, the judgment of God falls upon the Philistine cities (verses 5–6), leaving them too in a state of desolation. At last, having crushed many of Judah's traditional enemies, God would camp outside his temple in Jerusalem (verse 8), there to protect it from any further oppression.

Suddenly the warlike atmosphere of the first eight verses is exchanged for the tranquil tones of rejoicing in Jerusalem. The city is to rejoice at the advance of its king, triumphant and victorious, yet humble and riding upon an ass (verse 9). The arrival of the messianic king in Jerusalem seems to signal the dawning of a new age; the weapons of war would be abandoned in a new pursuit of peace, and the dominion of this King of peace would be world-wide.

But just as suddenly, the peaceful tone is transformed once again and replaced by martial poetry; the abrupt transitions may reflect originally separate units, but they have been welded together for a purpose. The new enemy is Greece (verse 13), which rose to world-wide power in the 4th century B.C. Once again, the enemy of God and his people will be defeated, so that God's flock might rest at peace in its land.

What are we to make of these dark visions, strident with the savagery of warfare, yet punctuated by the vision of world-wide peace? The question cannot be answered simply, but the outlines of the prophetic message can be partially discerned.

(i) *War*. For all people at all times, war is a painful and miserable experience. But war, and especially defeat in war, presented an additional difficulty to the chosen people. They believed themselves to be God's special nation, different in kind from other nations with their pagan gods. And they believed that through their role as a special nation, all the nations of the world would be blessed. But the reality of their historical experience was frequently at variance with their theology. Whatever the theology of foreign nations, the reality of them was that they were powerful military states which had frequently brought disaster and defeat upon both Israel and Judah in warfare.

Israel thus faced a dilemma. It existed in a world filled with war, and was more frequently victim than victor. In part it could understand its own devastation in war as a consequence of divine judgment, but it could not easily cope with the success of its pagan neighbours. And war, which was so patently out of harmony with a world believed to be created by God, seemed to continue for ever: would it never end?

Many of these themes are taken up in the visionary language of the prophet. Looking to the future, he saw the continuation of war, but in these verses there is a sense of the warrior God, through whose victories war would at last be brought to an end, and through whom justice would at last be meted out to the world's warlike nations. Such language cannot easily be translated into the theology of the future, but it is marked distinctly by both realism and idealism. The prophetic realism affirms clearly enough that war would continue to characterize human historical existence; the idealism sees beyond the violence to the dawning of an age of peace. But the alternation in scenes between war and peace, and then back to war once again, removes the possibility of any facile transition. The roots of peace are to be found in the fields of war. And the world-wide dominion of peace presupposes first of all the conquest of war itself. If we cannot grasp this fully and coherently, then perhaps we are sharing the prophet's own dilemma, but we can also seek to share with the prophet the absolute conviction that one day, in all probability beyond our own time, "he shall command peace to the nations" (verse 10).

(ii) *Peace*. The verses on peace (verses 9–10) are but a small window in the black wall of war which dominates this chapter as a whole. But the window opens onto a different world which, for all its alien character in our own or any other century, is at once understandable to us. Who has not longed, especially in times of war, to see the dominion of peace "from sea to sea" (verse 10)? It is something which most sensible human beings desire, yet this window-view of a world at peace is somehow other-wordly and unreal.

In the prophetic vision, it is a king who is instrumental in the dawning of the age of peace, and the coming king has a clearly messianic character. From the perspective of Christian interpretation, it is Matthew (21:5) and John (12:15) who shed light for us on this coming King, for they identify Jesus with him; the coming of Jesus somehow symbolizes the advent of peace between God and human beings. But we see, in the passion narratives, the reversal of ancient principles. War is the exercise of force, but Jesus, in establishing the new Kingdom, becomes the recipient of violence in the crucifixion. The war on the battlefield is to be exchanged for the warfare of the spirit. And gradually, as men and women find peace with God, they may bit by bit establish the kingdom of peace on earth. But we must be careful, even with this theological perspective, not to lose touch with reality. The world today is as much marred by violence and war as it was in the prophet's time, or in the early centuries of the Christian era. War remains the perpetual companion of civilization, and we must still share the hope of the biblical prophet that one day a better world will dawn.

THE COMING OF REDEMPTION

Zechariah 10:1–12

¹Ask rain from the Lord
   in the season of the spring rain,
from the Lord who makes the storm clouds,
   who gives men showers of rain,
   to every one the vegetation in the field.
²For the teraphim utter nonsense,
   and the diviners see lies;
the dreamers tell false dreams,
   and give empty consolation.
Therefore the people wander like sheep;
   they are afflicted for want of a shepherd.

³"My anger is hot against the shepherds,
   and I will punish the leaders;
for the Lord of hosts cares for his flock, the house of Judah,
   and will make them like his proud steed in battle.

⁴Out of them shall come the cornerstone,
    out of them the tent peg,
out of them the battle bow,
    out of them every ruler.
⁵Together they shall be like mighty men in battle,
    trampling the foe in the mud of the streets;
they shall fight because the Lord is with them,
    and they shall confound the riders on horses.

⁶"I will strengthen the house of Judah,
    and I will save the house of Joseph.
I will bring them back because I have compassion on them,
    and they shall be as though I had not rejected them;
    for I am the Lord their God and I will answer them.
⁷Then Ephraim shall become like a mighty warrior,
    and their hearts shall be glad as with wine.
Their children shall see it and rejoice,
    their hearts shall exult in the Lord.

⁸"I will signal for them and gather them in,
    for I have redeemed them,
    and they shall be as many as of old.
⁹Though I scattered them among the nations,
    yet in far countries they shall remember me,
    and with their children they shall live and return.
¹⁰I will bring them home from the land of Egypt,
    and gather them from Assyria;
and I will bring them to the land of Gilead and to Lebanon,
    till there is no room for them.
¹¹They shall pass through the sea of Egypt,
    and the waves of the sea shall be smitten,
    and all the depths of the Nile dried up.
The pride of Assyria shall be laid low,
    and the sceptre of Egypt shall depart.
¹²I will make them strong in the Lord
    and they shall glory in his name," says the Lord.

The echoes of war and peace continue in this chapter, but now a new metaphor has been introduced: it is the metaphor of the *shepherd*. Two chapters (10 and 11), though containing several originally separate literary units, are held together by this shepherd-metaphor, which is developed in several different directions, both positive and negative.

(i) *The lack of a shepherd* (verses 1–2). One basic role of a shepherd is to guide his flock to places where there is pasture for grazing. And the vegetation suitable for pasturing is in turn a consequence of God's gift of rain. This short passage begins with a reaffirmation of the ancient truth that God is the giver of the rains, which provide the crops and foodstuffs upon which human life depends. But human beings, in their perversity, seek the grounds of their survival elsewhere. They turn to the *teraphim* (household idols), to the diviners, and to the dreamers who claim special powers of prognostication, thinking that such false sources of leadership will bring them into the rich pastures of life. But in their search they are misled, and thus like sheep without a shepherd they wander around in the fruitless search for pasture-land.

The prophet diagnoses here an ancient blindness of the human race: needing guidance towards the rich potential of life, human beings perpetually turn to false leaders and those who claim much, but know nothing. Like sheep, human beings require guidance; they lack the natural instincts to know where to go. They have the right inclination in knowing they need a leader, but not the wit to choose the right leader. And so they wander, and they also suffer as a consequence of their lack of guidance.

There is an element of pathos in the prophetic description of the condition of his people, and by implication the condition of all people. On the one hand, there is God who provides rain and rich pasture-land. On the other hand, a flock of silly sheep elects to follow some of their own members in search of pasture, only to be led into the wilderness. The pathos and contrast point to one part of true wisdom: it is that, when we recognize we are lost, we should not follow those equally lost in the search for sustenance. Sheep cannot cease to be sheep, but they can learn that another sheep does not make for a good shepherd.

(ii) *Alien shepherds* (verses 3–5). Although the metaphorical language of sheep and shepherds continues, the sense of the metaphor is now radically changed. The word *shepherd*, in a variety of ancient Near Eastern civilizations, was employed to describe *rulers*, kings and governors. And the prophet indicates that the divine wrath was directed against such alien shepherds, for whom the welfare of the sheep was not a primary concern. The context suggests that these alien shepherds were the rulers of foreign nations who for so long had dominated the existence of the chosen people, both as a nation and in exile.

The focus of the message is initially the alien shepherds, rather than the sheep. Because they had not cared for their "flock", because they had shown no compassion for the welfare of their sheep, inevitably the divine anger would be exercised against them. And then the imagery of the passage changes suddenly and radically: under the new compassion of God for his people, they are transformed from a flock of sheep into a powerful army. They fight powerfully, because the Lord is with them (verse 5) and they crush those who formerly dominated them.

The words communicate two messages with respect to the alien shepherds, or false rulers. (a) In this context, the sheep are powerless and can do nothing for themselves; they need to be rescued. And the message is that false rulers, those who have no compassion for the persons entrusted to their care, will eventually be punished. Shepherd-ship is a position of responsibility; to fail in the proper exercise of that responsibility is to invite punishment. (b) False shepherds, false rulers, crush the potential of their charges. Under false shepherds, the people are no more than oppressed sheep. Under a true shepherd, they are transformed, as it were, into a powerful army. And the metaphor holds true of all persons, controlled by alien rulers or under the domination of the self; the potential of life cannot be released under such circumstances. Only when life is submitted to the Good Shepherd may there come also that freedom which releases the full potential of human existence.

(iii) *The true shepherd* (verses 6–12). In the latter half of this chapter, the language is dominated by the pronoun "I", reflecting the direct speech of God. God would strengthen the state of Judah and rescue "Joseph" (namely, the former northern state of Israel). Refugees and exiles would be returned to their homes, and those who used to be weak would become strong. Whereas the chapter opened with the people wandering like sheep (verse 2), the theme of this section is that of the wandering sheep being guided home again, to the place where rich pastures might be found. From among the distant nations, from both south and north (Egypt and Assyria, verse 10), God's dispersed people would be brought back: the message is one of redemption. And in the great return, the foreign oppressors would be judged, and the formerly oppressed would be made strong.

The key to the entire passage is in verse 6: "I will bring them back because I have compassion on them." It is compassion which distinguishes the true shepherd from all false shepherds. Compassion is a concern for the welfare of the sheep, rather than an attitude towards them which sees them only as a resource to be exploited. And in this language, we can begin to perceive the background to the New Testament imagery of the Shepherd. When Jesus said, "I am the good shepherd. The good shepherd lays down his life for the sheep" (John 10:11), he was drawing on the rich imagery of God the Shepherd in the Old Testament, of which the notion of God's compassion is a central part.

FURTHER REFLECTIONS ON THE SHEPHERD THEME

Zechariah 11:1–17

¹Open your doors, O Lebanon,
    that the fire may devour your cedars!
²Wail, O cypress, for the cedar has fallen,
    for the glorious trees are ruined!
Wail, oaks of Bashan,
    for the thick forest has been felled!
³Hark, the wail of the shepherds,
    for their glory is despoiled!
Hark, the roar of the lions,
    for the jungle of the Jordan is laid waste!

⁴Thus said the Lord my God: "Become shepherd of the flock doomed to slaughter. ⁵Those who buy them slay them and go unpunished; and those who sell them say, 'Blessed be the Lord, I have become rich'; and their own shepherds have no pity on them. ⁶For I will no longer have pity on the inhabitants of this land, says the Lord. Lo, I will cause men to fall each into the hand of his shepherd, and each into the hand of his king; and they shall crush the earth, and I will deliver none from their hand."

⁷So I became the shepherd of the flock doomed to be slain for those who trafficked in the sheep. And I took two staffs; one I named Grace, the other I named Union. And I tended the sheep. ⁸In one month I destroyed the three shepherds. But I became impatient with them, and they also detested me. ⁹So I said, "I will not be your shepherd. What is to die, let it die; what is to be destroyed, let it be destroyed; and let those that are left devour the flesh of one another." ¹⁰And I took my staff Grace, and I broke it, annulling the covenant which I had made with all the people. ¹¹So it was annulled on that day, and the traffickers in the sheep, who were watching me, knew that it was the word of the Lord. ¹²Then I said to them, "If it seems right to you, give me my wages; but if not, keep them." And they weighed out as my wages thirty shekels of silver. ¹³Then the Lord said to me, "Cast it into the treasury"—the lordly price at which I was paid off by them. So I took the thirty shekels of silver and cast them into the treasury in the house of the Lord. ¹⁴Then I broke my second staff Union, annulling the brotherhood between Judah and Israel.

¹⁵Then the Lord said to me, "Take once more the implements of a worthless shepherd. ¹⁶For lo, I am raising up in the land a shepherd who does not care for the perishing, or seek the wandering, or heal the maimed, or nourish the sound, but devours the flesh of the fat ones, tearing off even their hoofs.
¹⁷Woe to my worthless shepherd,
    who deserts the flock!
May the sword smite his arm
    and his right eye!
Let his arm be wholly withered,
    his right eye utterly blinded!"

The metaphor of the shepherd continues in this chapter, being the linking theme between three originally separate units. The meaning of several of these verses is extremely obscure, in part because of the brevity of the passages (verses 1–3, 15–17), and in part because of the difficulty of elucidating some enigmatic verses (especially in verses 4–14) which seem to presuppose a specific historical background.

(i) *The ruin of the shepherds* (verses 1–3). In a rich mixture of metaphors, this lyrical passage expresses the grief that will follow the collapse of the symbols of the world's greatest powers. Cedars, the kings of trees, will be destroyed by fire, so that other mighty trees, the cypress and the oak, will bewail their falling. If the cedars have been destroyed, then by implication no other tree of the forest is safe. (The references to place names, Lebanon and Bashan, specify places famous for the finest species of trees, rather than nations about to be judged.) The metaphor of the cedar alludes to the world's greatest powers, or perhaps their kings; such powers, for all their appearance of longevity and strength, were to be destroyed.

In verse 3 there is a change from the tree metaphor to two new metaphors, *shepherds* and *lions*; both, in context, appear to refer to human rulers, for both terms in the Bible and Near Eastern texts are used of kings. The kings would wail, for their people and their domains would be ruined.

The lack of an immediate context makes the passage difficult to interpret with precision. Yet in the larger context, the scene is suggestive of the violence and warfare that would precede the Kingdom of God. Those great rulers and kings of the world's nations, despite the apparent continuity of their reigns and the seeming invincibility of their strength, would be lamented in their collapse. The fall of the world's greatest symbols of strength was the intimation of the advent of one stronger than them all.

(ii) *The rejection of the good shepherd* (verses 4–14). The language and meaning of this prophetic oracle are particularly obscure. At the outset, the prophet is instructed to "become shepherd of the flock" (verse 4), and this he seems to do (verse 7). Perhaps the text is to be understood as an enacted prophecy, akin to those many cases in the Book of Ezekiel, where the prophet was instructed to perform certain actions which symbolized their own meaning.

The prophet's task seems from the beginning to be a dismal one, for the flock entrusted to him is described as "doomed to slaughter" (verse 4); his flock are destined for death and a future in the form of mutton, rather than a happy life in green pastures, growing on their skins wool for the shearing. But in addition to the prophetic shepherd, various other shepherds are alluded to, those why buy and sell sheep, and those who look after sheep, but only with an eye to profit. The metaphor embraces not only the shepherd as prophet, but also kings of the chosen people as well, presumably, as foreign kings, those who "buy" and "sell" the sheep. Nevertheless, despite the plethora of shepherds, it is the sheep themselves (namely, the people as a whole) who become the focus of the passage.

The good shepherd, who genuinely cared for the sheep, took two staffs, one with the symbolic name "Grace" and the other named "Unity"; the prophetic shepherd either represents God, or is God's agent. The two staffs represent God's concern for his people ("Grace") and his ultimate desire for them ("Unity", namely unity between the two states of Israel and Judah). The good shepherd, in fulfilling his duties, disposed of various incompetent shepherds, three in a month (verse 8). There have been long and inconclusive speculations amongst scholars as to which three rulers of the chosen people these three bad shepherds might be, but all that can be said with certainty is that, if three specific rulers were intended, we cannot be certain of their identity.

Now one might think that in circumstances such as these, the sheep would be happy and grateful. They were being tended by one who was genuinely concerned with their welfare, and he in turn was disposing of those incompetents who did not have the best interests of the sheep at heart. But not a bit of it: the sheep, who have seemed up to now to be merely innocent lambs in the whole affair, are revealed in their true character as both detesting the good shepherd and also as being detestable. And so the shepherd broke the staff called "Grace", indicating thereby that his (and God's) commitment to the sheep was ended; the covenant had been annulled. And the good shepherd also broke his contract with the other shepherds, the rulers of the people; his final wages, thirty shekels, were cast into the temple treasury, for he had worked on behalf of God. And so the second staff was also broken: there would be no brotherhood between the two states of Israel and Judah.

In spite of the obscurity of many of the details in this passage, the main themes of principle become clear. The words shatter the liberal illusion that, if only we had good leaders and good government, the people would be happy and responsive. The shepherd metaphor runs more deeply than at first appeared; human perversity and ignorance are so profound that human beings will not even accept good leadership if God gives it to them. There is a tendency among us always to destroy the good, for we cannot cope with it. Thus, from the perspective of the Gospel, even when the Good Shepherd came, the people for the most part did not want him. It became necessary for the Shepherd to lay down his life for the sheep, but the tragedy was that it was the sheep who required the death of their shepherd. The good news emerging from this dark scene is that, beyond the death of the Good Shepherd, the staff called "Grace" was restored; still the doors are open for human beings to recognize in God the true and eternal Shepherd.

(iii) *The worthless shepherd* (verse 15–17). Again, this short passage begins with the implication that the prophet is to enact a role, that of the worthless shepherd, but then no further details of the enactment are provided. The prophetic oracle, though, is firmly proclaimed: God is about to establish in the land a worthless shepherd who is entirely devoid of care or compassion for his sheep. In other words, a ruler was to be established, presumably over the chosen people, who would fulfil none of the responsibilities of his office towards his people, but would see them only as a potential source of exploitation and gain. The anticipation of the rise of the worthless ruler is followed promptly by a short song of vengeance, in which the poet calls for the wounding and blinding of this unworthy ruler of the people.

Again, the interpretation is difficult. It is quite possible that this message, when it was first declared, had the rise to power of a particular worthless person in mind. But if this were so, we cannot be sure who that person was. And perhaps the oracle follows the one that precedes it for a specific purpose: it may indicate that a consequence of the people's rejection of the good shepherd is the emergence of the worthless shepherd. Even from this negative perspective, the passage ends with a note of hope: worthless shepherds will fall beneath the divine curse (verse 17).

THE COMING DAY OF GOD

Zechariah 12:1–14

An Oracle

¹The word of the Lord concerning Israel: Thus says the Lord, who stretched out the heavens and founded the earth and formed the spirit of man within him: ²"Lo, I am about to make Jerusalem a cup of reeling to all the peoples round about it; it will be against Judah also in the siege against Jerusalem. ³On that day I will make Jerusalem a heavy stone for all the peoples; all who lift it shall grievously hurt themselves. And all the nations of the earth will come together against it. ⁴On that day, says the Lord, I will strike every horse with panic, and its rider with madness. But upon the house of Judah I will open my eyes, when I strike every horse of the peoples with blindness. ⁵Then the clans of Judah shall say to themselves, 'The inhabitants of Jerusalem have strength through the Lord of hosts, their God.'

⁶"On that day I will make the clans of Judah like a blazing pot in the midst of wood, like a flaming torch among sheaves; and they shall devour to the right and to the left all the peoples round about, while Jerusalem shall still be inhabited in its place, in Jerusalem.

⁷"And the Lord will give victory to the tents of Judah first, that the glory of the house of David and the glory of the inhabitants of Jerusalem may not be exalted over that of Judah. ⁸On that day the Lord will put a shield about the inhabitants of Jerusalem so that the feeblest among them on that day shall be like David, and the house of David shall be like God, like the angel of the Lord, at their head. ⁹And on that day I will seek to destroy all the nations that come against Jerusalem.

¹⁰"And I will pour out on the house of David and the inhabitants of Jerusalem a spirit of compassion and supplication, so that, when they

look on him whom they have pierced, they shall mourn for him, as one mourns for an only child, and weep bitterly over him, as one weeps over a first-born. [11]On that day the mourning in Jerusalem will be as great as the mourning for Hadadrimmon in the plain of Megiddo. [12]The land shall mourn, each family by itself; the family of the house of David by itself, and their wives by themselves; the family of the house of Nathan by itself, and their wives by themselves; [13]the family of the house of Levi by itself, and their wives by themselves; the family of the Shime-ites by itself, and their wives by themselves; [14]and all the families that are left, each by itself, and their wives by themselves."

Chapters 12–14, introduced once again by the expression "An Oracle" (or "burden"), comprise the second half of Part II and the final portion of the Book of Zechariah as a whole. The theme of the concluding chapters is to be found in the phrase "on that day", which is repeated over and again, including a mention in the last verse of the book. The phrase emphasizes the apocalyptic perspectives of these chapters; the prophet, whether Zechariah or some unknown successor, addresses the day towards which all of human history seems to be moving. As in the other apocalyptic passages in the prophet, the language is inevitably mysterious and difficult to penetrate. We must first read it and absorb its substance, before standing back and trying to grasp its deeper meaning.

Chapter 12 falls into two sections, the first describing an attack upon Jerusalem, the second portraying a tragic event, and its consequences, that took place within the city.

(i) *The attack on Jerusalem* (verses 1–9). God, who speaks these words through his prophet, is identified as Creator of heaven and earth and the One who imparts life to all human beings. These introductory verses are important, serving as a backdrop for what is to follow. The "day" which is the focus of this portion of the book is the time towards which all of creation inexorably moves, but we are reminded right at the beginning of the passage that creation is rooted in God. The God who is the source of creation also has the power to move the created world towards its consummation. And as, in the first acts of creation, order emerged from primeval chaos, so in the move towards consummation there are elements of chaos prior to the establishment of a final order "on that day".

A siege of Jerusalem, either literal or metaphorical, is anticipated in these verses. The nations of the world, including Judah,
gather around the capital city for attack, not knowing that God
has made the city impregnable. Just as a farmer, struggling to
remove an enormous boulder from a field, may hurt his back or
cause some internal injury, so too the nations arrayed against
Jerusalem would hurt themselves. The besieging armies, with
their mounted cavalry, would suddenly be struck as if by madness
in their approach towards the city. And the troops of Judah,
members of this unholy alliance, would quickly perceive that God
was with the city; understanding this truth, they would promptly
change sides in the conflict. The turncoat Judean troops would be
like a torch in a haystack, setting their former allies into chaos and
destroying the unity of attack. Through all this, Jerusalem would
remain unharmed, and the thrill of victory would go to the troops
of Judah, who belatedly had seen the error of their ways. God
would grant absolute protection to the city and its citizens, but the
nations of the world that had attacked Jerusalem would be
destroyed.

This apocalyptic scene of attack, counter-attack, and then victory, conveys an image of a certain world unity, to which initially
even some of the chosen people belong. The source of unity is to
be found in the common enmity against Jerusalem, and although
the reason for this enmity is not specified, it may be assumed to
rest in an antagonism towards God, whose presence in the world
was symbolized by the city. This future vision need not be understood literally, nor even as a prediction in any strict sense.
Rather, the prophet projects on the apocalyptic screen the elements of the reality he perceives in his present world. For all the
divisiveness of the world of nations, there is an underlying unity
in the pursuit of evil, which can be described in another way as
opposition to God. And this international opposition to God,
whether it lies in individual human hearts or in international
policies, must somehow be conquered before the Kingdom of
God can be established. The prophet's vision is a dark one, yet
also a realistic one: evil is so deep-seated in the world as we know
it that the Kingdom is impossible. Unless there is a conquest of
evil, there can be no victory of the good.

(ii) *Tragedy in Jerusalem* (verses 10–14). Within the city of Jerusalem, it seems that a terrible tragedy takes place, though the text is such that the precise nature of the tragic event is difficult to define. The citizens of the city have killed someone; whether it is an act of murder or of execution is unclear, though the latter is a more probable act for which, subsequently, an entire community might feel a sense of guilt. After the evil act has been done, the citizens suddenly perceive their guilt and then are overwhelmed by grief and seek forgiveness for what they have done. The whole community mourns, including the great families of the land (verses 12–13); both husbands and wives are stricken by genuine mourning as they perceive the enormity of the act, for which in part they were personally responsible. It is clear that they have been responsible for the death of a good man, though the identity of that man remains elusive.

A part of the consequence of this portion of the apocalyptic vision is to create recognition in the reader that, not only were the nations beyond the city wall drawn up in opposition to God, but even within the city, there was a failure to recognize the servant of God. There is a difference though: the citizens come to recognize in some manner the terrible nature of their deed, and in repentance turn to God for forgiveness.

Inevitably these verses evoke, in the Christian reader of the Book of Zechariah, the Passion narrative, with its description of the crucifixion of Jesus. Indeed, John quotes verse 10 in his description of the immediate aftermath of the death of Jesus (John 19:37), and the echoes of the scene continue to be heard in the Book of Revelation (1:7). In Christian theology, the death of Jesus Christ symbolizes human opposition to God, but more importantly also serves as a bridge towards the restoration of relationship between mankind and God. Thus, from the perspective of this ancient apocalyptic vision, the crucifixion represents both the mounting chaos that precedes the coming of the Kingdom of God, and also the possibility of a new peace of God beyond the chaos. But we can also see, from this perspective of Christian theology, how time is collapsed in apocalyptic vision. The crucifixion and the Christian Gospel do not exhaust the meaning of the vision; it still holds truth, albeit elusive, with respect to the future.

THE COMING OF HOPE

Zechariah 13:1–9

[1]"On that day there shall be a fountain opened for the house of David and the inhabitants of Jerusalem to cleanse them from sin and uncleanness.

[2]"And on that day, says the Lord of hosts, I will cut off the names of the idols from the land, so that they shall be remembered no more; and also I will remove from the land the prophets and the unclean spirit. [3]And if any one again appears as a prophet, his father and mother who bore him will say to him, 'You shall not live, for you speak lies in the name of the Lord'; and his father and mother who bore him shall pierce him through when he prophesies. [4]On that day every prophet will be ashamed of his vision when he prophesies; he will not put on a hairy mantle in order to deceive, [5]but he will say, 'I am no prophet, I am a tiller of the soil; for the land has been my possession since my youth.' [6]And if one asks him, 'What are these wounds on your back?' he will say, 'The wounds I received in the house of my friends.'"

[7]"Awake, O sword, against my shepherd,
   against the man who stands next to me,"
                                        says the Lord of hosts.
 "Strike the shepherd, that the sheep may be scattered;
   I will turn my hand against the little ones.
[8]In the whole land, says the Lord,
   two thirds shall be cut off and perish,
   and one third shall be left alive.
[9]And I will put this third into the fire,
   and refine them as one refines silver,
   and test them as gold is tested.
 They will call on my name,
   and I will answer them.
 I will say, 'They are my people';
   and they will say, 'The Lord is my God.'"

(i) *A fountain of forgiveness* (verse 1). To a city in mourning for a crime it has committed, there comes now a message of hope. Within the city, a fountain would be established whose perpetually flowing waters would cleanse the citizens from sin. Now that the external enemy of the city had been conquered and all threat removed, the inner life of the city could be tended to. And in part the forgiveness that was required was for the evil already committed within the city in an act of killing (12:10–14).

The imagery of a fountain flowing perpetually with waters of cleansing is a striking one: the source of the water, and therefore of the cleansing, was God. And who, like Pontius Pilate, has not tried to wash from his hands the stain of guilt and sin, only to find the stain remains when the water has been dried off? The sense of the need for cleansing is not uncommon among human beings, but finding the water that will truly cleanse is a more difficult task. And thus this prophetic word is full of promise: a part of the gift of God in the establishment of his Kingdom is the provision of a fountain of cleansing waters.

(ii) *A purifying of religion* (verses 2–6). Among the perpetual curses that afflicted the true faith in Jerusalem were the worship of idols and the prevalence of false prophets. Against these two perversions of religious faith, the word of God is now directed. The names of idols, which supposedly transformed lumps of wood and metal into divine beings, would be cut off; the idol-free faith of ancient Israel would be restored. And the false prophets, who in the past had made such a profit in selling their oracles as merchandise, would be eliminated. Indeed, prophecy would become a dishonourable profession, having been abused so frequently over the centuries by the doyens of deception; those who used to take pride in their profession would be revealed for the seedy characters that they were. The prophetic mantle would no longer be worn, and persons who used to practise the prophetic arts would go to any lengths to pretend they were farmers or simple labourers.

The result of this elimination of idolatry and false prophets would be a restoration of the faith to its purest form. The community as a whole would no longer be exposed to lies and falsehood, coming to them as if from God. There was hope, in other words, for a coming Kingdom in which God would be known and the truth would not be distorted.

(iii) *A purifying of leadership* (verses 7–9). The prose of the preceding verses is now replaced by lyrical poetry in which the shepherd metaphor is resumed. At first the section seems out of context, fitting more naturally with the collected passages on the shepherd theme in chapters 10–11. But the substance of this short oracle develops in its own way the thought of the section immediately preceding it. Just as false prophets would be dealt with, so too would false shepherds (or *kings, rulers*) in the establishment of God's Kingdom.

The shepherd no doubt represents a ruler of God's chosen people, though it is not possible to make a more specific identification. And the context presupposes that the shepherd is a false one, though this is not specifically stated in the text. The sword of the Lord would strike the shepherd, ending the false reign of pastoral care. But the prophet speaks with insight: inevitably the judgment of the shepherd would have negative consequences for the sheep, here referred to as lambs ("little ones", verse 7) as an indication of their innocence. Many of the sheep would perish, but the third that survived would emerge tested and stronger for the ordeal through which they had passed. The concluding words of the song (verse 9*b*) imply a full restoration of the Covenant and a new recognition of God as the Good Shepherd of his sheep.

Once again the prophet's sense of realism projects its shadow onto this canvas of the future. He perceives that false leaders must be dealt with if the people are to be restored to a full relationship with their God. But such things cannot happen without their consequences; the judgment of bad government inevitably spills over to affect the lives of those who are governed. The prophet will have nothing to do with bland words of comfort that only the guilty will be touched in the coming cataclysm. The world is not like that: innocent persons are constantly afflicted by actions of evil persons, and even the judgment of the wicked spills over into the life of God's "lambs". There is little comfort in this insight, though the prophet adds to it a constructive thought. As precious metals are purified by fire, so too the innocent may be purified and strengthened through the time of trial. And beyond the valley of suffering, the prophet foresees a time when God will say, "They are my people", and the people in turn will answer, "The Lord is my God" (verse 9). In these words may be found the entire essence of the transformed world towards which the prophet looks in his apocalyptic vision: the restored relationship between mankind and God would lie at the heart of the coming Kingdom. This vision, for all its qualifications and realism, was essentially one of hope for human beings.

THE APOGEE OF APOCALYPSE

Zechariah 14:1–21

[1]Behold, a day of the Lord is coming, when the spoil taken from you will be divided in the midst of you. [2]For I will gather all the nations against Jerusalem to battle, and the city shall be taken and the houses plundered and the women ravished; half of the city shall go into exile, but the rest of the people shall not be cut off from the city. [3]Then the Lord will go forth and fight against those nations as when he fights on a day of battle. [4]On that day his feet shall stand on the Mount of Olives which lies before Jerusalem on the east; and the Mount of Olives shall be split in two from east to west by a very wide valley; so that one half of the Mount shall withdraw northward, and the other half southward. [5]And the valley of my mountains shall be stopped up, for the valley of the mountains shall touch the side of it; and you shall flee as you fled from the earthquake in the days of Uzziah king of Judah. Then the Lord your God will come, and all the holy ones with him.
[6]On that day there shall be neither cold nor frost. [7]And there shall be continuous day (it is known to the Lord), not day and not night, for at evening time there shall be light.
[8]On that day living waters shall flow out from Jerusalem, half of them to the eastern sea and half of them to the western sea; it shall continue in summer as in winter.
[9]And the Lord will become king over all the earth; on that day the Lord will be one and his name one.
[10]The whole land shall be turned into a plain from Geba to Rimmon south of Jerusalem. But Jerusalem shall remain aloft upon its site from

the Gate of Benjamin to the place of the former gate, to the Corner Gate, and from the Tower of Hananel to the king's wine presses. [11]And it shall be inhabited, for there shall be no more curse; Jerusalem shall dwell in security.

[12]And this shall be the plague with which the Lord will smite all the peoples that wage war against Jerusalem: their flesh shall rot while they are still on their feet, their eyes shall rot in their sockets, and their tongues shall rot in their mouths. [13]And on that day a great panic from the Lord shall fall on them, so that each will lay hold on the hand of his fellow, and the hand of the one will be raised against the hand of the the other; [14]even Judah will fight against Jerusalem. And the wealth of all the nations round about shall be collected, gold, silver, and garments in great abundance. [15]And a plague like this plague shall fall on the horses, the mules, the camels, the asses, and whatever beasts may be in those camps.

[16]Then every one that survives of all the nations that have come against Jerusalem shall go up year after year to worship the King, the Lord of hosts, and to keep the feast of booths. [17]And if any of the families of the earth do not go up to Jerusalem to worship the King, the Lord of hosts, there will be no rain upon them. [18]And if the family of Eygpt do not go up and present themselves, then upon them shall come the plague with which the Lord afflicts the nations that do not go up to keep the feast of booths. [19]This shall be the punishment to Egypt and the punishment to all the nations that do not go up to keep the feast of booths.

[20]And on that day there shall be inscribed on the bells of the horses, "Holy to the Lord." And the pots in the house of the Lord shall be as the bowls before the altar; [21]and every pot in Jerusalem and Judah shall be sacred to the Lord of hosts, so that all who sacrifice may come and take of them and boil the flesh of the sacrifice in them. And there shall no longer be a trader in the house of the Lord of hosts on that day.

The worlds of both nature and history unite in these closing scenes which move towards the apogee of the apocalyptic message. The natural world moves and develops in a manner not normal by the laws of nature; the political world is caught up in a maelstrom outside the common experience of human history. Human language is here stretched to its utmost capacity to convey what is both mysterious and fantastic, ultimately beyond the powers of the author's ability to describe. What will be is beyond anything that has been; it will so far outstrip the knowledge gained from experience that it cannot be described in simple words. We have in this final chapter of the book a description of something that is in the last resort indescribable, but the prophet attempts to describe it anyway, for beyond the coming chaos he sees a new world arising from the ashes of the old. It is difficult to know whether the substance of this chapter is a sequel to the conflict in Jerusalem described in chapter 12; it is more probably another version of the same reality, superimposed on the former sketch. To complain that chapters 12 and 14 seem at points to contradict each other is to miss the main issue. The total reality, to which both chapters point, is greater than either of them or both of them together. Each chapter is, as it were, a snapshot of the coming Day of the Lord; each is taken from a different angle, with different foreground and background, but each one ultimately points to God's final victory and peace.

Once again the scene begins with conflict around Jerusalem. The people of the world have gathered together in an alliance, a kind of "United Nations", with their common goal being the destruction of Jerusalem, which seems somehow to threaten their common ground. The city is captured, houses are plundered, women raped, and it looks at first as if the victory is complete; half the survivors are sent into exile, the other half remaining in their homes. But then God enters the conflict and the tide of the larger battle is turned. A series of physical changes occur in the geography of the land, similar to those that might be caused by an earthquake but on a larger scale. The ridge called the Mount of Olives is split into two mountains by an east-west divide, and the former valley running from north to south is blocked at either end. The Lord now enters the Holy City accompanied by his retinue of divine beings.

The climate and physical environment change: there is no longer to be frost and cold, day or night. There would be perpetual light, and hence perpetual warmth. And in a city that always suffered from a precarious water supply, there would be a fountain of living waters flowing throughout the year. All these transformations in geography and the natural world mark the coronation of God as King over all the earth. For formerly hilly land of Judah would be levelled into a plain, while Jerusalem remained situated on hills rising above the surrounding plain. The city would be fully inhabited once again, despite the deportations that had so constantly reduced its population, and its citizens would live in perfect peace and security.

Then the focus of the scene shifts back from the city to those who had been its enemies. Many would suffer terrible deaths, afflicted by an outbreak of plague; others, in their desperate anxiety to escape, would kill their companions to improve their own prospects in the headlong flight. Horses, mules, and other beasts used in the transportation of armies would also die in the throes of plague. And from the rubble of the departing armies, great booty of silver and gold would be collected by the victors.

Despite the overwhelming nature of the defeat, a few persons from these foreign armies would survive; these survivors would somehow be converted and would come to recognize the true God. Year after year they would go up to Jerusalem, the city they had once so ruthlessly opposed, there to participate in the worship of God in the feast of booths, celebrating God's covenant and his gift of harvest. Those who refused to participate in this worship of God, giving thanks for harvest and provision, would suffer from drought and plague: if they would not give thanks, then there would be nothing for which to be thankful.

Within the city, there would be a new sense of God's presence, of his holiness and of the sanctity of the place which symbolized his presence. The temple would no longer be profaned by traders seeking to make a profit from visiting pilgrims; it would fulfil its true role as a house of worship. Thus does the vision end, with the focus on the temple and the interest in priestly matters. The temple would be functioning, so that human beings might fulfil the chief end of their existence, worshipping God and praising him for ever.

What does all this apocalyptic language mean? What message could it possibly convey to us in the 20th century? To read the verses as a series of mysterious predictions and try to flesh them out in the light of the evening news is surely to miss the point. The visionary language does nevertheless speak to our modern world.

(i) *The contemporary world.* Apocalyptic language reflects in a strange way the world of the visionary who utters the words. Although the language of apocalypse addresses the future, it reveals also the present, and the present from which such language emerges is usually a dark and bleak one. It is when human civilization is at its lower points that there emerges from the darkness the hope of a better world. The expression of hope tends to be tinged with realism; that is to say, the violence and conflict of the present world are projected into the future and made to be one of the obstacles which must be conquered before the day of the new world can dawn. But the realism in turn is totally penetrated by hope; there is rarely any evidence in the immediate world to suggest that the future will get better. Apocalyptic thinking, in other words, is rarely characterized by the liberal hope of man's perfectibility, but is marked rather by a deep faith in God's power to transform mankind and human history.

(ii) *The neglect of God.* There is an apologetic streak running through apocalyptic thought. All the great things that are believed about God seem frequently hollow and empty in the light of historical experience. It is not easy to affirm that God is Almighty when the world is in a shambles and the chosen people are a tattered remnant. Apocalyptic thought retains its faith in the full knowledge of God; it may not be easy *now* to believe in Almighty God, but ultimately the time will come when God's power is firmly established for all to see. And this conviction of the ultimate establishment of God's authority is a broad one; it embraces the Gentiles as well as the Jews.

(iii) *Faith and action.* There is a danger in becoming too obsessed with the apocalyptic portions of the Bible, a danger which is evident in certain areas of the contemporary Christian world. The times are ripe, near the end of the 20th century, for a fascination with apocalypse, but the danger of obsession is that balance may be lost. Apocalyptic writings quite rightly impart hope to the faithful in a hopeless time. They restore conviction in the biblical truth that God is ultimately sovereign in human history. But they may also impart to the unwary an attitude of *laissez-faire.* There is nothing we can do. History is moving inexorably towards its climax and we, as bystanders, can only watch with fascination. Such an attitude misses the mark by a wide margin. If we are to benefit from the vision, we must also accept its responsibility. History is also in large part the outworking of our own actions, and we are responsible for them. Faith in the vision of the future must be balanced by commitment to action in the present. And the faith will succour the action, helping us to realize, often despite all evidence to the contary, that not all that we do is in vain.

INTRODUCTION TO THE BOOK OF MALACHI

Malachi, the last of the Twelve Prophets and the final book of the Old Testament in its present ordering, brings to an appropriate conclusion our reflections on the message of the prophets of ancient Israel. The book reflects in many ways prophetic thought at the end of an era and it anticipates a different era yet to come. For the Christian reader of the Bible, there are intimations here of the transition from the Old to the New Testament world. And yet, as in the other prophetic works, the prophet was first and foremost a man of his times; if we would hear his message for later generations, we must first listen carefully to what he has to say to his own generation.

THE PROPHET AND THE TIME OF HIS MINISTRY

The introductory verse of the book (1:1) provides little by way of background information on either the man or the book. The work is described as an *oracle*, or *burden*, in a fashion similar to the two concluding sections of the preceding book (Zechariah 9:1 and 12:1), but the chapters of Malachi are quite different from the second part of Zechariah and have their own unity and distinctive style. The message of these chapters is addressed to "Israel", the word being used here in its broad sense to encompass all the chosen people of God.

The word *Malachi* has been the source of great debate. Is it a name, or a title? It means, translated into English, "my messenger", and the same expression is used in 3:1 where it is translated, quite properly, as "my messenger". Hence, many interpreters have supposed that Malachi is simply a title for an otherwise anonymous prophet, the title indicating clearly enough the prophetic function. But it is also quite possible that *Malachi* is simply a name, albeit a rare one, and that the use of the same Hebrew word in 3:1 is a play on the prophet's name, giving the message greater force. If it is a personal name though, we know nothing more about the prophet than may be inferred about him from the content of his short book.

The general period of the prophet's ministry can be determined from the substance of his writing. The date was approximately 460 B.C., and a little more than half a century had passed from the time of the ministries of men like Haggai and Zechariah. The rebuilding of the temple, which was so central an issue for the prophet's predecessors, was now a thing of the past; the restored temple stood and its worship was conducted on a regular basis. The chosen people were still a colonial people in the Persian Empire, but the rule was relatively benign and the international situation gave few grounds for concern.

For all the tranquillity of Malachi's world, it was not a particularly happy time for the chosen people. Times of international crisis bring with them their own stimulus to action and thought, but calmness can dull the spirits and destroy any sense of vitality. Israel floated on these still waters of international calm, with little sense of direction and the collapse of internal discipline. The high hopes of a preceding generation had been dashed; those who had expected the establishment of a new international order following upon the restoration of the temple had been sadly disappointed. The people had inherited a despondency which ill equipped them to cope with the drab and apparently unchanged world in which they lived. And for several decades, the prophetic voice had not been heard in calling the people back to the fundamentals of faith.

In such a world Malachi ministered, antedating and in some ways anticipating the later reforms of Ezra and Nehemiah. He was faced with a wall of apathy and indifference; he could not enlist for his purpose the fearful threat of war and conflagration. He spoke of the faith to a people for whom religion had become humdrum and who were lackadaisical in their observance of the ancient traditions. Malachi had an uphill task, but though he could hardly have known it at the time, he was laying the ground-work for his successors. The reforms of Ezra and Nehemiah, upon which the survival of the Jewish faith was to depend, pre-suppose the foundational work done by the virtually unknown prophet, Malachi.

THE MESSAGE OF THE PROPHET

It is never an easy task to deal with indifference and its con-sequences in the gradual slide towards an unstructured existence. When people cease to care, religion, morality, social customs and values all cease to function as the mortar that holds together a society and maintains an ancient faith. In Malachi's time, certain religious fundamentals were doubted. Did God really love Israel? Was there really justice in God's world? And these funda-mental doubts affected other areas of Israel's life. The priesthood and religious worship lost their integrity. Intermarriage became common, and with it the perpetual risk of an intermixing of the faith with pagan religions. These were the kinds of issues with which Malachi was faced.

But although there were urgent issues requiring the prophet's attention, like his immediate predecessors he addressed both his own time and the future world, for he perceived that the present had implications for the future. His work is not so dominated by eschatological or apocalyptic concerns as is that of Zechariah. But he speaks nevertheless of the future and intimates the coming of a messenger who would prepare the way for the Messiah. It is this dimension of the prophet's thought and work which enables the Christian reader to see his book as a bridge, linking the great bulk of the Old Testament with the narratives concerning John the Baptist and Jesus in the Gospels.

THE LOVE OF GOD

Malachi 1:1–5

[1]The oracle of the word of the Lord to Israel by Malachi.
[2]"I have loved you," says the Lord. But you say, "How hast thou loved

us?" "Is not Esau Jacob's brother?" says the Lord. "Yet I have loved Jacob ³but I have hated Esau; I have laid waste his hill country and left his heritage to jackals of the desert." ⁴If Edom says, "We are shattered but we will rebuild the ruins," the Lord of hosts says, "They may build, but I will tear down, till they are called the wicked country, the people with whom the Lord is angry for ever." ⁵Your own eyes shall see this, and you shall say, "Great is the Lord, beyond the border of Israel!"

The technique of the book of Malachi is that of disputation. Whether the disputation was rooted in some actual social context of dialogue and debate, or whether it is merely a literary form to communicate a message, remains uncertain, though the latter is perhaps more likely. The passage begins with a statement by God, declared by his prophet; this is followed immediately by the objection of the people, which in turn is probably the expression in words of an attitude prevalent amongst the people as a whole. The objection is then answered in some detail by a further statement from God.

The first disputation begins with a short, but pregnant statement: "I have loved you, says the Lord." The statement receives no further elaboration, but it summarizes Israel's entire history of covenant. In love God had called his people to a relationship of covenant, and in love he had been with them and guided them down through the centuries of their history. The love of God should have been evident to the chosen people as they reflected with understanding on their experience and history. But the objection to the opening statement indicates the jaundiced perception of reality that had overtaken the people: "How hast thou loved us?" The objection rings with petulance and perversity; the words are those of self-centred persons who can no longer perceive the love of God in their lives.

The objection is followed by a response which is designed to elicit acknowledgment of the initial statement from the audience. And the nature of the response seems at first curious: the prophet does not engage in a theological disquisition on the nature and proofs of love, but turns rather to a comparison of historical experiences. The comparison concerns Esau and Jacob, names which here stand for two nations, Edom and Israel, but which contain a reminder of the common ancestry of both nations: Jacob was loved, but Esau was hated. That is, to develop the covenantal overtones of the language, God chose Israel, in love, to be the nation through whom the world would see God's light; he did not choose Edom for any such special and privileged task. And Edom's experience of history, a consequence in part of its own legacy of evil, had been a devastating one: its land had been reduced to ruins. There may be an allusion in these words to the gradual eviction of the Edomites from their native land by the Nabateans, desert-dwellers who may be indicated here by the expression "jackals of the desert" (verse 3). For further information on the Edomites and their historical experience, see the introduction to the Book of Obadiah (in *The Twelve Prophets*, Volume 1, pages 195–197). Even if the Edomites were to determine to rebuild their shattered nation, they would be unsuccessful; they had become the object of God's wrath. All this, when it was properly understood, should create a new appreciation of God in Israel.

From this opening disputation, a number of interesting perspectives on the prophet's theology emerge.

(i) *Blindness to love.* Israel, by virtue of its response to God's opening statement, reveals how the passage of time and the contempt that comes from familiarity have blinded it to the love of God. Just as children from time to time may claim that they are not loved, in the face of a lifetime of parental love, so too did Israel. It had come to take for granted every sign of love, and thus ignored the signs, but the least little hardship or difficulty loomed as evidence of an unloving God. And so, when reminded of the love of God, the people responded in every attitude and word: "How have you loved us?"

The Church, no less than Israel, can be guilty of blindness to love. But it is an affliction which affects not only the religious life, but also the various forms of social interaction. A husband or a wife can take love for granted and forget in the end that it is there at all. And when love is taken for granted, the grasp of illusion replaces the caress of love; any little action, innocent in itself, can be taken for hate. And yet the saddest thing about blindness to love, whether in faith or social bond, is that it is in turn a symptom of the death of love in the one who is blind. Those who continue to love can see its signs in the partner every day; those who no longer love project their own failures onto their partner.

(ii) *The unpleasant comparison.* After the lofty introduction ("I have loved you"), we instinctively expect a profound analysis of the divine love. But what follows is at first sight strange and distasteful. "You think I have not loved you," God states. "Look at the Edomites, see how I have hated them, and then you will know you are still loved!" But to learn of the love of God by being shown the hate of God seems thoroughly to undermine the lesson.

Set in a larger perspective, the theology can be stated in something like the following terms. God loves all mankind; the purpose of God's love extends to all nations. Because of God's love for all nations, he chose one particular nation, Israel, through whom to communicate his love to all nations; that was Israel's *raison d'être* in being chosen by God. And thus Israel's chosenness, or election, is an example *par excellence* of God's love, both for Israel and, through Israel, for the nations of the world. But love can be rejected, whether by Israel or by other nations. Edom's inimical attitude toward Israel throughout their mutual history had, by implication, involved a rejection of Israel's God. Edom, by its attitudes and actions, had brought the "hate" of God upon itself by consistently refusing the love of God. But there is still more to the message than meets the eye.

(iii) *Love's warning.* Why is it that the short book of Malachi begins with a message of God's love? Is it merely to comfort the people who have forgotten that love? Is it simply to restore to its proper place a central element of Israel's theology? Or is it by way of warning? There is little by way of comfort and consolation in the chapters and verses that follow; Malachi goes out of his way to communicate an uncomfortable message to people and clergy alike. So perhaps the lesson on love is a warning, and the example of Edom a threat.

Israel, like so many of God's children, developed a tremendous sense of complacency from its theology of love. It could quickly lose from its conscious mind the truth that it was the object of God's love, but it could not come to think that its fate would ever become like that of Edom. But election love has a purpose. God loved the Israelites for themselves, but also he desired to love others through them. The failure to respond to divine love stymied both its goals. God could neither love his people, because they did not respond, nor could he love others through them. So why should Israel not become like the reprobate nation Edom? There was no good reason why Israel should remain a special nation.

The complacency that may arise from the comfort of being loved must always be disturbed. One cannot relax in the atmosphere of divine love, being loved and yet not loving, hoping nevertheless that the pleasant atmosphere will continue for ever. Love ever demands a response in kind, and if we truly love God, we cannot but seek to be the channels through whom God's love is made known to the world. Only then may all people proclaim "Great is the Lord!" (verse 5).

A CRITIQUE OF THE PRIESTHOOD

Malachi 1:6–2:9

6"A son honours his father, and a servant his master. If then I am a father, where is my honour? And if I am a master, where is my fear? says the Lord of hosts to you, O priests, who despise my name. You say, 'How have we despised thy name?' 7By offering polluted food upon my altar. And you say, 'How have we polluted it?' By thinking that the Lord's table may be despised. 8When you offer blind animals in sacrifice, is that no evil? And when you offer those that are lame or sick, is that no evil? Present that to your governor; will he be pleased with you or show you favour? says the Lord of hosts. 9And now entreat the favour of God, that he may be gracious to us. With such a gift from your hand, will he show favour to any of you? says the Lord of hosts. 10Oh, that there were one among you who would shut the doors, that you might not kindle fire upon my altar in vain! I have no pleasure in you, says the Lord of hosts, and I will not accept an offering from your hand. [11]For from the rising of the sun to its setting my name is great among the nations, and in every place incense is offered to my name, and a pure offering; for my name is great among the nations, says the Lord of hosts. [12]But you profane it when you say that the Lord's table is polluted, and the food for it may be despised. [13]'What a weariness this is', you say, and you sniff at me, says the Lord of hosts. You bring what has been taken by violence or is lame or sick, and this you bring as your offering! Shall I accept that from your hand? says the Lord. [14]Cursed be the cheat who has a male in his flock, and vows it, and yet sacrifices to the Lord what is blemished; for I am a great King, says the Lord of hosts, and my name is feared among the nations.

[1]"And now, O priests, this command is for you. [2]If you will not listen, if you will not lay it to heart to give glory to my name, says the Lord of hosts, then I will send the curse upon you and I will curse your blessings; indeed I have already cursed them, because you do not lay it to heart. [3]Behold, I will rebuke your offspring, and spread dung upon your faces, the dung of your offerings, and I will put you out of my presence. [4]So shall you know that I have sent this command to you, that my covenant with Levi may hold, says the Lord of hosts. [5]My covenant with him was a covenant of life and peace, and I gave them to him, that he might fear; and he feared me, he stood in awe of my name. [6]True instruction was in his mouth, and no wrong was found on his lips. He walked with me in peace and uprightness, and he turned many from iniquity. [7]For the lips of a priest should guard knowledge, and men should seek instruction from his mouth, for he is the messenger of the Lord of hosts. [8]But you have turned aside from the way; you have caused many to stumble by your instruction; you have corrupted the covenant of Levi, says the Lord of hosts, [9]and so I make you despised and abased before all the people, inasmuch as you have not kept my ways but have shown partiality in your instruction."

The opening theme of love, with its implicit warning, gives way now to a disputation on the nature of the priesthood and the legitimacy of the worship in which they are engaged. The passage begins obliquely with a rhetorical question concerning honour. A father is honoured by his son, a master by his servant, but by whom is God held in honour? Is he honoured in the worship conducted by the priests? Although the answer to that question should have been yes, the reality was that the actions of the priests were such as to imply that God was despised. The dispute develops further: "How have we despised thy name?" (verse 6), the priests ask. Their offerings have been polluted. Again the priests raise a question: "How have we polluted it?" (verse 7). And following the second question, there comes a detailed response outlining the failure of the priesthood.

By using blind, lame, and sick animals in their sacrifies to God, they have revealed their contempt for the worship of God. They wouldn't dream of using such defective beasts in a gift to their Persian governor (verse 8) for fear of the swift consequences. If you are going to give a gift, give a good one; a shabby gift undermines the whole purpose of giving. If the priests gave their second and third best to God, why should they look for any better in response from God? The divine exasperation with their shoddy worship is such that God indicates it would be better for the temple doors to be locked and the sacrificial fires unlit, than for this sham masquerading as true sacrifice to continue.

There follows a striking comparison, all the more remarkable given the particularistic and exclusivist traditions in ancient Israel. "From the rising of the sun to its setting", from east to west, God's name is said to be magnified in the worship of Gentile nations (verse 11). The purpose of the statement is to contrast the efficacy of Gentile worship with the profanity of Hebrew worship as conducted by the current generation of priests. The Gentiles, for all their ignorance, genuinely acknowledged the God of creation, whereas the Jews, in Malachi's time, had become weary with worship, turning up their noses at the tedium of it all. Such second-rate worship was unacceptable to God (verse 13); no worship at all would be better than bad worship, which did not recognize the kingship of God and was devoid of any sense of divine majesty.

The critique of the priesthood is followed by an intimation of judgment: if the priests would not lay to heart the prophetic message, then all their work would be cursed by failure. In daring language, the prophet describes the dung of the deformed sacrificial beasts being smeared on the priestly countenances (2:3). By their actions, the current regime of priests had broken the ancient priestly contract for honest service to God. They had failed not only in worship, but also in their educational tasks. Rather than teaching the faith honestly, they had purveyed a false knowledge of religion, thereby causing many people to stumble from the path of true knowledge. And so the priests, having by implication despised God in all their work, would themselves come to be despised and debased in the communities to which they belonged (2:9).

In this second disputation, Malachi highlights a number of critical points not common in the other prophetic writings.

(i) *Prophecy and the law.* Many of the prophet's predecessors had condemned temple worship from a quite different perspective. Before the exile, the temple worship had frequently seemed to flourish and abide by the law's stipulations, but it was all veneer: the people thought that worship alone was sufficient. Amos proclaimed on behalf of God, "I hate, I despise your feasts" (5:21), for, despite absolute propriety in the forms of worship, it was not accompanied by justice and righteousness in the life of the people. Amos, in other words, probably saw worship which was conducted properly, but was viewed wrongly by the people as a kind of insurance policy covering all other sins. Malachi, on the other hand, lived in a society which did not even take worship seriously, and the priests, who were responsible for the conduct of worship, were the worst offenders. Malachi's ideal would not be the abandonment of worship, but its return to the proper and ordained forms.

At heart, nevertheless, prophets like Amos and Malachi do not differ. Worship, properly conducted, is an expression of lives lived in the knowledge of God and in relationship with God. Worship is ordered into particular forms so that this knowledge of God may be given full and rich expression in the lives of the people. But all worship is subject to abuse from several directions. It is possible, as Amos perceived, to follow the proper forms of worship, but the worship as such be meaningless because those who worship have lost all knowledge of God. It is equally possible, as Malachi knew, for a people to be so far from God in relationship and knowledge, that worship becomes virtually

pointless. Nobody cared too much, for they had ceased to care
about God, but they kept the old forms of worship going for the
sake of tradition. They were considered unimportant, and so
second-rate sacrifices were good enough to offer in worship but,
when all was said and done, worship didn't matter. In both cases,
problems in worship reflect deeper problems in the lives of those
who worshipped. Only those who live in a continuing relationship
with God can worship him in spirit and in truth.

(ii) *The worship of the Gentiles.* Although Israel's role was to
be a light to the nations, few of Israel's prophets perceived any
light to exist already amongst the Gentile nations. Jonah tried to
broaden the vision of an exclusivist people by revealing to them
God's compassion for Nineveh and Assyria. And Malachi seems
to go further: he implies the acceptability of Gentile worship to
God (verses 11, 14). It is important to remember the context.
Malachi is not developing a "theology of other religions", but
drawing a contrast to demonstrate the inadequacy of the worship
of his own religion. But his point is no less important for its
incidental nature: he reveals an understanding of God, and of the
knowledge of God beyond the chosen people, that is remarkable
in its breadth. Whether he was referring to the religions of other
peoples in general, or whether he alluded to the Zoroastrian
faith, a monotheistic religion which was gaining ground in the
Persian Empire, cannot be known with certainty. It does seem
clear, nevertheless, that Malachi understood genuine worship of
God to take place outside and beyond the community of the
chosen people.

Christianity frequently claims to have left behind the more
exclusive traits of Judaism, but the reality is frequently different.
Judaism's role was to be a light to the nations; Christianity's role
was to preach the Gospel to all nations. But the two religions have
rarely found it easy, or even possible, to admit that there may be
genuine worship of God beyond their own communities. In part,
such an admission is difficult, because it may seem to undermine
the entire place of mission. But the glimpse of a greater truth
which Malachi affords us should not be set aside. The universal-
ism of mission should not blind us to the existence of the true
worship of God beyond our immediate walls.

(iii) *The importance of knowledge.* The priests had failed in both their major areas of responsibility: they had not conducted worship properly, and they had failed to instruct their people in the knowledge of God. A role model of the didactic responsibilities of the priesthood is provided in 2:6–7, but it was rooted in history, not contemporary reality. "The lips of a priest should guard knowledge, and men should seek instruction from his mouth." But the priests had not guarded their legacy of knowledge and had become ignorant, and so they had nothing to pass on to their people who required instruction. "Every priest of God is a priest of truth," Sir George Adam Smith wrote, "and it is very largely by the Christian ministry's neglect of their intellectual duties that so much irreligion prevails" (*The Book of the Twelve Prophets*, II, p. 361). Smith's comment was written at the end of the 19th century, echoing Malachi's lament, but little has changed at the end of the 20th century to make the comment any less apt.

MARRIAGE AND DIVORCE

Malachi 2:10–16

[10]Have we not all one father? Has not one God created us? Why then are we faithless to one another, profaning the covenant of our fathers? [11]Judah has been faithless, and abomination has been committed in Israel and in Jerusalem; for Judah has profaned the sanctuary of the Lord, which he loves, and has married the daughter of a foreign God. [12]May the Lord cut off from the tents of Jacob, for the man who does this, any to witness or answer, or to bring an offering to the Lord of hosts!

[13]And this again you do. You cover the Lord's altar with tears, with weeping and groaning because he no longer regards the offering or accepts it with favour at your hand. [14]You ask, "Why does he not?" Because the Lord was witness to the covenant between you and the wife of your youth, to whom you have been faithless, though she is your companion and your wife by covenant. [15]Has not the one God made and sustained for us the spirit of life? And what does he desire? Godly offspring. So take heed to yourselves, and let none be faithless to the wife of his youth. [16]"For I hate divorce, says the Lord the God of

Israel, and covering one's garment with violence, says the Lord of hosts. So take heed to yourselves and do not be faithless."

In most human societies, marriage is a fundamental social bond, one effect of which is to hold that society together; conversely, divorce not only breaks a particular social bond but, if it becomes widespread, can undermine the fabric of society as a whole. In ancient Israel divorce was permitted, though only under certain specific conditions (see Deut. 24:1–4), and remarriage was possible. But the law was designed to keep a tight control on the extent of divorce. Conversely, the high esteem in which marriage was held is seen in its character as a kind of *covenant*, the same word being used to describe Israel's faith and national constitution. As the covenant of faith lay at the heart of Israel's national life, so too the covenant of marriage lay at the heart of its social life.

In Malachi's time, the sanctity of marriage seems to have been largely eroded, and with it there was a massive increase in divorce and remarriages. This does not seem to have been simply an increase in laxity pertaining to marriage customs, but specifically a result of the social conditions in a post-exilic community. Those who had returned from exile came from Israel's distinguished families, but few of them had property or position in the new land to which they had returned. And it seems probable that divorce became common in Jewish marriages, so that the male partner could remarry a local woman, thereby establishing himself better in the community, and perhaps adding to his wealth and position. The consequences were two-fold. On the one hand, the social fabric was disrupted, and there was a large increase in the number of single, divorced women. On the other hand, the remarriages were a source of contention and trouble, for those whom the young Jews married were women of an alien faith, and thus, in those marriages, the ancient religion of Israel was gradually being lost.

This is the situation which Malachi addresses in 2:10–16, but the text of the passage is notoriously difficult to interpret. Given the style of disputation common to the book as a whole, verses

11–12 seem to intrude and delay the conventional disputational response (verse 14). And some of the verses, especially verse 15, are extremely difficult to translate from the Hebrew, as the foot-notes in the RSV make clear. It may be that, over the passage of time, earnest scribes, seeking to harmonize this passage with the conventional laws permitting divorce, introduced minor modi-fications. But for all the difficulties of the text, it is possible to recapture its general drift.

Behind the actual institution of marriage lies the fundamental theology of ancient Israel. There is one God, the creator of all life, who was known to his people in a relationship characterized by faithfulness. Marriage, too, was to be marked by this charac-teristic of faithfulness between partners. But, at two quite distinct levels, the growing prevalence of divorce had undermined the ancient tradition. (a) The increase in the incidence of divorce was a symptom in turn of a general increase in the characteristic of unfaithfulness in human relationships. (b) The reason for di vorce, namely remarriage to a person of a different religion, symbolized not only a decline in the religious faith of those men getting divorced, but it was also the "kiss of death" for the future of Israel's religion. Those who could so rapidly abandon the covenant of marriage for personal gain could equally rapidly abandon the covenant with God: both were acts of unfaithful-ness. And why should a people be surprised that God was no longer faithful in responding to their worship, when they in turn had long since ceased to be faithful to God and to one another (verses 13–14)?

Thus the prophet concludes: "I hate divorce, says the Lord" (verse 16). He is not a legislator, drafting a new law for his community, making divorce illegal and impossible. He is a prophet, expressing with absolute clarity the divine displeasure when divorce has become a run-of-the-mill routine in a declining society. While divorce is always sad, representing the break-up of a relationship, it is saddest when it is taken the most lightly. When divorce becomes an easy convenience for one partner, smoothing the path to worldly success, marriage begins to lose its meaning. And the growth of divorce actions in Israel also indicated a growing callousness of the human spirit; the terrible hurt and ruined life of one partner were of no consequence in the other partner's pursuit of ambition. And so, not unnaturally, there comes the divine declaration: "I hate divorce". The ruined lives, the collapse of hopes, and the loss of faithfulness make it a hateful practice.

Yet at the end of this disputation, it is the wider implications of prevalent divorce that are stressed. "So take heed to yourselves and do not be faithless" (verse 16). Certainly the injunction includes those persons who so casually accepted divorce. But it is wider than that, indicating the importance of faithfulness in all forms of relationship, both with fellow human beings and with God. Faithfulness in all relationships is a part of the mortar that holds a human society together. And in Israel, faithfulness towards God, reflecting his prior faithfulness, was the foundation upon which all human relationships could be built.

JUSTICE AND JUDGMENT

Malachi 2:17–3:5

17You have wearied the Lord with your words. Yet you say, "How have we wearied him?" By saying, "Every one who does evil is good in the sight of the Lord, and he delights in them." Or by asking, "Where is the God of justice?"

1"Behold, I send my messenger to prepare the way before me, and the Lord whom you seek will suddenly come to his temple; the messenger of the covenant in whom you delight, behold, he is coming, says the Lord of hosts. 2But who can endure the day of his coming, and who can stand when he appears?

"For he is like a refiner's fire and like fullers' soap; 3he will sit as a refiner and purifier of silver, and he will purify the sons of Levi and refine them like gold and silver, till they present right offerings to the Lord. 4Then the offering of Judah and Jerusalem will be pleasing to the Lord as in the days of old and as in former years.

5"Then I will draw near to you for judgment; I will be a swift witness against the sorcerers, against the adulterers, against those who swear falsely, against those who oppress the hireling in his wages, the widow and the orphan, against those who thrust aside the sojourner, and do not fear me, says the Lord of hosts."

The disputation continues with another statement from the prophet, on behalf of God, followed by the people's reaction. "You have wearied the Lord with your words," the prophet says. "How have we wearied him?" the audience respond, meaning with what words have we caused such a response? And so the prophet answers with two examples (verse 17b), which are not so much direct quotations as they are expressions in words of the typical attitudes and actions of the people. They act as though they think God considers evil to be good, or as though there is no justice in God's world. They have become, by their attitudes and actions, functional atheists, not bothering to deny the existence of God, but destroying any link between God and justice, or between the Almighty and good and evil.

The prophet's message concerns justice and judgment; it has little explicit concern for confession and repentance, even if those actions might be an appropriate response to his proclamation. God announces that he is sending a messenger to prepare the way for his own advent. In the light of the New Testament, this messenger is identified with John the Baptist (Mark 1:2), though the original sense of the words is probably more general and only later developed in detail (see further the postscript, 4:4–5). But there is also a word play involved here, for *Malachi* means *my messenger*. The prophet does not seem to identify himself explicitly with this forerunner of God, though his own message is in itself a prior announcement of the coming of God. The coming one is a "messenger of the covenant in whom you delight". The words involve irony, for though Malachi's audience delighted in the covenant's blessing, it was of the covenant's judgment that they would hear. Any hope the people might entertain at this announcement of God's coming to his temple is abruptly halted: "who can endure the day of his coming, and who can stand when he appears?" (verse 2).

There follows a description of God seated in judgment (verses 2b–4), which quickly confounds the delusion that God has confused good and evil and no longer acts in justice. The metaphors of the scene are mixed. On the one hand, God is a fuller, whose alkaline "soap" makes dirty garments white. On the other hand, God is a refiner of precious metals, whose hot fire removes all impurities from silver and gold. The metaphors illustrate the double thrust of the purpose of the coming God. He comes both to purify the faithful and to eliminate the unfaithful. Following the purification, the worship of the chosen people will be acceptable to God once again, but the longer word is preserved for the description of divine judgment (verse 5). Sorcerers, adulterers, oppressors, and all those who in their lives and professions have no reverence for God, will fall victim to his judgment. They are not a part of the silver and gold to be purified, but a part of the dross to be cast away.

Malachi's vision of this fearful advent of God combines, as so frequently in the prophets, present relevance and future perspective.

(i) *Present relevance*. Although he does not explicitly call for repentance, Malachi was certainly concerned to speak plainly to all those evil persons categorized in verse 5. The sorcerers who played on superstitions and desires, the adulterers whose licentious lives made mockery of the notion of faithfulness, the oppressors who exploited the weak and underprivileged for their own advantage: all these persons were anathema in Israel's society. They corrupted whatever they touched, they extinguished the torch of justice towards which the oppressed looked with longing, and so false was their sense of values that good and evil could no longer be distinguished in society as a whole. Even when such rampant evil cannot be contained, it must be denounced, and Malachi raised his voice in denunciation. But the very act of the prophet's proclamation changed the shape of society: when few knew any longer the distinction between good and evil, one man affirmed the good and declared the final end of evil. And even when a society is so far gone that reform seems impossible, it is still essential that some lonely voices declare with courage what is good and what is bad. Therein lay the present relevance of the prophet's message.

(ii) *Future perspective.* Malachi also had a message concerning God in the world's future. His language is less vivid than that of Zechariah, but his vision nevertheless is a frightening one. God would not abandon his people; some would be refined and purified, and they would continue in the proper worship of God. But the evil-doers, like dross, would be disposed of on the judgment day. And to those who spoke openly of their evil, confident that God would never act, Malachi's words are aimed in such a way as to puncture confidence: "Who can endure the day of his coming?" The fire of judgment would be unquenchable, and it is a message echoed in the later preaching of Jesus, whose coming was anticipated by the Baptist (Matt. 3:1–12). Justice and judgment go hand in hand together; and the message of justice and judgment may always bring hope to the oppressed, but to the oppressors who have the courage to hear it, it sounds a note of warning and fear.

THE ROBBING OF GOD

Malachi 3:6–12

> [6]"For I the Lord do not change; therefore you, O sons of Jacob, are not consumed. [7]From the days of your fathers you have turned aside from my statutes and have not kept them. Return to me, and I will return to you, says the Lord of hosts. But you say, 'How shall we return?' [8]Will man rob God? Yet you are robbing me. But you say, 'How are we robbing thee?' In your tithes and offerings. [9]You are cursed with a curse, for you are robbing me; the whole nation of you. [10]Bring the full tithes into the storehouse, that there may be food in my house; and thereby put me to the test, says the Lord of hosts, if I will not open the window of heaven for you and pour down for you an overflowing blessing. [11]I will rebuke the devourer for you, so that it will not destroy the fruits of your soil; and your vine in the field shall not fail to bear, says the Lord of hosts. [12]Then all nations will call you blessed, for you will be a land of delight, says the Lord of hosts."

The disputation begins once again with a statement from God containing criticism of the people: "You have turned aside from my statutes and have not kept them." But the criticism, despite its accompanying call for repentance, is not very specific, and so the people ask, "How shall we return?" In the second part of the divine declaration, the charge is stated more precisely: "You are robbing me." But still the audience protests and requires further clarification: "How are we robbing you?" And then there follows an elaboration of one particular area in the community's life in which their actions were tantamount to the robbery of God.

The robbery took place in the area of tithes and offerings. An ancient part of both law and tradition required of the Hebrews that they return a portion of what was given to them to God the Giver. The tithe represented a return of one tenth of all provision. But the failure to give was not merely a lapse in religious duty, but amounted to a form of robbery: what rightfully belonged to someone else was being taken by another. The consequence of the nation's robbery was the experience of the divine curse: if they knew not how to give, they would receive less and less. The prophet then enjoins the people to bring the full measure of their offering to the temple; such action would result not only in there being "food in my house" (verse 10, for the feeding of the temple's support staff), but would also test God with respect to his ability to provide more abundantly. There is a promise attached to this message, which is concurrently a challenge and a call to repentance. If the people would give, they would discover God's bounty; he would control the pests that destroyed the crops, and the vineyards would bear an abundant harvest. The blessing on the land would be of such a kind that all surrounding nations would observe it and comment on the happy estate of the chosen people.

The prophet's message brings out some fundamental perspectives with respect to the matter of giving.

(i) *Attitudes to property*. The prophet, employing a rare Hebrew verb, describes the actions of the people as a form of *robbery*. In keeping their tithes and offerings to themselves, they acted as if they owned all that they had. Their attitude towards property was not one of stewardship, according to which their possessions were held as a sacred trust from God, but one of ownership. What they had belonged to them; it was up to them to decide whether any portion of it should be given to God. And there is an irony in the situation: they actually had much less than they might have had, in part because their selfish and tight-fisted attitudes towards property had reduced their capacity for growth.

The prophet urged them to consider how they should use *God's* property, while the people wondered what they would do with *their own* property. In this, their thinking was fundamentally flawed, and the flaw in turn undermined their relationship with God. To think that property and wealth belong entirely to oneself is to presuppose that we, by our own efforts, earn all that we have. This view, because it is partly true, is easy to accept, but it is essentially a deception. We work to earn what we have, and we may be rewarded for our labours; but the health and strength to work, and indeed the opportunity to work, are all a part of God's gift to us in life. Thus, however hard we work, and however rightfully we reap our rewards, there is a distinct sense in which none of it would be possible without God. Our attitude towards property and wealth should therefore always involve an acknowledgment of God's role in its acquisition, and this acknowledgment in turn will relax the tightness of our hold on that which we possess. The totally self-centred view of wealth, and the egotistical pride that may arise in its accumulation, are a recipe for stinginess. Generosity arises from a proper attitude towards wealth and property, in which we recognize the blessing and provision of God in its receipt.

(ii) *Attitudes to God*. The person who is stingy with wealth, refusing to give to God or to other persons, betrays a deep-seated lack of belief. Such persons do not really believe that God, if there is a God, has had any hand in making and giving them what they are and what they have. The proud and confident self-made person has at bottom little faith. And having little faith, such a person sees no need to give generously to the temple and to the support of God's larger work in the world.

Small giving and small faith go hand in hand together, and indeed the former may be a symptom of the latter. But the prophet makes something else clear: small giving and small faith lay the foundation for small receiving. Persons who do not give generously are ill-equipped to be the recipients of generosity. The positive point which the prophet makes is a delicate one, prone to misunderstanding. It is that the one who gives generously to God may receive bountifully from God. It cannot be reduced, as sometimes happens, to a formula for success in business: if you give such and such, you can be sure that your profits will rise phenomenally year after year! The principle is rooted more in the health of the relationship a person has with God. It is in the nature of rich relationships that the partners want to give to each other from what they have. But when one partner is stingy, that meanness inevitably affects the quality of the relationship and affects the capacity of the other partner to give. The generous giving to God from a full heart naturally results in the rich blessing of the One with whom we have a relationship. The blessing may be in physical or spiritual form, but is none the less real in either kind.

(iii) *Attitudes to others*. A nation that does not give to God reveals not only its spiritual temper, but also its social attitudes. The meanness reflected in the faith inevitably becomes a characteristic of the citizens' attitudes towards one another. And it is a social truth, as well as a theological one, that a nation marked by meanness is unlikely to prosper. Generosity, in turn, may affect the entire temper of a nation. The joy and practice of giving freely, towards both God and the needs of fellow citizens, create health in the human community and the more even distribution of wealth.

Malachi addressed a community stingy at heart, and its failure to give to God and temple became a blight on the nation's personality as a whole. But sadly the prophet did not address a rare or unique social situation. The Church, through many generations, has recreated in its life the conditions of Malachi's time, making his message ever timely.

GOOD AND EVIL

Malachi 3:13–4:3

13 "Your words have been stout against me, says the Lord. Yet you say, 'How have we spoken against thee?' 14 You have said, 'It is vain to

serve God. What is the good of our keeping his charge or of walking as in mourning before the Lord of hosts? [15]Henceforth we deem the arrogant blessed; evildoers not only prosper but when they put God to the test they escape.'"

[16]Then those who feared the Lord spoke with one another; the Lord heeded and heard them, and a book of remembrance was written before him of those who feared the Lord and thought on his name. [17]"They shall be mine, says the Lord of hosts, my special possession on the day when I act, and I will spare them as a man spares his son who serves him. [18]Then once more you shall distinguish between the righteous and the wicked, between one who serves God and one who does not serve him.

[1]"For behold, the day comes, burning like an oven, when all the arrogant and all evildoers will be stubble; the day that comes shall burn them up, says the Lord of hosts, so that it will leave them neither root nor branch. [2]But for you who fear my name the sun of righteousness shall rise, with healing in its wings. You shall go forth leaping like calves from the stall. [3]And you shall tread down the wicked, for they will be ashes under the soles of your feet, on the day when I act, says the Lord of hosts."

In the final disputation, the prophet pinpoints the cynicism that permeates the community to which he belongs. The people's words, the prophet claims, have been opposed to God. When they ask in what way they have spoken against God, he replies once again by expressing in words the attitudes typified by the people's actions and their way of life. Their sense of values indicates clearly that no one considers the service of God to be worth while or important. Ordinary persons have abandoned ancient principles for a more empirical approach; since arrogant and evil persons seem to prosper, without any response from God, why not join them? So the community's values have been totally reversed: the admirable persons are those who prosper while ignoring the faith, whereas the righteous poor are only to be despised for their ignorance and folly. Such an attitude is an insult to God, confusing good and evil, abandoning the good in the headlong rush to pursue evil.

The response to this reversal of values moves from the present moment into the area of eschatology. A society may decide to abandon the distinction between good and evil, but God never abandons it. Beyond the horizon of time as we know it, there lies a judgment in which good and evil are still the criteria of what is acceptable and unacceptable to God. The righteous, who in their living expressed reverence for God, had their names recorded in God's book, from which the evidence would be read out on the judgment day. However absent God might appear to be from a society's life, he was in reality present, observing how people lived and noting those who did good and those who practised evil.

The scene then shifts from the God who records human actions to the God who comes to judge the world. The day is one of contrasts. Those who have embraced evil will be burned as stubble, their lifetime's accomplishments proving to have little enduring value on the day of testing. On the other hand, the good, so depised and forlorn for much of their lives, will greet the judgment day as the dawn of a new age, their God rising with the brightness of the sun in a world that has seemed for so long to be dark in the divine absence. As calves frolic in the field, full of the joy of life on an early summer morning, so too would God's people rejoice in his presence. And the righteous, who for so long had been trodden under by the wicked, would be God's agents on that day in treading upon their former evil oppressors.

Malachi ends his disputations by establishing a larger context within which to understand good and evil, those fundamental parameters of all human living. Life must be directed by a knowledge of good and evil in faith and action, for the knowledge of God creates this polarity in human understanding. But when faith in God is abandoned, the distinction between good and evil becomes gradually more fuzzy. The moral absolutes are abandoned for a series of ethical compromises, in which personal success and benefit are the principal criteria of decision-making. And when the pursuit of evil seems to bring its immediate and rich rewards, then the former abandonment of the distinction between good and evil is seen as a kind of emancipation: such distinctions are fine for children, but now that we have come of age, we no longer need such a simplistic morality! And when such changes in perception sweep through a society, the first to suffer will be those who cling to the old notions; they have become, in a new world, the natural victims of oppression by those who embrace evil.

There are no simple solutions to such widespread changes in human society, and tragically the confusion and perversions of the notions of good and evil are as common in our century as in Malachi's. The prophet's response takes the form of reminder and warning. He reminds human beings that, although they find it convenient to forget the difference between good and evil, God does not forget. Massive social change does not change the nature of God. And he warns human beings that evil always culminates in its own judgment. Whether one views such judgment, in an internal and spiritual sense, as a time in which evil persons recognize all their achievements for the worthless stubble that they are, or whether one projects it against the canvas of future judgment, the coming of God's day is inevitable. But, with remarkable insight, the prophet perceives that the day which will dawn with such despair for many will also be a day in which the humble will celebrate the rising of the "sun of righteousness".

POSTSCRIPT: THE COMING OF ELIJAH

Malachi 4:4–6

4"Remember the law of my servant Moses, the statutes and ordinances that I commanded him at Horeb for all Israel.

5"Behold, I will send you Elijah the prophet before the great and terrible day of the Lord comes. 6And he will turn the hearts of fathers to their children and the hearts of children to their fathers, lest I come and smite the land with a curse."

The short book of Malachi ends with retrospect and prospect, both impinging upon the prophet's present time. As these are the last verses not only of Malachi, but also of the Book of the Twelve Prophets, not unreasonably their authenticity has been questioned. It is possible that they reflect an editorial addition from the hand of the editor of the Book of the Twelve. But the verses also combine law and prophecy in a manner typical of Malachi and they may well be authentic. Thus, it may be that the Book of Malachi was placed at the end of the collection of the Twelve Prophets, because its concluding words summarize so aptly not only its own substance, but also the message of the prophets as a whole.

In retrospect, the people are enjoined to remember the law of Moses, given so many centuries in the past but establishing for all time the fundamental dimensions of the relationship between God and Israel. The commandments given to Israel at Horeb (Mount Sinai) were never intended to be a burden, but rather were a gift which could lead to fullness of life.

In prospect, the advent of Elijah is announced, whose coming would precede and prepare "the great and terrible day of the Lord". The prospect warns that God's judgment day must surely come, but that it will not be without its signs and warnings. In a society that has degenerated so badly that one generation is set against another, God's prophet would return to set things right before the actual coming of the Lord.

Moses and Elijah represent here two of the great foundations of the Old Testament, law and prophecy. The law established the norms of life in relationship with God; the prophets served as the conscience of Israel, constantly calling back God's people from the error of their ways to their first and true relationship. And thus it is no coincidence that, on the Mount of Transfiguration, it is with Moses and Elijah that Jesus converses (Mark 9:2–8). For the Gentile reader of the Old Testament, Jesus brings to completion the substance of its message. Like Moses, Jesus brings to us the possibility of a life lived in a relationship of covenant with God. Like Elijah, he calls us back from the false ways to which we have turned. And thus the promise of the law and the message of the prophets take on for Gentiles new and continuing meaning in the person and ministry of Jesus Christ.

FURTHER READING

Books marked * are more suitable for initial study.

L. C. Allen, *The Books of Joel, Obadiah, Jonah and Micah* (The New International Commentary on the Old Testament) (Eerdmans, 1976)

*J. G. Baldwin, *Haggai, Zechariah, Malachi* (Tyndale Old Testament Commentaries) (Inter-Varsity Press, 1972)

D. R. Hillers, *Micah* (Hermeneia Commentaries) (Fortress Press, 1983)

*D. R. Jones, *Haggai, Zechariah and Malachi* (Torch Bible Commentaries) (SCM Press, 1962)

*J. Marsh, *Amos and Micah* (Torch Bible Commentaries) (SCM Press, 1959)

*R. Mason, *The Books of Haggai, Zechariah and Malachi* (The Cambridge Bible Commentary on the New English Bible) (Cambridge University Press, 1977)

*H. McKeating, *The Books of Amos, Hosea and Micah* (The Cambridge Bible Commentary on the New English Bible) (Cambridge University Press, 1971)

G. A. Smith, *The Book of the Twelve Prophets*, Volume II (The Expositor's Bible) (Hodder and Stoughton, 1899)

R. L. Smith, *Micah–Malachi* (Word Biblical Commentaries) (Word Press, 1984)

*J. D. W. Watts, *The Books of Joel, Obadiah, Jonah, Nahum, Habakkuk and Zephaniah* (The Cambridge Bible Commentary on the New English Bible) (Cambridge University Press, 1975)

See also the list for Further Reading in *Twelve Prophets I*.